THE ESSENTIAL GUIDE TO WILLS, ESTATES, TRUSTS, AND DEATH TAXES

THE ESSENTIAL GUIDE TO WILLS, ESTATES, TRUSTS, AND DEATH TAXES

Alex J. Soled

an AARP Book
published by

American Association of Retired Persons
Washington, D.C.

Scott, Foresman and Company
Lifelong Learning Division
Glenview, Illinois

This publication is designed to provide accurate and authoritative information in regard to the subject matter covered. It is sold with the understanding that the publisher is not engaged in rendering legal, accounting, or other professional service. If legal advice or other expert assistance is required, the services of a competent professional person should be sought.

Copyright © 1984 Scott, Foresman and Company, Glenview, Illinois
American Association of Retired Persons, Washington, D.C.
All Rights Reserved
Printed in the United States of America
 23456-KPF-8887868584

Library of Congress Cataloging in Publication Data

Soled, Alex J.
   The essential guide to wills, estates, trusts, and death taxes.
   "An AARP book"
   Includes index.
   1. Estate planning—United States—Popular works.
2. Wills—United States—Popular works.   3. Trusts and
trustees—United States—Popular works.   4. Inheritance
and transfer tax—Law and legislation—United States—
Popular works.   I. American Association of Retired
Persons.   II. Title.
KF750.Z9S6   1984   346.7305′2   83-20408
ISBN 0-673-24809-7   347.30652

CONTENTS

WILLS

Types of Wills

Courts

TERMINOLOGY

ESTATES

General Information

Administration of an Estate

TRUSTS

DEATH TAXES (ESTATE AND INHERITANCE) INCLUDING GIFT TAXES

APPENDIX

INTRODUCTION

While most of us realize that it is necessary to devote a good deal of time and attention to the acquisition of property during life, we do not realize that an equal or greater effort must be made to preserve and dispose of property after death.

After death, we are no longer present to guarantee that the property we acquired during life

- passes to the ones we intend to benefit with the least possible delay,
- is received by our loved ones with the lowest possible death taxes, and
- quickly becomes income-producing or, if the property is not income-producing, provides our loved ones with benefits as soon as possible.

To accomplish these objectives you must plan now. A knowledge of the basic laws dealing with property, taxes (both federal and state), and estate administration becomes essential. Knowing the ground rules will help you plan to quickly and economically transfer all of your property on your death, whether modest or substantial in amount.

This book will provide the information you need to participate actively in your own estate planning. It does so in a question-and-answer format that anticipates the most frequently-asked questions and answers them in a way that can be understood easily. The book is not intended to teach you to do it yourself. Rather, it is written as a guide for you, the lay person, so that you may ask the appropriate questions of professionals who can help you. The question-and-answer format will help you understand this complex process. When dealing with wills, trusts, estates, and death taxes there are many pitfalls to be avoided before one can accomplish a quick and economical transfer of property. The reader should not assume that he or she can arrange the transfer without professional help.

The Essential Guide to Wills, Estates, Trusts, and Death Taxes is organized to permit selective use, allowing you to refer quickly to specific topics. A comprehensive table of contents and a complete index are included. The information contained in this book will also help you determine whether a professional you consult is really trained to be of assistance. If the professional does not know the answers to most of the questions raised in this book, go elsewhere.

The problem of how to plan for the efficient distribution of your hard-earned dollars and property deserves your attention now if you wish to guarantee that the distribution will reflect your wishes and will occur with the least expense, complications, or delay.

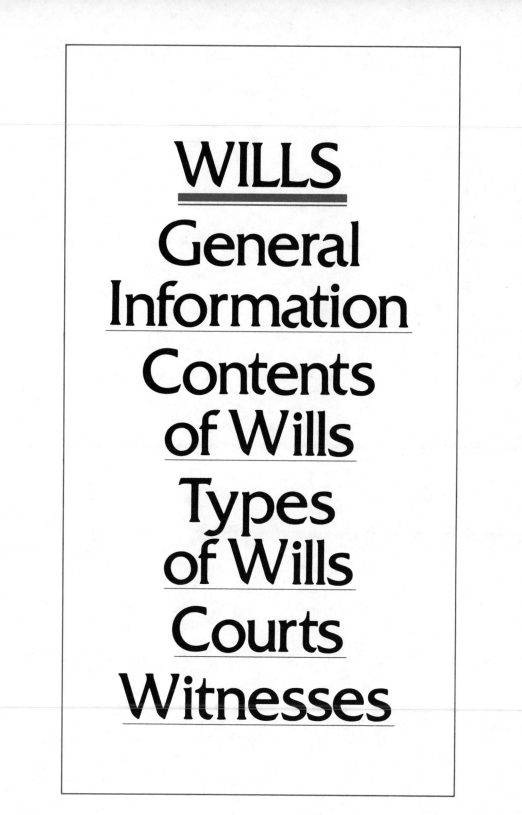

WILLS

General Information

Contents of Wills

Types of Wills

Courts

Witnesses

WILLS

GENERAL INFORMATION

What is a will?

A declaration, usually in writing, which disposes of one's property after death.

What is a *testator*?

A male who makes a will.

What is a *testatrix*?

A female who makes a will. For clarity, this book will usually refer to the testator (the male version); however, this reference also includes the testatrix.

What property can be disposed of by will?

All property of any kind owned solely by the one who makes the will (the testator).

Can a testator by will dispose of property which is not owned solely by him?

No. Consider this: can I provide in my will that the car that you (the reader) own shall be left to my daughter? Certainly not! Why is this so? Simply because your car does not belong to me and is not mine to give away.

Let us reverse roles. Can you give away to your son, by your will, the car that I own? Again, no! Again, the reason is that you cannot give away property that does not belong to you.

Assume you bought six U.S. Series E Savings Bonds some years ago. Last year, you added your daughter's name to the bonds. By registering the bonds in this manner, you provided that on your death the bonds would be paid to your daughter (the words used are "payable on death," abbreviated "p.o.d.").

You now prepare a will. Because of a change in family circumstances, you provide in the will that the bonds be paid to your son. Will your son become the owner of the bonds on your death? Certainly not!

Why not? Because at the *moment* of your death, ownership of the bonds shifted to your daughter. Since your will could only dispose of property owned by you at the *moment* of your death, at that moment you no longer owned the bonds.

Of course, during your lifetime you could have made the changes by re-registering the bonds and substituting your son's name for your daughter's.

When does a will become effective?

When the testator dies and the court having jurisdiction accepts the will as the valid instrument that expresses the final wishes of the testator. The procedure leading up to and including acceptance of the will is called "probating the will."

What does *testament* mean and what is the difference between the separate words *will* and *testament* and the phrase *last will and testament*?

In earlier times, *testament* referred to leaving personal property (property other than real estate) on death, and *will* referred to leaving real property (real estate) on death. When the same instrument left personal as well as real property, the instrument was commonly referred to as the "last will and testament."

Today, the term *will* refers to personal property as well as to real property. Because of custom and the laws of some states, it is recommended that the phrase *last will and testament* be used.

What is meant when it is said that a will is *ambulatory* and *revocable*?

Ambulatory means that it does not take effect until death.

Revocable means that it is capable of being revoked. To *revoke* a will means to cancel, dissolve, or declare it to be of no force or effect.

A will only takes effect on the death of its maker (the testator) and every will may be revoked by its maker. Thus, if you make a will, you may change it as many times during your lifetime as you wish, or you may revoke it.

Should I have a will?

Yes, the object of a will is to dispose of one's assets as desired. The lawyer's role is to advise the client and to prepare the necessary documents so that this objective (distributing assets as one desires) may be accomplished with the least delay and at the lowest possible tax cost and expense of administration.

When a person dies without a will (*intestate*), the laws of the state in which that person resides at the time of death direct how his or her solely-owned assets shall be disposed of. In other words, the state makes a will for you! State laws which leave your property to those specified in such laws are known as "laws of descent and distribution." (Solely-owned assets are commonly referred to as *probate assets*, that is, assets that are administered under the supervision of a *probate court*. For a full discussion of this subject, see the material beginning on page 40.)

By way of illustration, under Maryland law, if you have a wife and minor children and you die intestate, your wife inherits one-half of your property and your children inherit the other half. You must then ask yourself if this is the type of distribution that you wish. In the back of this book we have set forth a summary of the current laws of descent and distribution for all 50 states plus the District of Columbia.

If your children inherit half your property, they are entitled to receive the property as early as age 18. I am of the opinion that it is unwise to give large sums of money to children at age 18 since at that time in their lives they may not have learned how to handle large sums. Appropriate language in a will can delay their receipt of large sums until they are older.

In most states, a person under the age of 18 years is considered a *minor*. While a minor, a person usually does not have the legal capacity to enter into contracts. In the eyes of the law, the minor is considered to be under a legal disability. This legal disability disappears when the minor attains legal age (referred to as attaining *majority*). When property is left to a minor, complications arise during the time the money is held for the benefit of the minor.

Frequently, it is necessary to appoint a guardian of a minor's property. Without a will, the appointment of a guardian for a minor's property usually requires filing with the court a surety bond. With a will, you can appoint guardians of the property of minor children without requiring a bond. Premiums for the surety bond are costly and are payable from the assets of such child. Also, the minor's funds frequently may not be spent for the minor's benefit without securing a court order.

A will permits you to designate an executor of your choosing, and you need not rely upon state law, and eventually the courts, to appoint an executor. In the absence of a will, any court-appointed executor must post a bond. The premium cost varies with the size of the estate and is an estate expense. In some areas of the country, if a bond is required, the bonding company will properly require that all transfers of property be countersigned by the company with the attendant delays associated with that procedure.

If you are the sole owner of a business, at the moment of your death this asset (the business) becomes the property of your estate. The laws of most states prohibit an estate from owning or running a business.

This may then require the liquidation of the business at an inconvenient time. A will can permit the continuation of the business if so desired by you.

In some states, there is a requirement that a business be incorporated in order for the estate to run it. This will entail additional expense.

At the outset, you may think that all of your property is jointly-owned and that there is no necessity for a will. In reality, you may have forgotten about property, you may later have inherited additional property that is not jointly-owned, or you may have sustained personal injuries resulting in the recovery of sums of money that could be a valuable asset of your estate and should really be disposed of by provisions of your will.

However, assuming that all your property is jointly-owned with your spouse and that your spouse survives you, your spouse would certainly need a will since she or he would become the sole owner of all of the property. If your spouse does not have a will, the property of which she or he is the sole owner would be inherited in accordance with the laws of descent and distribution. You may say that your spouse can, as soon as you die, go out and have a will made. Consider, however, the possibility that you die together in an automobile accident or a plane crash. Also your spouse may have a stroke immediately after your death and be incapable of making a will.

Making a will can frequently enable you to save death taxes by appropriate planning and will clauses.

I wish to have a valid will. What is required?

The laws of most states require that you be of a certain age, usually 18; that you be of sound mind; and that the formalities required by law be followed.

Usually, this means

1. that there be a written instrument;
2. that you sign the instrument, or some other person signs for you in your presence and by your express direction;
3. that it be attested and signed by two or more credible witnesses in the presence of the testator.

In several states, step 2 requires that you identify the instrument as being your will and also that you specifically request the witnesses to serve as such. Another name given to step 2 in these states is *publication* of the will. Sometimes this step is referred to as *execution*.

Shouldn't I execute several copies of the will so that, if I lose the original, one of the copies can be probated?

No. As a general rule, if copies are executed, every copy must be produced in court. If all executed copies are not produced, the law assumes that the will was revoked. It is much simpler to preserve one original signed document in a safe place.

Assume you execute the typewritten ribbon copy (the original) and also two carbon copies or perhaps two photocopies of the original. On death the original only is submitted to the court for probate. One or two signed copies cannot be found. The laws of virtually every state provide that if *all* of the executed documents cannot be produced, there is a presumption that the will was revoked.

This same rule applies if the copies are submitted to the court for probate. In the absence of the original will, the presumption is that the will was revoked. (A *presumption* is a technical rule of evidence as to what conclusion is to be drawn from the stated facts. As it applies to wills, if an executed document is missing, the conclusion drawn is that the will was revoked.) The presumption can be overcome. For example, if we can show that the original will was at all times in your attorney's hands, that he never turned it over to you, and that he cannot explain its disappearance, then if the executed copies are produced, probate will normally be approved for the copies of the will.

Where should my will be kept?

In most states, your will should be kept in your safe deposit box at a bank, provided that the box is rented in joint names with your spouse, at your lawyer's office, or at the trust company (if you have named one as your executor). In some states, the clerk of the probate court will hold it for safe-keeping in a sealed envelope. There will be a nominal fee for this and only you or your duly designated agent can secure possession of it during your lifetime.

However, in some states, such as New York, if your will is in a bank safe deposit box and the box is rented in your name either as sole tenant or as joint tenant, the box will be sealed on your death. In such states, entry to the box may not be made until the state tax commission representative is present. A substantial delay could result.

In all other states, when the box is rented in the decedent's sole name, bank representatives will seal the box when they learn of the death. In such cases, a court order will be required to open the box. Usually, the order is limited to looking for and removing the will; the box is then re-sealed.

What you should do:

1. If you reside in a state in which the state tax representative need not be present when the box is opened, rent the box in the names of yourself and your spouse as joint tenants. On one person's death, the other may properly open the box.

2. If you reside in a state in which the state tax representative must be present, place your will in a box rented in your spouse's name and vice-versa. Or, if you control a family-owned corporation, have the corporation rent the box and place the will there. In this case, be sure your spouse has corporate authority to enter the box.

3. Leave the original will with your attorney or bank (if named as executor) and

keep your receipt in a place known to your family.

I can't find my original will. I think I left it with my lawyer but I can't remember his name. How can I revoke my will?

Execute a new will and declare that the new will revokes your old will.

How else is a will revoked?

While the laws of each state determine how a will is to be revoked, a will generally is revoked as follows:

1. By your subsequent valid will which says directly or indirectly that it revokes an earlier version. (Naturally, it is desirable to say so directly.)

2. By you, the testator, cutting, tearing, burning or mutilating the will, or by having someone else do this in your presence with your consent.

3. By a final divorce or an annulment of your marriage. (Bear in mind the difference between a final divorce and a separation.)

4. If, after the execution of the will, you as testator marry and a child is born of the marriage, or one is adopted, provided that the child is not provided for by the will. In some states, *either* your marriage or the birth of a child causes the will to be revoked.

My will was executed ten years ago. My wife and children are all living. I do not need to bother with the will anymore, right?

Wrong! A will should be reviewed every three to five years or even more often if your finances or family situation changes.

When you first executed the will, your children may have been minors. You might have designated your mother as the guardian for the children. Ten years later, is she still physically able to care for the children?

Did you perhaps provide for trusts for your children and have they by now demonstrated financial maturity so that you would wish them to receive their shares of your estate outright?

Has another child been born to you and your spouse, one for whom you failed to provide under your will? In some states, when a child is born after a will is executed (known either as an *after-born child* or as a *pretermitted child*) and you have not provided for such child in your will, all or part of the will is deemed to be revoked.

Have the amount and titling of your assets changed so that a will which was logical and fiscally sound ten years ago is no longer appropriate?

Give me some examples of what you mean.

1. Your mother was designated guardian of your minor children when she was 62. She is now living in a nursing home in frail health. Your oldest child is now 20 and your youngest child is 12.

   Your mother should be replaced as guardian of your youngest child by your oldest child.

2. When you wrote your earlier will, your two children were uncertain about what they wanted to do and wanted time to travel and think. Your daughter is now an attorney, happily married, and has one child. Your son is an engineer and head of a large industrial unit.

   Your earlier will and your spouse's will left all the property after your spouse's death to a bank, as trustee. The wills provide that the trustee may distribute income to the children, and, on the death of both the remaining property is to be held in trust. It now appears that the children are mature and should receive the property outright.

3. When your will was written your sole assets were a home, some savings, and property in West Virginia. These assets were worth $125,000. Both you and your spouse provided that your children receive everything outright. Oil now has been discovered on your West Virginia property and the property is worth a great deal of money. You should consider whether or not your children should inherit the property outright on the deaths of you and your wife. It may be advisable to give them their shares at five-year intervals.

I lived in New York when I executed my will. I now live in Maine. Must I have my will rewritten?

While not necessary, it is wise to have your lawyer review the will.

If the mechanics of executing the will (the "formalities") were in accordance with New York law, then Maine law says that the document will have full force and effect in Maine. Every state has a similar rule.

However, the laws of one state creating, defining and regulating property rights (as distinguished from the procedural requirements—the "formalities") may be different from those of another state. It is therefore wise to have a lawyer review the will to point out any problems due to differences in the laws of the state to which you moved.

What laws apply to a decedent's property?

Generally, the state laws governing the decedent's domicile determine rights to personal property, but the laws of the state where real property is located determine rights to that real property.

The laws of a particular state may change this general rule.

CONTENTS OF WILLS

Please tell me what, in your opinion, a will should contain.

1. State your full name. If you are known by any other names, list them.

   Comment: Your name is Mary Smith and you own stock registered in the name of Mary A. Smith. Your estate may have difficulty re-registering the stock unless it can be shown that Mary Smith and Mary A. Smith are the same person. It is far simpler to prove the fact when it is clarified by the will.

2. State where you consider your principal residence to be.

   Comment: The court that has principal jurisdiction over your will and the property disposed of by your will is the court located in the place where you have your principal residence. (Technically, your principal residence is referred to as your *domicile.*)

   There are tax reasons for making this statement of your residence. The general rule of death taxation is that with respect to all of a decedent's property, other than real property, the state in which you reside has jurisdiction to impose taxes. (A *decedent* is someone who is dead.) Hence, by clarifying your place of residence, you simplify for the estate representatives the determination of which state has the proper authority to tax your property. This also simplifies the decision as to which court properly has jurisdiction over the administration of the estate.

   It should be noted, too, that even when you declare where your residence is, a state other than the one in which you declare you live is free to ignore your statement and to make its own determination as to your residence. There are times, though rare, when two or more states try to tax your estate. Declaring where you reside will be helpful in preventing two states from trying to impose death taxes on your estate.

3. State that the will revokes and supersedes (takes the place of) all prior wills and codicils (a *codicil* is an instrument that revokes, changes, or adds to the terms of a will).

   Comment: This should be done even if you do not remember having an earlier will. Why take the chance that an earlier will was not revoked and still has legal effect?

4. Give your instructions with respect to the disposal of your body and funeral arrangements.

   Comment: In many states, the representatives of your estate may not spend above a certain amount for your funeral without special authority given by your will. If this authority is not given by your will, it may become necessary to secure a court order. Giving instructions will avoid the expense and delay of requesting a court order authorizing the amount of money that has already been spent on your funeral or the amount desired to be spent. Without appropriate language in the will, the court has the discretion to deny the necessary permission.

Also, if you wish to be cremated or to donate your body or any of its parts (eyes, kidneys, etc.) to medical science for research or transplantation, you should clearly so provide.

If you want your body to be used for scientific purposes, you should carry with you a written expression of your wishes. Otherwise, by the time your will is located, it may be too late to carry out your instructions since you could already have been buried or cremated. Obviously, if you have a surviving spouse, he or she will know of your wishes. Eye banks, kidney foundations, medical societies, and hospitals can provide printed forms which you can sign, have witnessed, and carry with you. Some states' drivers' licenses also contain optional directions for body or organ disposal.

---

5. Do *not* direct the payment of all "just debts."

Comment: Too many wills are written with the testator's direction that the estate pay all "just debts." The law is clear that debts *must* be paid, regardless of what is said in the will. So why say anything about debts?

You may then ask, what harm is done by a reference to "just debts?" The answers are:

a. You may owe the federal or state government money for past income taxes. The law may prohibit the collection of such taxes because the statute of limitations ran out on the debt. (A *statute of limitations* is a law that imposes limits on the time period during which someone may sue or collect debts; such a statute also applies to the federal and state governments.) But while these statutes of limitations may prevent taking action with respect to debts, they do not prevent you from voluntarily paying debts. The question raised is, when you direct by your will the payment of "just debts," have you voluntarily agreed to pay these "outlawed" debts and, therefore, is your estate then required to pay them?

If you do not wish your estate to pay debts on which the statute of limitations ran out, why say so?

b. You may owe money on a mortgage. You may have left property to a cousin but the property may be subject to a mortgage for which you, and then your estate, are legally liable.

Do you wish to have your estate pay off the entire mortgage? If you do not, then why state in your will that all your "just debts" should be paid?

Using such language could be cause for a court suit to determine exactly what you meant—an unnecessary expense and possible result you did not intend.

6. Direct the passing of your household furnishings, paintings, silverware, art objects, automobiles, etc., to your spouse, if living, and if not living, to your then-living children.

Comment: In many states, when a residence is owned by a husband and wife as joint tenants or tenants by the entirety, the contents of the residence are considered owned in the same fashion. In such a case, the survivor will become the automatic owner on the spouse's death.

This rule (whereby the survivor becomes the automatic owner) does not apply in all states and usually does not apply when residence is owned by you in your name only, nor does it usually apply to automobiles, a boat, or other valuable vehicle, such as a recreational vehicle. When the survivor does not become the automatic owner, and if the testator did not specifically bequeath these objects, there could be serious and substantial adverse income tax consequences. These consequences could arise when the survivor acquires ownership of these assets.

A detailed explanation of these rules will be found in this book beginning on page 152.

7. Dispose of the "rest, residue, and remainder" of your estate. (The words *rest* and *remainder* have been interpreted by the courts to mean the same thing as *residue.* Customarily, lawyers refer to the balance of the testator's property, after specific bequests, as the rest, residue, and remainder of that person's property.)

Comment: Residue is what is left after something is taken out. We want to be sure that the will disposes of *all* your property. If everything is not disposed of, the remaining property must be disposed of as *intestate* (undisposed of by will) property. State law will determine who will inherit intestate property. To avoid having state law determine who will inherit part of your property, and to dispose of your property as *you* wish, your will should state who will inherit the residue of your estate.

Under the topic of *death taxes* later in this book, we will discuss what may be desirable from the tax point of view. However, in this section we wish to establish what the will should contain to be sure that your loved ones receive what you intend them to receive.

To illustrate, we will discuss several different situations.

a. When you die, your parents, wife, and three children survive you.

Assume that you wish to leave some property to your parents to supplement their incomes. You might then leave $100,000 to trustees in trust, and direct them to pay the income from the $100,000 to your parents for life; on their deaths to pay over the trust property to your wife outright; and if she is not then living, to pay the same to your children. When your will is prepared, we obviously do not know who will be living on the date of your death. The language of the will should therefore take care of all possibilities. In this case, the language of your will should be substantially the following:

"If either of my parents survives me, I give and bequeath the sum of $100,000 to Jane Doe, my wife, as Trustee. My Trustee shall pay the net income [the balance of the income remaining after all expenses are deducted] therefrom to my parents, in equal shares, or all to the survivor of them surviving me, so long as each shall live, and in addition, my Trustee may give, at any time or times, to either of my parents during such parent's lifetime, such sum or sums from the principal of the trust, including the whole thereof, as, in the absolute discretion of my Trustee, may be deemed necessary, advisable or desirable for the health, maintenance or support of my parents or either of them.

"Upon the death of the survivor of my parents, the trust shall terminate and my Trustee shall pay over and distribute the trust, as then constituted, to my said wife if then living and if not then living to my children then living, in equal

shares, or all to the survivor of them then living."

You should consider the following:

If neither of your parents is living at the time of your death, there would be no reason to create the trust. Therefore, you will note that the language of the will states that you give the sum of $100,000 to your trustee only if either of your parents survives you.

On the death of your parents, the trust terminates (ceases) and the trust property is paid over to your wife, but only if she is *then* living. "Then" refers to the date when the survivor of you and your parents dies, since there will be no trust if neither of your parents survives you. I have seen wills that inappropriately say that the trust property shall be paid over to someone's wife if she survives *the testator*. She may have survived the testator but dies before the death of the survivor of your parents. For example, assume you died in 1970, your parents died in 1980, and your wife died in 1975. If the will uses the (incorrect) language that the property shall be paid over to your wife if she survives you (the testator), this could cause two major problems.

First, if your wife is not living when your parents die, the property will be paid over to her estate. By reason of this the property will be needlessly subject to death taxes in *her* estate, and needlessly subject to delay and expense since the property will be administered as part of her estate.

Second, if your wife remarries and dies without a will, and she is not living when your parents die, your property may be required to be paid over to her second husband. This will, of course, reduce the amount of your property that your children will receive.

Third, if both of your parents die after your death and your wife is not *then* living, you may perhaps wish to leave the property to *your* brothers and sisters or perhaps to a charity. However, if you leave the property to your children who survive *you* (rather than restrict the bequest to such of your children as are *then* living), the property may be left to one of your children's spouses. This happens because even though your children are not living when the survivor of your parents dies, they were living when *you* died. The law then requires their interests under your will to be paid to their estates. If the interests are paid to the ones who are entitled to inherit such child's estate, they may then belong to such child's husband or wife. Leaving your interests to a *child's* husband or wife may be in accordance with your wishes. But if it is not, then provide that a child receives a share only if he or she is living at the time of the death of the survivor of your parents.

b. When you die, your wife and three children survive you.

In this case the language of your will should provide substantially as follows (remember, we are not now taking into account any tax results):

"All the rest, residue, and remainder of my estate, I give, devise, and bequeath to my wife, Jane, if she survives me, and if she fails to survive me, to my children surviving me, in equal shares, or all to the survivor of them surviving me."

Please note that the language here does not take into account the fact that a child may die before you but has children (your grandchildren) surviving you. If you wish to leave property to the child or children of your deceased children, language similar to what appears in the next example should be used.

c. When you die, your wife, three children and two grandchildren survive you.

The language of your will should provide substantially as follows:

"All the rest, residue, and remainder of my estate, I give, devise, and bequeath to my wife, Jane, if she survives me, and if she fails to survive me, to my issue surviving me, per stirpes."

Here, you would have to recall two things. First, the word *issue* means all your descendants. This includes children, grandchildren, great-grandchildren and so on. Second, the words *per stirpes* (which is further explained on pages 55–56) explain the portions that your descendants receive. The older generation takes a share to the exclusion of younger generations and the younger generations take only the share that their ancestor would have taken if he/she were alive. For example, your three children are named Arthur, Benjamin, and Cathy. Arthur dies before you but leaves two children surviving you. By using the quoted language, Arthur's two children (your grandchildren) each would inherit a one-half portion of the one-third share of your estate that Arthur (the ancestor of your grandchildren) would have inherited had he lived at the time of your death.

If you wish to leave property only to your children, then you should say:

". . . to my children surviving me, in equal shares, or all to the survivor of them surviving me."

d. When you die, only your wife survives you.

The language of your will should provide substantially as follows:

"All the rest, residue, and remainder of my estate I give, devise, and bequeath to my wife, Jane, if she survives me."

It is always advisable to name your wife because you may have remarried after you signed your will. The wife you had when you first signed your will may have died before you. Therefore, if the language you used in your will only states that you leave your entire estate to your "wife," there could be questions raised about whether you intended your second wife to inherit your property.

An important factor in writing a will is to eliminate questions as to what was intended. By naming your wife, there can be no questions about your intentions.

You could certainly argue that if you remarry you will redo your will. But what if you never get around to doing so or go off on a honeymoon with your new wife (before you have a new will) and die in an automobile accident? In this case you obviously will not have clarified the matter.

e. When you die, only your three children survive you. The language of your will should provide substantially as follows:

"All the rest, residue, and remainder of my estate I give, devise, and bequeath to my children surviving me, in equal shares, or all to the survivor of them surviving me."

Here, should only two children survive you, then the two children inherit your entire estate. If only one child survives you, then this one child inherits your entire estate.

f. When you die, only your brothers and sisters survive you.

The language of your will should provide substantially as follows:

"All the rest, residue, and remainder of my estate I give, devise, and bequeath to my brothers and sisters surviving me, in equal shares, or all to the survivor of them surviving me."

As in the case of paragraph *e*, only those among your brothers and sisters who are living on the date of your death will inherit from you.

The language used in each of the preceding situations is designed to be a guide only and is not intended to be complete. It is strongly recommended that a lawyer be consulted.

---

8. Provide for the disposal of *all* your property in the event, however unlikely, that none of your referred-to family members survives you.

   Comment: Every well-written will should state what happens in the event that *none* of the persons you name, or refer to, survives you. (Professionally, this is referred to as providing for *remote contingent beneficiaries.*) For example, you, your husband, and your two children are killed in a plane crash. Who will inherit your property and your husband's property? Proper consideration to this possibility would suggest that appropriate language be inserted in both wills to take care of this situation.

---

9. Consider the source of the payment of death taxes. If no special provision is set forth in the will as to what assets are to be used for payment of death taxes, with certain exceptions, each asset is required to pay a proportionate part of the tax. This may not be in accordance with your wishes.

---

10. If you have a minor child or children, you should appoint a guardian of the person and property of your children. The general rule throughout the United States is that the surviving parent has the power and authority to appoint a guardian for minor children in case of the survivor's death. Many people forget that the oldest child, if he or she is not a minor, may serve as a guardian of minor children.

    I have used language similar to the following in wills I have written for clients:

    "I nominate, constitute and appoint my then oldest legally competent child to be the guardian of the person and property of all children of mine who may be minors at the time of the death of the survivor of my spouse and me."

So that I can be aware of possible problems in the will I now have or in the will I am planning to have, please advise me what problems you have encountered or learned about in the course of your professional career.

---

1. Gifts to charity.

In the legal profession, when the word *gifts* is used in connection with leaving property on death, it really means the same as a *bequest* (leaving personal property by will) or a *devise* (leaving real property by will). When used in a will, the term gift is not limited to the kinds of transfers most people are accustomed to making during their lifetimes, either at Christmas or for birthdays, weddings or other occasions.

When making a gift by will to charity, the precise name and address of the charity should be used. Too frequently, there are two charities with similar names. When you die, you are no longer there to tell which you meant and your wishes may not be carried out as you had hoped. So if there are two charities with similar names the court will decide which you meant. Apart from the problem of which charity will eventually receive the property, the court process involved is very costly because lawyers will be hired for each charity and for your estate, and each lawyer usually receives a legal fee. Sometimes a legal fee is paid from the assets in your estate. This determination depends upon the laws of your state as well as the discretion of the court.

In some states, when certain members of your family are living, you may not leave to a charity any property that is larger than a certain percentage of your estate. You should check this with your lawyer. Also, in some states you may not leave property to a religious organization when you die within a certain period of time after your will is executed. The reason for this last rule is a historical one and is designed to protect the testator from undue pressures from the representatives of the religious organization.

---

2. You leave your property to your children.

If you have an adopted child, is it your wish to have this adopted child included among the words "child or children"? If you have a child who, in turn, adopted one or more children, is it your wish to include these adopted children (of your child) among those included in any gifts you make to grandchildren? If, during your marriage, a child is born to your wife by artificial insemination and you are not the donor of the semen, do you intend such child to be included among your children?

In most states, by statute, the word "child" is defined to include adopted children (as well as illegitimate children under certain circumstances). Yet, if one of your children is adopted, be certain that he or she will inherit the property you intend such child to inherit based on the laws of the state. It is therefore wise to consult your lawyer about the answers to these questions.

---

3. You make a gift to your issue.

When you refer to your *issue*, the word includes all your descendants. But the real question here is whether you wish to leave your property to descendants living at any time during your lifetime or only to those living when you die.

For example, you have three children who are named Al, Bob, and Cathy. Al had one child and Bob and Cathy each have three children. Al and his child both died before you. Is it your intention to leave property to the estate of Al or perhaps the estate of Al's child, even though they are not living at the time of your death, because they come under the definition of "issue"? Undoubtedly not.

There are certain rules of construction that lawyers and the courts follow which state what happens when you leave *class gifts* (class gifts are gifts to a number of persons who are not named but who fit a general description). The usual rule of construction in the United States is that when you make a gift to a class, in this case to *issue,* the persons who inherit are those who are living at the time of your death. However, why leave these interpretations open to question, or to possible changes in the law or in court rulings?

Be specific!

If you wish only Bob and Cathy to inherit your property you can arrange this by saying in your will that you leave your property to "my issue surviving me, *per stirpes.*" By adding the words *per stirpes,* you have indicated in a shorthand way that if Bob or Cathy is living, then the children of Bob and Cathy do not inherit the parent's share.

By stating "to my issue surviving me," you have indicated that those who inherit property from you must be living at the time of your death. Thus,

since Bob and Cathy are both living, they would inherit your property, but neither Al's estate nor Al's child's estate would inherit your property. Unless you clarify your wishes it is possible for Al's estate to inherit a share. His share may then be inherited by his wife, since his wife may be entitled to inherit all or part of Al's estate.

What has just been stated is meant by way of illustration and is not intended to be a recitation of all possible similar problems.

---

4. You leave your property to "A and his children."

I have reviewed wills in which this language was used. It is not specific enough.

I would imagine that you meant to leave your property to A if he is living at the time of your death but if he is not living, then to his children if living at the time of your death. However, too often wills are written with imprecise language and the courts then have the problem of trying to understand what your intent was.

Did you really mean that if A has three children living at the time of your death and A is also living, your property would be divided into four shares? Or did you mean that A receives all of it if he is living at the time of your death and that if he is not living his children inherit his share? Or did you mean that A inherits one-half and his three children inherit the other half?

To complicate this matter further, assume that A at one time had four children, one of whom is now dead. Was it your intention to leave one part to this dead child's estate?

Because of imprecise language, the answers to these questions are not clear. It is obvious that the will should be more specific. It is suggested that you state that you "give, devise and bequeath all of my property to A if he survives me and if he fails to survive me, to his children surviving me, in equal shares, or all to the survivor of such children surviving me."

---

5. *You leave your property to your brother, John, and his wife, Mary, if both survive you.*

The problem here is that you do not specify the shares that each owns nor do you specify the form of ownership.

If both of them are living at the time of your death, do they inherit your property in equal shares or as joint tenants with the right of survivorship? If they own the property equally, then on the death of one of them the other does not inherit all the property remaining; however, if they own it as joint tenants the survivor of John and Mary will own it all.

Do not leave the determination of what you intended to a court; clarify this in your will.

---

6. *You leave all your tangible personal property to your brother, Frank, if he survives you.*

By definition, *tangible* refers to something that you can touch and feel. Usually when tangible property is left to someone by will, what is meant is household goods—flatware, clothes, furnishings, etc. All too frequently people forget that they own other "tangible" property. For example, is it your intention to leave your brother, Frank, your automobile or perhaps your 40-foot speedboat? What about your Moped, bicycle, or perhaps your expensive golf cart? They, too, are tangible personal property.

More importantly, you may be the owner of a stamp collection or a valuable painting worth $30,000. Is it your intention to leave this to your brother?

Your will should be specific and clarify what you mean. It is not necessary to itemize each item and this is usually *not* done, but you should consider the preceding comments before you and your lawyer write your will.

I have also reviewed wills in which the lawyer who wrote the will wrote that the testator leaves all of his *personal property* to an individual. The lawyer forgot (or never knew) the distinction between *tangible personal property* and *personal property*. The term *personal property* is much broader than *tangible personal property*. For example, if you own stocks in a company, savings bonds, passbooks, or certificates of deposit, these items would be personal property. When the clause of the will is read, the context of the gift indicates that the intention was to leave the personal household furnishings (tangible personal property) and not *all* personal property. Yet, because wills are invariably strictly construed, when the term *personal property* is used, most courts state that they are bound by the language the testator used and are not free to speculate as to what was meant. Therefore, if you use the phrase *personal property,* this language could be binding on the disposition of your property.

---

7. *You leave a house to your cousin Fred.*

The house has a mortgage. The mortgage could have been placed on the house after you wrote your will or perhaps even before you wrote your will. In many states, the law provides that when property is specifically left to someone by will and the property has a mortgage on it, the person receiving the property is entitled to have the mortgage paid off from the balance of your estate. This is known as *exoneration.*

But aside from this rule, you should consider whether this result is what *you* wish. Is it your intention to have the balance of your estate pay off the mortgage at the time of your death so that Fred receives the house free from the mortgage? Or is it your intention that Fred receive the property *subject to* the mortgage (in other words, Fred will have to pay it off)?

Since it is your property that you are leaving, your wishes should prevail and this matter should be considered by you and included in your will.

8. *You are angry with your sister, Joan, because you felt that when your father died and she took the grandfather clock, she cheated you. Your will recites that you direct that Joan shall receive nothing from your estate because she cheated you years ago.*

This statement is libelous and Joan can sue your estate for damages. The damages she can recover may be the entire amount of your estate.

A will is an inappropriate place to express such sentiments.

---

9. *You leave your entire estate to your first cousin William. Your will states that you request William to use the funds for the benefit of all your cousins.*

The question that arises here is whether the language you used in your will is clear so that William *must* use the property for the benefit of the cousins. In other words, have you imposed a trust upon the property so that the property is not really owned by William but is held by him for the benefit of your cousins? Or are you really expressing the hope that he *may* do so, but that the decision is strictly at his discretion?

For example, you leave your property to your husband. You then state that it is your "wish and will" that your husband give your daughter, Kathy, $10,000 when she marries to help set up her household.

When Kathy marries is your husband *obligated* to pay her $10,000? Does the language "wish and will" mean that your request is mandatory or is it merely the expression of a hope that is not legally binding on your husband?

While the courts always wish to determine and enforce the intention of the testator, bear in mind that the will is probated after your death and that you are not here to clarify your wishes. It is therefore important for you to be specific in your will. Whether your wishes are mandatory and legally binding or merely expressions of a wish, which is not binding, should be made clear by appropriate language.

(The technical term used by the courts when the language is not binding is *precatory*.)

---

10. Every will should take into account the effect of death taxes. This is done by either directing the source from which death taxes shall be paid or deciding to do nothing about such direction.

The general rule is that if nothing is said about death taxes, the property inherited is reduced by its proportionate share of death taxes. A simple example of this rule is where A inherits $75,000 from your estate and B inherits $25,000. If the total tax is $12,000, then A's share of the tax will be $9,000. This is because A inherited three-quarters of the total of $100,000 and his share must therefore bear the burden of three-quarters of the taxes.

Since three-quarters of the total tax of $12,000 is $9,000, this amount will be allocated to A's share.

I know of a situation in which an individual died with considerable wealth. The only property owned by the testatrix in her individual name—that is, the only probate asset—was a farmhouse with the surrounding land, worth approximately $75,000. Everything else the testatrix owned was in joint names. The death taxes of this particular estate amounted to $60,000.

The will of this testatrix directed that all death taxes be paid from the rest, residue, and remainder of her estate. She also provided that the farmhouse was to be held for the benefit of her long-time employee and friend, Mary, who was the housekeeper. Mary was to be able to live in the house rent-free for her lifetime and without the payment of any repair or insurance expenses. The only expense Mary would have would be for utilities and property taxes. The testatrix felt that with the small savings that Mary had, plus Social Security and lifetime cash gifts that she made to Mary, Mary was well provided for. However, all her plans were spoiled since the will directed that taxes be paid from the rest, residue, and remainder of her estate. Because the only property in the rest, residue, and remainder of her estate was the farmhouse, this farmhouse had to be sold to pay death taxes. This was a sad end to a situation in which someone did not consider or understand the consequences of the particular tax clause.

What the testatrix should have done was to set aside money to pay the death taxes or to have said nothing about them at all. If nothing were said about taxes, everyone who received property on the death of the testatrix would have had to pay a portion of the taxes imposed on the estate. That is, even those who inherited jointly-owned property would have had to pay a proportionate part of the taxes. Then perhaps one acre of the land inherited by the housekeeper could have been sold to raise the cash to pay her proportionate part of death taxes, leaving the farmhouse and most of the land intact for Mary's benefit.

---

11. **You leave 1,000 shares of Exxon stock to your son, Jimmy. At the time you made your will, you owned 1,000 shares. Since then, there have been two stock splits. In addition, you reinvested the dividends by purchasing additional shares of Exxon stock. At the time of your death, you own 8,000 shares of Exxon stock.**

Is it your intention that your son receive only 1,000 shares as you stated in your will? Or is it your intention that he receive all shares owned on the date of your death or all the shares that originated with the original 1,000 shares that you owned?

The laws of most states originated with the laws of England. During the course of history, the courts of England as well as of the United States have had to decide literally thousands of cases involving meanings of wills. During this time, rules, called *rules of construction,* have evolved. These rules of construction were designed to help the courts decide what the testator meant in each case. Yet it is obvious that there is no rule of construction that is as precise as clear instructions from you, the testator. If what you meant by the direction in your will was that Jimmy shall inherit all the shares of Exxon stock owned by you on the date of your death, then say so.

There is a further problem if, on the date of your death, you do not own any shares of Exxon. This problem arises because of a rule of law known as *ademption.* In general, this rule states that where specific property is left to someone and on the date of death the property is no longer owned by the testator, the legatee receives nothing because the gift is considered to be *adeemed* or "wiped out." In this case clarification is needed as to whether you as testator left your son the 1,000 shares of stock owned when you executed the will. In other words, was there a specific bequest? If so, since the 1,000 shares were not owned on the date of death the gift would be adeemed. On the other hand, did you as testator intend that your son receive 1,000 shares of Exxon stock on your death, whether or not you owned the shares on the date of your death? That is, is the executor required to go out and purchase 1,000 shares of Exxon stock?

If it is your desire as testator that your son receive the equivalent of the value of the 1,000 shares as of the date of your death, whether or not you own these shares on the date of your death, you should be specific and say so in your will.

---

12. **You make a gift to your daughter, Suzanne, if she is an adherent of the Jewish faith at the time of your death.**

Theological authorities, just as lawyers, judges, etc., have varying opinions as to what constitutes being an "adherent of the Jewish faith." Do you intend to leave property to your daughter only if she is practicing the dietary laws at the time of your death? Is it your intention that your daughter be required to observe the Sabbath as set forth in the Bible? Your daughter may have married someone outside the Jewish faith. If she did marry outside of the Jewish faith but was nonetheless an adherent of the Jewish faith in important respects, was it your intention that she should or should not inherit any part of your property?

Suppose you provided in your will that your estate was to be divided among your nieces and nephews who survive you *and* were Catholics who abided by the laws of the Roman Catholic Church. Would a niece who practiced artificial birth control be entitled to inherit a share of your property? Was it your intention that instead of abiding by all the laws of the Catholic Church

she would inherit a share if she were a practicing Catholic?

By failing to be clear as to what you mean it may be necessary to have a court decide what you intended. A court proceeding is costly and time-consuming. In addition, the court may reach a conclusion which may not be in accordance with your wishes.

---

13. **By will you leave property in trust for the benefit of your children.**

Many problems can arise in this type of situation. For example, you provide that the trust shall give income to your son, John, but the will fails to mention when the trust terminates (ends). In such a case, John may never receive principal and he would receive income only during his lifetime. Then, on John's death, the problem arises as to who is then entitled to the trust principal when the trust terminates.

If you provide that the trust terminates on John's death and the trust principal is to be distributed to John's children, Chris and Richard, in equal shares, the will should clarify whether they must be living at the time of John's death. If this is not specified, the laws of most states provide that if a descendant is dead at a time when he is entitled to possession of any property, his estate would inherit his share. This occurs because of a law known as the *anti-lapse statute*: the share of the dead person does not "lapse" or fail, but is nonetheless inherited by that person's estate. Therefore, if Chris dies before

John but has a husband who is living, it is possible for Chris's husband to inherit all of her share or perhaps one-half of her share. This result may follow (1) if Chris left a will leaving all her property to her husband or (2) under the laws of intestacy (if she left no will) which specify who will inherit all of Chris's property interests. (Most states provide that when an individual dies without a will, survived by a spouse and children, the surviving spouse inherits one-half the property left by the decedent.)

In most cases it is natural for people to leave their property to their spouses and then to their descendants, but not to spouses of their descendants. If Chris has children you would undoubtedly wish them (your grandchildren) to inherit *your* property before Chris's husband does so. If Chris has no children, it is possible that you would wish Richard to inherit Chris's share before Chris's husband does so.

The appropriate language to use for you to benefit your descendants would be language similar to the following:

"The trust shall terminate upon the death of my son, John. Upon termination, my Trustee shall pay over and distribute the trust principal, as then constituted, to my then surviving issue, per stirpes."

You will notice that the suggested language does several things.

a. It specifies what property shall be distributed (namely, the principal then held).

b. It specifies that the ones who shall inherit are those living at the time of John's death (to "my then surviving issue"; the word *then* refers to the date of John's death).

c. It specifies how the division shall be made by the use of the phrase *per stirpes* (Chris's living children inherit the one-half share that Chris would have inherited had she been living at the time of John's death).

Another example: You provide for disposition of the trust principal to your son, John. You provide that he shall receive one-third of the trust principal at age 21, one-third at age 25, and one-third at age 30.

Is this correct? No! Why isn't this correct? Because the language used does not dispose of all the property. An illustration will readily show why this is so.

Assume the property is at all times worth $10,000. Then at age 21, John will receive $3,333 (1/3 of $10,000), leaving a balance of $6,667. At age 25 he will receive 1/3 of $6,667 or $2,222, which leaves a balance of $4,445. Finally at age 30, he will receive 1/3 of $4,445 or $1,482, which leaves a balance of $2,963. This balance of $2,963, you will note, is left in the trust and you have not made provision for its distribution.

Appropriate language should take care of this situation.

Another example: You provide that all the trust property is held until

John dies or attains age 35, whichever occurs earlier; but if John dies before age 35, the property shall be distributed to his wife, Mary.

At the time you created the trust under your will, John was married to Mary. However, when John dies, say at age 34 (before he is entitled to all of the principal), he is no longer married to Mary, having been divorced from her for the last six months. It would seem to me that no consideration was given to whether or not Mary would be John's wife at the time John died. Appropriate language should therefore be inserted to take care of this situation.

In addition, language should be inserted that requires Mary to be living at that time. If this is not done and you live in a state where there is an *anti-lapse* statute, then Mary's estate would inherit the property. In this case *her* closest relatives would inherit the property. This means that if there are no children of John and Mary then living (your grandchildren), *her* parents and *her* brothers and sisters would inherit *your* property.

Perhaps you provide that all the income shall be distributed to your son, John. No provision is made for distribution of principal.

Were you alive and your son in need of large sums for his health, support, or education, you would obviously pay whatever was needed. Why then limit distributions from the trust to income only? If no provision is made for distributing any sums from the principal, the trustee would be unable to distribute principal. Giving the trustee discretion to distribute principal should be considered by you when the will is prepared. If it is your desire to be restrictive in this regard, this can be done by limiting the trustee's exercise of such discretion to "emergency needs" for your son's health, etc.

---

14. By will you leave property in trust for the benefit of your wife, Joan, and on her death the property is to be paid over to her children.

As obvious as it may seem, you will note that this provision does not take into account the fact that your wife may remarry and have additional children by a second husband.

The will here leaves the property to her children and is not limited to your descendants. If it is your desire to leave your property to *your* descendants, then say so directly or by using language similar to the following:

"If my wife, Joan, survives me, the trust shall terminate on the death of my wife, Joan. On termination the trust principal, as then constituted, shall be paid over and distributed to the children then surviving of the marriage of my wife, Joan, and me, in equal shares, or all to the survivor of such children then living."

15. *Other major problems.*

It should be clear that a will disposes of property owned by you at the moment of your death. Assume that the principal asset you own is a stock certificate representing the ownership of one-third of the stock of a family-owned corporation. Your two brothers own the other two-thirds of the stock.

The stock was inherited from your parents and for the last 20 years or so you and your brothers ran the business in harmony. Each of you took an equal salary which gave each of you a good living. If the business were sold to an outsider each of you would receive approximately $250,000.

On your death you leave your entire estate to your wife of 25 years. What is the most important asset you leave to her? The stock certificate. What can she do with the stock certificate? Will she receive income from it? Since the stock certificate only represents a one-third interest in the corporation, the other stockholders really control the business. The economic benefits from the corporation are controlled by your two brothers. They can withdraw all or most of the profits in the form of salaries and other employee benefits. They may declare no dividends on the stock, preferring instead to use the money in the business. Can your wife sell the stock to an outsider? Legally yes, but who would buy it when the stock really has no current value?

Can your wife compel your brothers to sell the business to an outsider so she will have at least the benefit of the use of the $250,000? The answer is no.

This seemingly valuable asset is really almost valueless because it may give your wife no present income or capital. The stock is then only a piece of paper that seemingly represents something worth $250,000 but in reality does not.

What should have been done?

a. A stockholder's agreement should have been entered into which *requires* the corporation or the other stockholders to purchase the stock of any deceased stockholder. In this way the stock would be sold to or redeemed by the corporation or the other stockholders. The estate would then receive $250,000 and in turn your wife would really receive what you thought she should receive, namely $250,000.

This agreement is commonly referred to as a *Buy-Sell Agreement* or a *Stockholder's Redemption Agreement*. The purpose of this agreement is to turn a piece of paper, the stock certificate, into an asset worth its proportionate share of the business. Without the agreement, the stock has little economic value. Your brothers would then end up owning 100% of the business without any interference or claims by your wife.

b. An agreement could have been entered into whereby your wife would be entitled to be employed by the corporation at the same salary as your brothers or perhaps she would be entitled to a continuation of your salary as a form of deferred compensation based on your past employment.

It must be recognized that a stock certificate represents only a percentage ownership of a corporation. Unless this stock represents a majority interest in the corporation or has contractual rights, the actual dollar value of the stock is severely limited.

The point to be noted here is that while a will may be well-written and have provisions that are 100% suitable, unless care is taken to see how the will will work with the assets you own, all your plans may not work out.

I have seen several situations that turned out to be disastrous for the testator's family. The will was beautifully written and well thought out. What the maker of the will forgot was how to implement its provisions. For example, in one instance the principal asset owned was stock in a successful restaurant. The decedent was the owner of 40% of the stock. He was the manager and received a yearly salary of $45,000 plus the use of a car.

When he died the other stockholder hired another manager, his nephew, for $60,000 per year and the stockholder took for himself a salary of $30,000 as a part-time employee.

After paying these salaries the corporation had no profits to be able to pay as dividends. The wife of the 40% stockholder inherited his stock but could not turn it into cash. All she had was a piece of paper (the stock certificate) that said she owned 40% of the stock of the corporation that owned the restaurant.

If the restaurant were sold, her share would have come to $160,000 but she had no way of forcing the 60% stockholder to make the sale. Had there been a stockholder's agreement or employment agreement, she would have been protected. The will therefore was, as a practical matter, worthless.

The lesson to be learned is that one should look at one's assets and see if they have economic value apart from the will. If not, try to make them productive after your death.

These principles also apply to other potentially valuable interests such as partnerships. An example will illustrate what is meant.

Suppose that during lifetime Hal was a one-third partner with his two cousins in a large resort hotel operation. Hal was in charge of the food operation, one cousin was in charge of the front desk and grounds, and the other cousin was in charge of the office and finances. The business was started by an uncle long dead. The three cousins each lived on the premises with their families, rent and tax free, and each drew a salary of $80,000 yearly. Not bad!

There was a short partnership agreement. After all, nothing elaborate was needed among cousins. To keep the business in the family the agreement provided that as long as any of the cousins lived, the partnership would continue. Nothing else of importance was in the agreement.

When Hal died the two remaining cousins voted to hire their two sons to replace Hal at an annual salary of $40,000 each. Hal's wife was not an employee and was asked ever-so-politely to vacate the premises.

As in the past, after salaries, cars, etc., the partnership had no profits to distribute to Hal's widow and family. The one-third partnership interest which, on a financial statement had great value because of the value of the land and buildings, had little value to Hal's family.

Hal's family could not compel the partnership to dissolve or to sell its land and buildings. Nor could his family derive any income from the partnership; there was none.

Had Hal, or his advisors, given any thought to this situation, he would have realized that a will is like a funnel. The funnel is only as good as the assets one can "pour" into it. In this case the partnership interest was not well protected.

From time to time people change their minds about the amount of property they wish to leave someone. Assume you leave $10,000 to your good friend and neighbor, Sybil. After a bitter argument you decide to eliminate this bequest to her. You take out the original of your executed will, and in ink you cross out the statement about the bequest to her. You also decide to change two other gifts at the same time. The gift to your godchild, Eunice, is increased from $10,000 to $20,000 and the one to your cousin, Franklin, is reduced from $7,500 to $5,000.

The gifts to Eunice and Franklin were changed by your crossing out in ink the figures in your existing will and inserting the new amounts.

Your acts create problems. Some states require that for a will to be valid the formalities of execution must be strictly complied with. Also, different state laws set forth how a will is to be revoked. When you strike out a gift or change its amount, what has really happened? The act may be a revocation of part of the will.

Some states permit a revocation of part of a will. Thus, in these states the gift to Sybil can be revoked. In those states that do not permit a partial revocation, striking out Sybil's name and the dollar amount or the entire sentence will really have no legal effect.

When you changed the amount, you did not insert the new amount with the formalities required for execution of wills. In those states which permit a partial revocation of a will, a further complication arises. Since the new amount has no legally binding effect, the question is whether you intended that the prior gift (the gift of $10,000 to Eunice) really be revoked, but only if the $20,000 gift becomes legally binding. Or did you intend to revoke the old gift completely whether or not the new gift was valid?

It may be easier to answer the last two questions when an amount is increased than when it is decreased. I would be of the opinion that in the case of the gift to Eunice, in which the amount is increased but the increase is not effective, you would have wished Eunice to have at least the lower amount. However, I am not so sure of the answer in the case of the gift to Franklin. In this case you reduced the gift from $7,500 to $5,000. Would you rather that Franklin receive nothing instead of $7,500? After your death you are not here to explain to the court what you meant. Even if the court does decide the question in the way you would have wished, a court proceeding is an expensive matter, far more expensive than it would cost to redo your will or prepare a codicil. (See page 51 for a definition of codicil.)

Enough has been said here to convince you, I hope, that once a will is executed, no changes should be made in it without consulting with your attorney. Usually the easiest way to make changes is to do so by codicil.

I have a bank account whereon I have named my sister Jane as joint owner. At the present time, I really would want to leave the money in this account to my sister Mary. Can I do so by will?

No. A will only disposes of property individually owned by you at the moment of your death. When you have a joint bank account, at the moment of your death the joint owner becomes the sole owner. Therefore, your will does not operate to affect ownership of this account. (There is an exception to this rule in New York with respect to *Totten Trusts,* and there may be exceptions for certain kinds of bank accounts in certain states. Your lawyer should be consulted.)

I have named my sister Jane as the beneficiary of my life insurance. I now wish to name my sister Mary as the beneficiary in place of Jane. Can I do so by will?

No. The insurance company which issued the policy is bound by the contract that you made with it to pay the beneficiary you named on the form provided to you. At the moment of your death, you do not own this policy or its proceeds; at the moment of your death the owner becomes the named beneficiary.

If you do not name a beneficiary at all, the contract with the insurance company, with rare exceptions, provides that it will pay over the insurance proceeds to your estate.

If the proceeds are paid over to your estate, then of course you will have the right to dispose of the proceeds by your will.

I have named my sister Jane as the person to whom all my U.S. Series E Bonds will be paid on my death. I now wish to name my sister Mary as the beneficiary. Can I do so by my will?

No. The payment of the proceeds of U.S. savings bonds are governed by United States Treasury regulations. These Treasury regulations provide that the proceeds will be paid to the beneficiary you designated during your lifetime. Whatever you write in your will with respect to leaving these bonds to someone is not legally controlling and would not be effective to accomplish what you want to do.

What do I do to make the changes that I desire?

In the case of the bank account, you should go to the bank and fill out a new signature card, instructing the bank as to what you wish done with your money on your death. If you are named as the only owner of the account, then on your death the proceeds will be paid over to the executor of your estate and in this case, the language of the will would control the executor in terms of how this money is left.

For the insurance policy, contact your insurance agent or the home office of the insurance company and ask for a change of beneficiary form, then insert the name of the beneficiary you desire, sign the form, and mail it to the agent or the insurance company. The change will be recorded by the company which will then send you an acknowledgment that this has been done. This is the simplest way to handle the matter. The insurance proceeds can of course be paid to your estate and in such a case, the language of the will will take care of who gets the proceeds.

In the case of the savings bonds, a change of beneficiary form is available at the bank or at the regional office of the Federal Reserve Bank. If you follow the instructions on this form, you can make whatever changes you desire.

Lately I have not been getting along too well with my second wife. I would rather leave all my property to my children. Can I do so?

Usually not.

For the purpose of this discussion, we must first assume there is no written agreement between you and your current spouse providing what happens to your property upon the death of either of you. If there is such an agreement, it is really a contract that is binding on you. If you break the agreement, the court will enforce it even after your death and may require the executor of your estate to satisfy its provisions. This type of agreement is called a *pre-nuptial agreement* (when it is entered into before marriage).

In general, each state has its own laws as to what amount of your property *must* be left to your spouse. Except for such laws, every person is generally free to leave his or her property to whomever he or she wishes.

At one time, many state laws protected the wife by giving her *dower* rights in the property of her deceased husband. These dower rights took many forms. As a rule, a dower right took the form of giving the wife an interest for life (called a *life estate*) in the real property owned by her husband at any time during the marriage. The protection of the laws was extended to such an extent as to give such dower rights even if the husband disposed of the property during his lifetime.

Incidentally, this is why a wife may have been asked to sign a deed in the past when property was sold. The effect of signing was to give up any dower rights in the property.

Protection for the husband, similar to dower rights, was extended in the form of giving him *curtesy* rights in the property of the deceased wife.

The majority of states now have abolished or greatly modified dower and curtesy, and have instead given certain rights to the surviving spouse. (Remember, *spouse* refers to one's husband in the case of a wife and to one's wife in the case of a husband. *Surviving* refers to the one who outlives the other.)

These rights take different forms in the several states. Usually they provide that the surviving spouse is entitled to a certain percentage of the estate of the dead spouse. If this is not given by will, then the surviving spouse can elect to take the minimum share provided for by that state's law.

An example of this situation would be when the husband dies first and leaves the following assets:

A house that is jointly owned with right of survivorship to his wife and is worth	$150,000
An insurance policy insuring his life with his wife named as beneficiary. She receives from the insurance company the face amount of	$200,000
Stock of a corporation that is worth	$300,000
	$650,000

The husband's will leaves his wife $75,000 and the balance to his children by a first marriage. I pointed out earlier that the will is effective to dispose of property owned by the husband individually at the moment of death. It is clear that the wife will become the sole owner of the house since it was titled in her name and her husband's name as joint tenants with right of survivorship. She survived him and at the moment of his death she became sole owner.

The proceeds of the insurance policy, or $200,000, will be paid to his wife by the insurance company since she was named as the beneficiary of the policy.

Let us assume that Maryland law applies here. Maryland law states that a surviving spouse (whether male or female) may elect to take, instead of property left by will, one-third of the probate estate if there are surviving issue and one-half if there are no surviving issue. Here the wife was left $75,000 under the will, but actually received a total of $425,000 by reason of the husband's death (the house plus the insurance proceeds plus the $75,000 bequest). Yet the law now permits the wife to elect against the will. She will therefore be entitled to receive $100,000 (instead of the $75,000 bequest) which is one-third of the $300,000 he left in his probate estate, in addition to the house and the insurance proceeds.

(The effect of death taxes has not been taken into account in order to simplify this illustration.)

I have left my spouse $150,000 by naming her the beneficiary of my pension plan. Since I own in my own name $100,000 in stocks and bonds, may I leave all $100,000 to my children?

Probably not.

The laws of the several states usually provide that the property individually owned by you is the property that is subject to the laws dealing with the minimum share your spouse is entitled to. Regardless of the amount of property (other than individually owned property) which you leave your spouse, your spouse is still entitled to the "minimum share" provided for by state law from your *individually* owned property (the property controlled by the terms of your will).

The stocks and bonds are individually owned by you and the laws of most states provide that your spouse would be entitled to her statutory or minimum share from these assets.

I live in California. Do these rules as to how much I must leave my spouse apply to me, too?

No, but the rules as to what you own are different, too.

California, together with Arizona, Idaho, Louisiana, Nevada, New Mexico, Texas, and Washington, has *community property* laws. In general, these laws provide that all property acquired by either the husband or wife during the marriage is community property. (The marriage is considered something like a partnership or "community"; this community property is in general limited to property acquired during the marriage.) The following are usually excepted from being considered community property:

1. All property owned before marriage.
2. All increases, profits, and income derived from property owned before marriage.
3. Property acquired by either the husband or wife by gifts, devise (that is, inherited under the terms of a will), or descent (that is, inherited from someone who dies without a will).

The important legal effects of property being considered community property are:

1. Each party to the marriage is considered to own one-half of such property.

2. One party to the marriage cannot dispose of any part of the community property to third parties during his or her lifetime without the consent of the other party.

3. On the death of one party to the marriage, the dead party (the decedent) may be restricted from leaving his or her share of the community property to whomever he or she wishes.

In community property states, the general rule is that, on death, one spouse may dispose of his or her share of community property as he or she wishes. With respect to property that is not community property, the law varies from community property state to community property state. It is therefore wise to consult an attorney in your state for the answers to your questions.

I remarried 15 years ago. Since then, my children will not talk to me. I wish to leave them nothing under my will. May I do so?

Yes.

In every state except Louisiana, you may disinherit children and leave them nothing. Louisiana requires that you leave some property to your children.

If I wish to leave my children nothing in my will, must I name them and leave each $1?

In most states, no. However, in a good number of states, if a person dies leaving children who are not named or provided for in the will or otherwise, the children not named are entitled to take some share of your estate as though you died without a will (*intestate*).

Even in those states where you need not name a child whom you disinherit, you should do so when a child is born after you make your will. If you do not do so, the child will take that part of your estate as though you died intestate.

In general, if a child is left nothing by will, it is wise to name the child. This advice is based on the general rule that in order to make a will you have to be legally competent and of sound mind. As pointed out earlier, the courts have adopted a simple test to see if someone is competent. The test determines whether the person has a general knowledge of his or her affairs and knows the natural objects of his or her bounty. A child is usually the natural object of one's bounty.

Therefore, if your children are not named as the ones to eventually inherit your estate, an argument can be raised by them that you were not competent to make a will.

To be more specific, let us discuss the following example. You are a widower who became infatuated with a lady 25 years younger than you are. You have lived with her for two years and wish to leave her all your property because she has made you so happy. Your children will receive nothing. If you do not mention your children in your will, they may contest the will. They can state that since you did not provide for the natural objects of your bounty, your children, you were not competent to make your will. If the court decides that you were not competent, you will have died intestate (without a valid will) and all your property will go to your children.

Generally speaking, the question of your competence is one for the trier of fact, which would be a jury or a judge. If the jury or judge can be convinced of your incompetence, the one you wished to benefit, your lady friend, may not be benefited.

What can you do to prevent this result in this situation? Simply name your children and leave them each $1. They can still claim you were incompetent, but cannot do so on the basis that you were not aware of the natural objects of your bounty.

I was married years ago. The marriage ended in divorce. I want to treat my children by my first marriage equally with my children by my second marriage but I want to be certain my first wife receives none of my property directly or indirectly. Please advise what can be done.

I must first assume that there is no agreement between you and your first wife whereby you agree to leave her some of your property by will. If there is such an agreement and you do not fulfill your agreement, your first wife will then be a creditor of your estate. If there is a separation agreement, you should show it to your lawyer for his review in preparing your will.

The principal problem arises if you leave, say, 20% of your estate to your two children by your first marriage. If you leave this percentage to them as outright owners they may do with the property as *they* see fit. They can then give the property to their mother (your first wife). Also, we must assume that a child of yours could die without leaving a spouse or children surviving him or her. If the child dies without a will (remember, the child may be legally incapable of making a will because of age), in most states the surviving parents inherit all of such child's property. In each case, then, the child's mother (your first wife) would essentially be inheriting *your* property.

Consider leaving such children's shares in a trust and either not giving them any income during the life of their mother (which is designed to prevent their mother from benefiting from such income) or giving them income but not giving them principal until the death of their mother.

My husband died without a will. We have two children. Under the laws of my state, I inherit half the property and my children inherit the other half. I am the estate's personal representative. One of the items owned by my husband when he died was a 26-foot power boat worth $50,000. I will be retitling the boat next week so that I will be the sole owner of it, giving my children an equivalent amount of cash. Later on, after all taxes are paid, the estate will

be distributed. Should I transfer ownership of the boat to myself now?

The answer to this question depends on what income the estate has and the timing of the distribution. It is therefore important that you should first have your accountant or lawyer analyze what the taxable income of the estate will be. To the extent that there is income from the estate during the period in which you distribute the boat to yourself, you may be legally required to report the income for income tax purposes. The explanation that follows will clarify this statement.

While an estate, if large enough, is required to pay death taxes, it may *also* be required to pay income taxes. For example, an estate sells the business it owns and collects $100,000 by reason of the sale. The estate's representative invests the $100,000 in a certificate of deposit at a bank. The interest from the $100,000 is $10,000 per year. This $10,000 is income that is subject to federal income tax.

Now let us assume that the estate distributes the $10,000 to the beneficiary who is entitled to this income. The estate will now receive a deduction for the $10,000 and will have no taxable income. However, the beneficiary will be required to report the $10,000 as income and pay the appropriate income tax on this amount.

The technical tax name given to what income the estate or the beneficiary must report for income tax purposes is *distributable net income* or *DNI*. (DNI does not quite mean the same thing as taxable income. But for purposes of this book we

will be treating DNI as though it meant taxable income.)

Not everything that an estate receives is part of its taxable income. An example of this is the prior situation in which the business was sold. The $100,000 received would not be taxable income if the business was valued at $100,000 for estate tax purposes. (Why not? Because the amount received was equal to its basis, that is, its value for estate tax purposes. There is no income when something is sold for the same amount as its basis; all that occurs is the recovery of principal.)

One further rule: An estate's taxable income is figured on its income for its taxable year. Most of us report our income on a calendar year basis. This means that whatever money or property we receive as income between January 1 and December 31 of any year is our taxable income for that year. An estate is considered to be a new taxpayer that comes into being on the date of the decedent's death. At this time, the estate has the right to pick its taxable year. The estate representative has the choice whether to have the estate's taxable year end on December 31 or at the end of any other month. Once the choice is made, a change cannot easily be made.

Now let's apply these rules to your question about transferring ownership of the boat. Let us assume your husband died on February 15. Assume, too, that the income of the estate will be $48,000 per year on the average, or $4,000 per month.

If the estate chooses December 31 to close its taxable year, then it will have income of $42,000 (the income for February being only $2,000, since it is for one-half month). If you distribute the boat, worth $50,000, to yourself on February 28 of the year your husband died, the law will require you to report all of the income of the estate generated during this period as your income. Since the income of the estate for the period ending December 31 is $42,000, you (the beneficiary) will be required to report this $42,000 as your income. As a general rule then, bear in mind that any distribution by an estate constitutes taxable income to the extent there is any taxable income in the year when the estate makes such distribution.

To pursue this matter further, assume that you distribute to your children $50,000 ($25,000 to each) in cash and that it is also distributed on February 28. Since the income of the estate is $42,000 (remember— we referred to this as distributable net income or DNI) the law now requires that this income be apportioned among you and the children. Since you received 50% of the total amount distributed, you would report 50% of the $42,000 of DNI, or $21,000, as income in your taxable year ending December 31. Each of your children would also report $10,500.

If no distribution is made by the estate, then the $42,000 of income is taxable to the estate at its applicable rate. When the $42,000 is taxed to you (or to you and the children), the estate gets a deduction for this amount and the estate will have no income tax to pay.

To answer the question—there should be an analysis of your other income and the other income of your children. Then your accountant or your lawyer would prepare tentative income tax returns for the estate, you, and your children, showing what the total taxes would be both ways—that is, if a distribution is made and if a distribution is not made. The method that produces the lowest tax would be most advisable.

The reader should be aware of two possible variations to the above. The first one, based on the facts just given, is to have the estate pick a taxable year that ends February 28. If the estate income (DNI) for this short period is only $2,000, and the boat worth $50,000 is distributed on February 28, you would be considered to have income of only $2,000. The balance of the value of the boat, or $48,000, would not be considered to be income. The reason for this is that you are only taxable on income to the extent of the estate's taxable income (DNI) for its taxable year. Since the estate's DNI here was $2,000, this is the limit of the income that you will be taxed on.

The second possible variation is for the estate to select as its taxable year the period ending January 31 of the following year. In this case the income for the 11 1/2 months (from the preceding February 15) would presumably be $46,000. If the boat is distributed to you on February 28, while you would be required to report $46,000 as your income, the income would have to be reported by you only in the following year. This is possible because of another rule that says that income received from an estate is income to the beneficiary only in the year of the estate ending within the beneficiary's year. This enables you to defer paying taxes for a substantial period of time.

The reader should note that the rules just mentioned also apply to the taxation of income from trusts.

These rules are complex and their application to your situation requires the assistance of an experienced accountant and a lawyer.

The reader should be aware of an important exception to the taxability of distributions from an estate. The exception provides that when a will bequeaths a specific item or cash, referred to as a specific legacy, the recipient is *not* considered to have received any taxable income from the estate. For this reason we suggest that (1) there be a will and (2) the will specifically bequeath tangible personal property to the extent desired.

TYPES OF WILLS

I have heard about a *joint will*. What is it?

One document which is usually signed by husband and wife, and which represents the will of each party. This document is sometimes referred to as a "joint and mutual" will.

In a joint will the terms usually provide that the one who dies first leaves everything to the other. Then, on the death of the second party, everything is left to specified persons, usually children.

A joint will sounds like a good idea. A joint will could save me legal fees. Also, it saves the bother of having two pieces of paper. Do you approve of joint wills?

No.

First, it takes more time for the lawyer to draft (write) a joint will than to draft two separate wills. The more time it takes, the higher the legal fee. Second, many state courts have found that a joint will is really a contract for the survivor to leave his or her property the way the will read on the death of the first of you to die. In such cases, there could be substantial adverse tax consequences. If you really want to contract to leave your property a certain way, then say so and ask your lawyer to prepare an appropriate agreement.

What is a *self-proved will*?

In many states, when a will is probated the witnesses must appear personally before the court, or a representative of the court, to testify to the facts relating to the execution of the will.

In an attempt to simplify this procedure the laws of many states now provide that when an affidavit is signed by the witnesses setting forth the facts about the will's execution, their personal appearance in court is not necessary. A will that is submitted to a court for probate and has this affidavit attached or presented separately is called a self-proved will.

Sample Affidavit

An example of such an affidavit is as follows:

STATE OF ....

COUNTY OF .... ss.:

Each of the undersigned, individually and severally, being duly sworn, deposes and says:

The within will was subscribed in our presence and

sight at the end thereof by .... ,

the within named testator, on the ....

day of ...., 198 .... , at

....

Said testator at the time of making such subscription declared the instrument so subscribed to be his last will.

Each of the undersigned thereupon signed his name as a witness at the end of said will, at the request of said testator and in his presence and sight and in the presence and sight of each other.

Said testator was, at the time of so executing said will, over the age of eighteen years, and, in the respective opinions of the undersigned, of sound mind, memory and understanding and not under any restraint or in any respect incompetent to make a will.

Said testator, in the respective opinions of the undersigned, could read, write and converse in the English language and was suffering from no defect of sight, hearing or speech, or from any other physical or mental impairment which would affect his capacity to make a valid will. The will was executed as a single, original instrument and was not executed in counterparts.

Each of the undersigned was acquainted with said testator at such time, and makes this affidavit at his request.

The within will was shown to the undersigned at the time this affidavit was made, and was examined by each of them as to the signatures of said testator and of the undersigned.

The foregoing instrument was executed by said testator and witnessed by each of the undersigned affiants

under the supervision of .... , attorney-at-law.

_____

_____

Severally sworn to before

me this ....

day of ....,

198 ....

_____
     Notary Public

What is a *living will*?

A living will is a separate document in which a person, while competent to do so, expresses a wish that his life should not be prolonged by artificial, extraordinary, or heroic measures. This type of will does not involve disposing of one's property.

Is a living will legally binding?

It probably is binding in those states that have laws dealing with this subject. The states that have enacted such laws are Alabama, Arkansas, California, Idaho, Illinois, Kansas, Nevada, New Mexico, North Carolina, Oregon, Texas, Vermont and Washington. The District of Columbia also has such a law. These laws are variously called *natural death acts, right to die laws,* or *living will laws*. Such a will may be legally binding and enforceable in other states as well, but this is not as clear and as certain as in those states that have laws on the subject.

What does such a will look like?

The form most used has been prepared by an organization called Concern for Dying (250 West 57th Street, New York, New York 10019). A copy follows:

To My Family, My Physician, My Lawyer and All Others Whom It May Concern

Death is as much a reality as birth, growth, maturity and old age—it is the one certainty of life. If the time comes when I can no longer take part in decisions for my own future, let this statement stand as an expression of my wishes and directions, while I am still of sound mind.

If at such a time the situation should arise in which there is no reasonable expectation of my recovery from extreme physical or mental disability, I direct that I be allowed to die and not be kept alive by medications, artificial means or "heroic measures." I do, however, ask that medication be mercifully administered to me to alleviate suffering even though this may shorten my remaining life.

This statement is made after careful consideration and is in accordance with my strong convictions and beliefs. I want the wishes and directions here expressed carried out to the extent permitted by law. Insofar as they are not legally enforceable, I hope that those to whom this Will is addressed will regard themselves as morally bound by these provisions.

Signed _____

Date _____

Witness _____

Witness _____

Copies of this request have been given to

_____

_____

I have heard about *holographic wills*. What does that term mean?

Generally, a holographic will is a will that is *entirely* in the handwriting of a testator and is signed and dated. The laws of each state specify when and under what conditions such wills may be made.

The main difference between wills that are holographic and other wills is that, when permitted, holographic wills need not have attesting witnesses. Many states permit such wills only when a testator is in the U.S. Armed Services and makes the will while outside the United States.

What is a *noncupative* will?

Oral wills are also called *noncupative wills*. While all states require that the will be in writing, there are cases in which this requirement is waived. The usual exception is when a will is made on one's deathbed, in which case an oral will is permitted. An oral will is one in which the testator states his final wishes in front of appropriate witnesses. (The laws permitting oral wills also usually require three witnesses, death within a certain period of time after making such a will, and certain other conditions.)

COURTS

What is meant by *probate*?

Probate is the procedure required by law whereby the court having jurisdiction accepts (or rejects) the instrument as being the will of the decedent.

What does one's probate estate consist of?

Property owned by the testator in his own name as sole owner at the moment of death. The will disposes of this property, and this property is therefore the *probate estate*.

While the testator may own one or more policies of life insurance insuring the testator's life, if a beneficiary was named, that beneficiary becomes the sole owner of the insurance proceeds at the moment of death. Therefore the will of testator has no control over ownership of the proceeds. If the beneficiary is the estate of the testator, then the provisions of the will would control the ownership of the proceeds. During his or her lifetime the owner of the policy has control over who is named as beneficiary.

Lawyers, the courts, and others will sometimes refer to the probate estate as the "estate."

What do you mean by the court having jurisdiction?

Jurisdiction is the legal authority granted by state law to an appropriate court to exercise its power over the particular subject matter.

Why is it necessary to give any court jurisdiction over my property?

The right to leave property by will to the person or persons of one's choice is not a constitutional right. This right is given by state law. State law requires that before ownership of property is turned over to the person or persons you name in your will, all debts you may have and also all federal and state death taxes must first be paid. The courts are given jurisdiction to see that these objectives are fulfilled.

It is important to emphasize the required end-result of court jurisdiction over wills. It is

1. to establish entitlement to ownership of property or the benefits from it and to transfer ownership of property to the person or persons entitled to it,

2. to see to it that the ones entitled thereto do indeed receive the property or as directed, the benefits from the property,

3. to pay all debts due from the deceased person whose estate is being administered and to give creditors time to

notify the estate's representative of the existence of such claims, and

4. to pay all federal and state death taxes that are due.

What is the name of the court that has jurisdiction?

Each state gives the court a different name. In some states it is called the *Orphans' Court*, in some the *Probate Court*, *Surrogate's Court*, the *Prerogative Court*, or the *Court of Ordinary*.

Sometimes, the language used in a will has to be clarified by the courts to determine what the testator meant. In such cases, jurisdiction may be given to courts (other than those named above) to answer the questions raised. The power given to these other courts may be in addition to or instead of the courts first named. The courts that have such jurisdiction are called by various names. Some of the names used are *Superior Court*, *Circuit Court*, or *Supreme Court*.

What happens to a will which is not accepted by the appropriate court?

The will is not legally binding on anyone. However, members of the family may consider themselves morally bound by the wishes expressed in the will.

If the will is not accepted by the court, it is as though the maker of the will died without a will (*intestate*). In this case, state law determines who is entitled to the property owned by the decedent.

What do I do to be certain that my will is accepted for probate?

Be sure that you follow the law of the state in which you live or in which you sign your will. Each state has its own requirements as to what is necessary to have a valid will. An example would be the requirement that the testator be of a certain minimum age. Among the requirements are those related to the procedure that must take place when the will is signed. Required procedures are sometimes called *formalities*. They *must* be followed strictly.

What is the procedure to be taken on someone's death so that ownership of the decedent's property shall pass to those named in the will or, if there is no will, as provided by state law?

When there is a will the procedure to accomplish this is known as the *probate process*, and the process varies from state to state. In general, courts have a printed form usually called *petition for probate*. *Probate* means "to prove" and probate is the means whereby an instrument is proven to the satisfaction of the court as being the decedent's will.

When a petition is filed with the court, the court, through its employees, sends notices of the petition to all the interested persons named in the petition, or the petitioner does so. Interested persons are those named in the will, those who would inherit property if there were no will, and in some states, those who are named in a prior will or codicil. This gives those persons an opportunity to challenge the probate of the instrument that the court is asked to accept as the will of the decedent.

This procedure is designed to determine if the instrument that is offered for probate really represents the will of the decedent. If the instrument is not accepted as the will of the decedent, then it is as if the decedent died without a will.

The person who files the petition is usually the person or persons named in the will as the *executor* or *personal representative*.

After the will is probated, the property owned by the decedent is administered under the general supervision of the court that approves the probate of the will.

If the decedent dies *intestate* (without a will), a petition is submitted to the court requesting that the court issue an order giving the petitioner legal authority to represent the estate of the decedent and act on its behalf. This petition is usually called a petition for *letters of administration*. As when there is a will, after the petitioner is appointed the court will supervise the administration of the estate's property.

Once the court approves the petition (either to accept the will or appoint the petitioner as the estate representative when there is

no will), it will issue an order. The order will accomplish the following:

When there is a will

1. it will accept the document as being decedent's will;

2. it will appoint the legal representative of the estate, called the personal representative.

When there is no will it will appoint the legal representative of the estate, called the personal representative.

When there is a will the personal representative is required to administer and dispose of the estate property in accordance with the terms of the will. When there is no will the personal representative is required to administer and dispose of the estate property in accordance with state law.

The court procedure involved when one dies with a will is similar to the procedure if one dies without a will. To simplify the explanation, the following discussion will generally refer to both procedures as though the decedent died *testate* (with a will).

Is anyone else required to receive notice of the petition for probate?

Yes. In some states, the persons notified are also those who are adversely affected by a will or any codicil.

For example, assume that in your will you leave a gift of $5,000 to your friend, Jack Horner. You later execute a codicil whereby you reduce the amount of the gift to your friend, Jack, to $2,000 or you eliminate this gift entirely. Jack is adversely affected by the codicil. In many states, Jack would be considered a person who must be notified of the petition to probate the will and codicil.

Who submits the petition for probate?

Generally, it is submitted by the executor or personal representative named in the will. The petition could also be submitted by a surviving spouse or a child. Basically, any interested person can submit the petition.

When the decedent dies without a will, state law specifies which person or persons are entitled to petition the court to be appointed as the personal representative. In general, those persons most closely related to the decedent are the first ones entitled to be appointed. When more than one person is equally entitled to be appointed (such as children), the court may appoint all or may choose among them.

I have received a notice from the court that my mother's will is about to be probated. My mother left her entire estate to my sister. At the time my mother executed her will, she was living in my sister's house. I feel that the will should not be probated because the will represents my sister's wishes rather than my mother's. What can I do about this?

See a lawyer.

It should be noted that not everybody may come into court to object to the probate of a will. Those entitled to do so are usually interested persons adversely affected by a codicil.

When one does object to the probate of a will, documents are filed with the court contesting the probate of the offered document as being the will of the decedent. In some states, this procedure is known as *caveating a will*. (*Caveat* is Latin for "let him beware"; therefore, a *caveat* is a notice to the court to beware and not to accept the instrument as the will of the decedent.) The procedure is similar to any court trial and the one who objects to the probate of the will has the burden of proof to support his or her contentions.

What are the grounds for contesting a will?

The grounds for contesting a will can generally be divided into two parts: mechanical defects and substantive defects.

A document becomes a will only when it is admitted to probate. In order to be probated, it is essential that the document be executed in compliance with the formalities of state law. A failure to follow any of the formalities would be considered a mechanical defect.

Most states require that the will be signed in the presence of witnesses, that the witnesses be considered *testamentary witnesses* (in most states they have to be asked to serve as testamentary witnesses), and that the witnesses sign the will in the presence of the testator and in the presence of each other. If any of these formalities is not present, the instrument may fail because it does not represent the will (intent) of the decedent.

For example, you are home ill and you sign your will in the presence of your brother who serves as a witness. Your brother then takes the will and alone goes next door to your neighbor and asks your neighbor to serve as a witness. You are not present when your neighbor signs as a witness. This will would be defective because you did not sign the will in front of both witnesses who, in turn, did not sign in your presence and in the presence of each other.

Another example: when you signed the will, six pages had been typed and were ready for your signature. The witnesses signed as they should have. The next day, upon rereading your will, you noticed that on page three of the signed will you made a gift to your friend of $3,000 and you really meant to leave your friend only $1,500. Rather than go back to your attorney, you retyped page three with the exact language of the first will but substituting $1,500 for $3,000. This will is defective because the formalities of execution were not satisfied. Some courts would admit to probate everything except page three or they might admit to probate everything except the change.

How would anyone know about these mechanical defects?

If called upon in court, the witnesses would have to testify about the facts. Also, copies of the will may be in existence and the copies may show variations between what is offered as the original and the copies. These are some of the ways that mechanical failures can be disclosed.

What do you mean by substantive defects?

In order for a document to be accepted by the courts as a will, the person signing the same must be of sound and disposing mind and capable of executing a valid deed or contract. If any of these elements is missing, there would be a substantive defect.

Give some examples of substantive defects in a will.

You may show that your mother signed her will by reason of fraud or by undue influence exercised upon your mother by your sister. Your mother may have been senile and without the mental capacity to execute a will. Your mother may have thought that she was executing an agreement of some sort rather than her will.

With respect to undue influence, you would perhaps want to show that in a prior will you were treated equally with your sister, that the attorney who drafted your mother's first will was her attorney of many years standing and that the attorney who drafted the last version of the will was your sister's personal attorney, or that your sister placed unfair pressure on your mother to sign a will leaving everything to her.

The preceding is not intended to be a complete statement of the law on this subject. Books have been written about how to contest wills and it is important that you consult your lawyer if you wish to contest a will.

The important thing to remember is that each state has a time limit during which you *must* file the appropriate papers to contest or *caveat* (serve notice to the court) the probate of a will. If the time limit is not strictly observed, you would not be able to contest the probate of the will even if you had a good case.

The court has now accepted the will for probate, or if there is no will, has approved the petition for appointment of the estate's personal representative. What happens now?

If you are appointed the personal representative you will need to establish your legal authority to "step into the shoes" of the estate; therefore, the court will issue a document under its seal called *letters of administration, letters testamentary,* or some other similar name.

Some courts issue *certificates of letters* (as they are called) evidencing your authority. In some states, you must order (and pay for) certified copies of the letters which you will need to submit to various banks, stock transfer agents, and others who ask for them. These certificates or certified copies of letters are evidence that you are the legal representative of the estate and as such, are legally entitled to act on its behalf, to secure possession of the estate assets, and to have temporary ownership of the property during the time the estate is being administered.

Before the letters are actually issued, the filing of a bond may be required.

A word of explanation about a bond: The purpose of a bond is to insure the estate beneficiaries and the taxing authorities against losses due to improper administration. The laws of most states require the filing of a bond for every estate unless waived. By choice, most wills that appoint a personal representative waive this requirement. However, when a decedent dies intestate there is no will that permits the bond to be waived. Therefore, in the majority of states, when a person dies intestate a bond will be required.

When a bond is required, the amount of the bond may be equal to the estimated value of the estate, twice the amount of the estate, or, for example, some in-between amount. The premium cost of a bond of $100,000 is approximately $460 per year until the estate is closed. The cost of a bond is one reason why it is important to have a will that can waive the bond.

WITNESSES

Tell me more about witnesses. Would it be advisable to have three witnesses?

The states of New Hampshire, South Carolina, and Vermont *require* three witnesses. However, even these states provide that a will is valid with only two witnesses if the will was executed in a state which allows only two witnesses. For example, New York law provides that a will executed there needs only two witnesses. Thus, a Vermont resident may execute his will in New York with only two witnesses, and the courts of Vermont will accept the will. If you own real estate in New Hampshire, South Carolina, or Vermont (where three witnesses are required) and are a resident elsewhere, it is advisable to have three witnesses.

Can my husband be a witness to my will?

In most states, there is no legal objection to this. In some states, such as New York, however, a witness is legally prevented (disqualified) from inheriting any property under the will when that witness is necessary to prove the will. For example, if there are only two witnesses to the will and one of them is your husband, the will is valid but your husband may not inherit anything under the terms of your will.

On the other hand, many states do not permit an interested person to become a credible witness. An interested person becomes a disqualified or incompetent witness. In states that apply this rule the will would *not* be valid; the witness may not even waive his rights to receive property under the terms of the will so that he can become a qualified witness.

In general, it is preferable to have two disinterested witnesses. These witnesses should be persons who can testify in court if it is necessary to prove that all legal formalities in connection with the execution of the will were satisfied.

What do you mean by *interested persons*?

An *interested person* is an individual who has a direct and immediate financial interest in establishing the validity of your will. For example, if you were to leave $10,000 to your sister in your will, she would be an interested person because she would have a financial interest in assuring that the will is probated.

The laws of many states provide that an interested witness is not a competent witness.

What happens to my will if the laws of the state in which I live and make my will provide that an interested person is

an incompetent witness, but an interested person becomes one of the two required witnesses?

Since your state requires two competent witnesses and the interested person becomes an incompetent witness, your will does not have the required number of witnesses. Therefore, the will cannot be admitted to probate and will have no binding legal effect.

Please explain these phrases:

YOU SIGN THE INSTRUMENT, OR BY SOME OTHER PERSON . . .

The usual procedure is for you, the testator, to sign the instrument using ink and signing your full name. If you are unable to write your name, you may place an "X" mark or your initials on the instrument as long as it is later shown that you intended the document (instrument) to be your will. If you cannot do that—for example, if you had a stroke and your hands are paralyzed—you can have another person sign your name. The other person must sign at your request and in your presence. In a few states, having another person sign at your request and in your presence may not be acceptable, so a lawyer should be consulted.

IT BE ATTESTED AND SIGNED BY . . . WITNESSES

Generally this means that the witnesses must intend to act as witnesses and in doing so must fulfill all the statutory requirements necessary to the legal execution of a will.

THE WITNESSES BE CREDIBLE

The word *credible* is the equivalent of *competent* and means a person who could legally testify in a court to the facts to which he or she attests.

Please give me an example of what you consider to be the correct language to use when the witnesses sign their names to my will. I understand this language is called an *attestation clause*.

The foregoing instrument, contained on this and the ( ) preceding typewritten pages, was on the date last above written, signed, sealed, published and declared by the above-named Testator, (insert name), as and for his Last Will and Testament, in the presence of us, who at his request, in his presence and in the presence of each other, have hereunto subscribed our names as witnesses.

_____ Address _____

_____ Address _____

_____

(If the person making the will is a female, substitute the word *Testatrix* for *Testator* and, of course, *her* for *his*. Also, if the will is executed in a state that requires three witnesses, add another line on which the third witness is to sign.)

Do the witnesses have to know how I disposed of my property?

No. All that is required is that they see you sign the document. In some states, they do not even have to see you sign as long as you acknowledge to them that the signature is yours.

TERMINOLOGY

TERMINOLOGY

Abatement: The reduction of a legacy because there is not enough property in the estate to pay it.

Ademption: When someone is left specific property by will, and on death the property is not owned by the decedent, the gift fails (is adeemed). For example, I leave you my wristwatch. On my death, I do not own that watch. The gift is adeemed.

Affinity: Relationship by marriage.

Ancestors: Those in your bloodline from whom you are descended. Your mother and father, their parents and grandparents, and so on, would be your ancestors.

Bequest: Technically, leaving personal property by will. Today, this also refers to leaving all types of property by will.

Class: When property is left to a number of persons who are not named but who fit a general description, the property is left to a "class." For example, bequests to your grandchildren or your issue would be a gift to a "class."

Codicil: An instrument which revokes, changes, or adds to the terms of a (prior) will.

A codicil must be executed with all the formalities of a will.

Collaterals: Relatives who trace relationship to an intestate (one who dies without a will) through a common ancestor. These relatives are neither descendants of the intestate nor ancestors of the intestate.

For example, your mother's brother (your uncle) is a collateral, as are your uncle's children (your cousins).

Consanguinity: Relationship by blood.

Descendants: Persons who have been born through someone's bloodline. The term includes every generation downward from the individual. For example, your father is not *your* descendant, but your children, grandchildren, and great-grandchildren are.

Descent and distribution: The laws of a state that set forth who inherits your intestate property and in what proportions. (Remember, *intestate* property refers to property not disposed of by will. Sometimes, too, when an individual dies without a will, we refer to that individual as having died intestate.) These laws are sometimes known as statutes or laws of descent and distribution.

Devise: Leaving real property by will. The person who receives real property by will is called the *devisee.*

Distributive share: The share of property that someone inherits when one dies intestate. It is possible for someone to inherit all of the intestate's property. For example, assume someone dies intestate, and has no spouse and only one child. In most states, the child inherits the entire estate. This (the entire estate) would be the child's distributive share.

Executor: The person or trust company which legally steps into the shoes of the decedent, temporarily owns all the decedent's property, and represents the estate in the eyes of the law. In some states, the title given to the executor or executrix is *personal representative.* Throughout this book the author uses the terms *executor* and *personal representative* interchangeably. You may appoint more than one person to serve as executor. If the executor is a trust company, it can serve as sole executor or co-executor.

Gifts, dispositions, passes, bequeaths: These words are really shorthand ways of describing the act of having ownership of property transferred from the testator to the one the testator wishes to benefit. The lawyer or author of law books would describe the property left by you to your loved ones as the *gifts* (the word *gifts or gift* has different meanings in different settings; here, we are only talking about gifts by will) made by you or the property that "passes" on death from you, or the "disposition" made by you of your property or the fact that you "bequeathed" your house to your spouse. You would be called the *transferor* and the one who receives the property would be called the *transferee.*

Grantor or settlor: The person who creates a trust during lifetime. When the trust is created by will, the creator of the trust is called the *testator,* which is the same name given to the one who makes a will. Sometimes the grantor is referred to as the *donor* or *trustor.*

Heirs: In most states today, the word means those who inherit property from those who die intestate (without a will). For example, if your will left all your property to your heirs, your property would be inherited by the same people, and in the same amounts, as if you died without a will.

The word *heir* usually means the same as *heirs at law* or *lawful heirs.*

Interested person: An *interested person* is defined by state law. In most states, it is a person who would inherit the property when someone dies without a will.

Inter-vivos trust: A trust created during lifetime, sometimes called a *living trust.*

Intestate: Someone who dies without a will. A person who dies with a will and fails to dispose of *all* his individually-owned property is referred to as leaving property by *intestacy.*

Issue: All descendants of a particular person. The term includes—in addition to children—grandchildren, great-grandchildren, and so on.

Lapse: The principle of law which provides that when a person who is left property by will (a legatee) dies before the testator (the maker of the will), neither the legatee nor the legatee's estate is entitled to receive the inheritance, since it "lapsed."

However, many state laws provide that when a person is named in a will or a class is indicated, even where the named person or any person who is part of the class dies before the testator, their respective estates inherit the share left to the person or class. This type of law is commonly referred to as an *anti-lapse statute*.

For example, you leave all your property to your children, John and Mary. If Mary dies before you, the bequest to her would lapse. However, if the state has an anti-lapse statute, then her estate would inherit the share of property she would have inherited had she lived. In this case, the property would in turn be inherited by those she named in her will (or if she died without a will, by those who would inherit her property under state law).

On the other hand, if you state in your will that you leave all your property to John and Mary if they survive you (or are alive on your death), then Mary's estate will not inherit her share. This is so since your will provided that they must be alive on the date of your death.

Many states have adopted variations of this lapse or anti-lapse rule which must be considered when a will is prepared.

Legacy: Leaving any type of property by will.

Legacy, demonstrative: A legacy of a certain amount to be paid first from a particular source. If the source is not sufficient to satisfy the legacy, then it shall be paid from the rest of the estate if there is sufficient property. For example, you leave someone the sum of $1,000 but direct that this sum shall first be paid from your savings account at the First Federal Savings and Loan Association. If, on the date of your death, the account balance is only $600 but your estate has other property valued at $80,000, then the person who is left $1,000 is entitled to the balance of the savings account plus $400 from the other property.

Legacy, general: A legacy or devise by will which is paid out of the general assets of the testator's solely-owned property but not from any specifically designated portion of it. For example, if by your will you leave someone the sum of $1,000 and do not limit this legacy as coming from a specific savings account, then the amount shall be paid from the general assets of the testator's estate.

Legacy, specific: A legacy of a particular article. For example, leaving your diamond bracelet or your new automobile to someone is making a specific legacy.

Legatee: The person who receives property by will.

Next of kin: There is disagreement as to the meaning of this phrase. The preferred view is that it means those who are the nearest *blood* relations. Thus, a surviving husband would not be included under this definition. Some courts interpret "next of kin" similarly to "heirs," that is, those who would inherit property if you died without a will.

Personal representative: See *Executor.*

Per stirpes and per capita: As a technical definition, *per stirpes* means "by the roots" or "by representation." It really refers to a method of distributing property. When the *per stirpes* method of distributing property is used, a group inherits the share to which their ancestor would have been entitled had such ancestor lived. This method is also referred to as a *per stirpital* method of distribution.

For example, assume you leave all your property to your "issue surviving you, *per stirpes.*" Assume you have three children named Ann, Betty, and Charles. Ann and Betty are dead, but Ann has four children (your grandchildren) living at the time of your death. Betty has one child (also your grandchild) living at the time of your death. Charles has no children.

Ann's four children share equally the one-third share that Ann would have received if Ann had survived you. Betty's child inherits the one-third share that Betty would have received if Betty had survived you, and Charles inherits one-third. Note that here the word *issue* includes all your descendants, children as well as grandchildren.

Per capita means "by the head." It also refers to a method of distributing property. Thus, each member of the group inherits equal shares.

For example, assume you leave all your property to your "issue surviving you, *per capita.*" Assume the same facts as in the prior example. That is, you have

three children, Ann, Betty, and Charles, and Ann and Betty are dead, etc. In this case, at the time of your death there are six persons living in the group. (The group consists of your issue.) These six persons are Ann's four children (your four grandchildren), Betty's one child (your grandchild), and Charles (your child). Your property would be divided into six equal shares.

The distinction between these two methods of distributing property, as applied to the prior example, is that when the property is left *per stirpes,* the property is divided into three equal shares (and Ann's four children share one of those three equal shares), but where the property is left *per capita,* the property is divided into six equal shares. Also note that under the *per stirpes* method a living parent inherits to the exclusion of his living descendents. Under the *per capita* method each living descendant would inherit an equal share of the estate.

The following illustration will help to clarify these rules.

Example and comparison, of distribution of property per stirpes *and* per capita.

Example: Three children, Ann, Betty, and Charles. At the time of your death. Ann is dead but has four children who survive you. Betty is dead at the time of your death but has one child who survives you. Charles is alive at the time of your death and has no children. (For convenience we refer to the children as A, B, and C and their children (your grandchildren) as A1, A2, A3, A4, and B1.)

Per stirpes method of distribution	Per capita method of distribution

A	B	C
A1	B1	
A2		
A3		
A4		

A	B	C
A1	B1	
A2		
A3		
A4		

Estate is distributed as follows

		Estate is distributed as follows		
A1	1/12		A1	1/6
A2	1/12		A2	1/6
A3	1/12		A3	1/6
A4	1/12		A4	1/6
B1	1/3		B1	1/6
C	1/3		C	1/6

If Charles had three children (C1, C2, and C3) and Charles and all his children were alive at the time of your death, the estate would be distributed as follows:

Estate is distributed as follows | *Estate is distributed as follows*

A1	1/12		A1	1/9
A2	1/12		A2	1/9
A3	1/12		A3	1/9
A4	1/12		A4	1/9
B1	1/3		B1	1/9
C	1/3		C	1/9
			C1	1/9
			C2	1/9
			C3	1/9

Sound mind: In general, this means that you, the testator, can understand the nature of the business in which you are engaged at the time you make your will, that you have a recollection of the property which you intend to dispose of, and that you understand the importance of the different persons who are or should be the natural objects of your bounty. For example, your spouse and children would be considered to be the natural objects of your bounty. Your close friends would not.

Spouse: A husband or wife.

Testamentary trust: A trust created by will. To create such a trust, there must be a direction to deal with property that is identified as the subject of the trust and to specify the beneficiary or beneficiaries who have certain rights and privileges in the trust property.

Testator: A male who makes a will. A female who makes a will is called a testatrix.

Trust: A device used for disposing of and managing property. Technically, it is the name applied to the relationship created between two or more persons, when one of them—the trustee—holds property for the benefit of another. The one for whose benefit property is held is called the *cestui que trust* or "beneficiary."

Written instrument: While it is clear what is meant by "written," the writing need not be in ink or by typewriter. If a pencil is used, this will satisfy the law, but pencil is not recommended. Pencil writing can be erased easily and someone can readily insert names, change dollar amounts, and commit other frauds.

ESTATES

General Information

Administration of an Estate

ESTATES

GENERAL INFORMATION

What does my estate consist of?

An estate generally consists of two parts:

1. Property owned by you outright in your own name as sole owner.

2. Property not owned by you outright in your own name as sole owner but in which you have some financial interest.

What is the practical difference between the two types of property ownership?

Property owned by you outright in your own name as sole owner has these characteristics:

1. Ownership of the property passes to whomever you designate in your will.

2. The property is usually subject to supervisory control by the courts.

3. The property is always subject to federal and state inheritance, estate, or similar taxes.

Property not owned by you outright in your own name as sole owner but in which you have some financial interest has these characteristics:

1. Ownership of the property does not usually pass to another under your will.

2. The property is usually not subject to supervisory control by the courts.

3. The property may or may not be subject to federal and state inheritance, estate, or similar taxes.

For example, if the title to property is registered in your name as sole owner, the property is an item that can be disposed of by will. (By "disposing of" property, we mean stating who becomes the owner after your death.) But if you, the testator, have the property registered in your name as joint owner with another, then on your death the *survivor* becomes the sole or individual owner of the item. Since the survivor becomes the owner at the moment of your death, your will cannot dispose of the property because it is not then owned by you.

Give me some examples of the two categories of property in an estate.

One category includes bank accounts (checking and savings), certificates of deposit, savings certificates, etc., for which you are shown as sole owner of this property. If stock is owned by you individually (in your sole name), whether the stock is in a publicly held company or in a privately held company, you may effectively dispose of it by will.

On the other hand, if you are listed as a joint owner of stock or bank accounts, the survivor becomes sole owner on your death. In such a case, you do not own the stock or the bank account at the moment of your death, and thus cannot dispose of it by your will. Proceeds of life insurance, when you have designated a beneficiary other than your estate, would also be treated as property that you cannot dispose of by your will. This is so because at the moment of your death the person named as beneficiary becomes the sole owner of the proceeds.

ADMINISTRATION OF AN ESTATE

What is meant by *administration* of an estate?

An estate consists of property owned by a deceased individual at the moment of death and owned only in the decedent's name. The process involved in collecting the assets belonging to the estate, safekeeping and investing these assets, paying the estate's debts, taxes, and expenses, and distributing the balance of the estate to those entitled thereto, is called *administering* an estate.

This entire process is sometimes referred to as *settling* an estate.

Where is an estate administered?

In the county of the state where the decedent was domiciled at the time of his or her death. The term *domicile* refers to that place where a person has resided with the intent to make that residence his or her fixed and permanent home. A person may have several residences (for example, one or more vacation homes) but only one domicile. For simplicity, we will usually refer to a person's *residence* but we will mean *domicile*.

The place of principal residence (domicile) is the place where the principal administration (sometimes referred to as *domiciliary administration*) takes place. When a decedent also owns property located in another state, administration of this other property frequently will be required in the other state. When this occurs the administration is called *auxiliary* or *ancillary* administration, which means administration that is secondary to the principal place of administration.

What is a *public administrator*?

When someone dies *intestate* (without a will) the laws of every state provide that certain persons are entitled to administer the estate. These laws generally set forth who is first entitled to this privilege. Usually this means that the spouse is first entitled, then children, then grandchildren, then parents, and so on.

If none of these persons is alive or able to serve, some states have a publicly-appointed official who then serves as administrator of the estate. This official is called the *public administrator*. Each of the counties of New York has a public administrator.

The public administrator's duties are similar to those of a personal representative or an executor: to collect the estate property, to pay all outstanding debts, to pay all due taxes, and to distribute what remains to those who are legally entitled to it.

What is a *fiduciary*?

The word describes someone who has a relationship with another which involves a duty to act for the benefit of the other party. The one who has this duty is called the *fiduciary*. Thus a guardian of your children, the trustee of a trust created under your will, or the executor of your estate, among others, is considered to be a fiduciary.

Instead of the court appointing an executor, I have read somewhere of courts that appoint fiduciaries with names such as *administrator cum testamento annexo, administrator de bonis non* and *administrator cum testamento annexo, de bonis non*. What are they?

If a will does not name an executor or if the executor does not serve and there is no successor executor appointed or capable of serving, the court appoints an individual or trust company to serve in this capacity. This fiduciary is called *administrator cum testamento annexo,* which means "administrator with will annexed."

In some states when someone dies intestate, the fiduciary appointed to administer the estate is called an *administrator*. (In other states, the title of the person who is appointed to administer the estate, whether or not there is a will, is *personal representative*.) If the administrator fails to complete his administration for some reason (death, resignation, incapacity, or removal), the court appoints an individual or trust company to serve in this capacity. This fiduciary is called *administrator de bonis non,* which means "administrator of goods not administered" (that is, not administered by the previous administrator).

If an executor fails to complete his administration of the estate and there is no successor executor appointed or capable of serving, the court appoints an individual or trust company to serve in this capacity. This fiduciary is called *administrator cum testamento annexo, de bonis non,* which means "administrator with will annexed, of goods not administered" (that is, not administered by the previous administrator).

Whom do you recommend to be my named fiduciary?

As *guardian*: A relative or friend, even your oldest child, who has the interest, warmth, love, and intelligence to take care of your children and has the ability (physical and financial) to do so. The guardian I have just described refers to the guardian of the person. This guardian determines where the minor child lives, goes to school, what dental care is administered, etc. The guardian of the property fulfills functions similar to a trustee. While each of these functions can be performed by different people, I am of the opinion that, if you trust someone with custody of your child, you should trust him or her with custody of that child's funds. Therefore the guardian of the person

should be the same person as the guardian of the property.

As *trustee*: One or more persons, a bank, or a trust company with the skill, experience, and intelligence to manage funds and possibly business enterprises over a possibly extended period of time.

State laws limit those who may serve as trustees, some states being more restrictive than others. Not every bank has the legal authority to act as a trustee. Sometimes banks which are authorized to serve as trustees have a name that indicates this power, such as Mercantile-Safe Deposit and Trust Company of Baltimore, Maryland, or Union Trust Company of Maryland. Some banks are well qualified to serve as trustees but their names do not disclose this power, such as the Maryland National Bank.

Your spouse or one of your children would be suitable, provided that this person either has the ability to manage the trust property or the experience or skill to select a suitable attorney, bank, broker, or accountant to assist with the several tasks. An attorney or accountant would be a good choice depending, of course, on experience and ability. A bank or trust company, serving alone or with a member of your family, the attorney, or the accountant, would be suitable.

As *executor* or *personal representative*: The duties of this individual are usually of a relatively short duration as contrasted with those of a trustee who may serve for an extended period. Nevertheless, the comments about the trustee are applicable here. The only possible exception is that there is less need to have more than one person serve as trustee.

A fiduciary is entitled to commissions or fees for serving in that capacity. Such commissions or fees are paid from the assets that the fiduciary administers. When appointing someone, this should be taken into account.

I wish to appoint my sister as guardian of the person and property of my minor children. You said that the guardian should have financial ability to serve. My sister's heart is big but her purse is small. Are you suggesting she not be appointed?

No, but funds may be needed for your children's care. If you left enough property, the income from the property would be adequate to take care of the children's needs. On the other hand, if you died without accumulated earnings or property, the guardian would need the means to feed, clothe, and educate your children.

You should be realistic and face this problem while you are alive and should plan accordingly. Consideration should be given to purchasing life insurance for this purpose.

What does a guardian do?

There is a difference between a *guardian of the property* and a *guardian of the person.*

The guardian of the property of a minor is the one who manages funds or property. The guardian of the person determines where the child lives, what schools he attends, what clothing and medical care he receives, etc. In other words, the guardian of the person stands in the shoes of the deceased parents. When preparing wills, we of course do not know whether the husband or wife will be the survivor. It is therefore desirable for each parent to state his or her wishes as to who shall be the minor children's guardian. Any such designation will take place after the death of both parents. Hopefully, both parents can agree upon a suitable person. Also, if possible, it is advisable to name one or more successors to the named guardians.

If a testamentary trust is created under your will, you should appoint one or more trustees to administer the trust property. It is also advisable to name one or more successor trustees. (Note: A trust company may be appointed to serve as sole trustee or as a co-trustee.)

What is a *personal representative*?

A *personal representative* is the individual or individuals, a trust company, or a combination of these, who legally steps into the shoes of the decedent, temporarily owns all the decedent's property, and represents the estate in the eyes of the law.

In some states, the name given to the personal representative is *executor* (if a male) and *executrix* (if a female).

Who appoints the personal representative or the executor?

The testator has the privilege to name the personal representative. (The *testator* is the one who makes the will.) The court will then issue an order confirming the appointment. If the testator does not name a personal representative or if he names him and the person cannot serve, state law provides whom the court may appoint. (Technically, the testator nominates the personal representative and the actual appointment is made by the court.)

If the decedent dies without a will or if the document is not accepted as the decedent's will, state law dictates whom the court may appoint.

I have appointed my friend John to serve as my personal representative. Under what circumstances would he be unable to serve?

Clearly, John has to be alive and willing to serve. The usual situations prohibiting him from serving are: he has not reached the age of majority, he has been convicted of a serious crime, he is not a United States citizen, or he is perhaps a judge of a court. In some states, such as Florida, a non-resident is prohibited from serving as a personal representative unless the person named is closely related to the decedent.

Do you have any recommendations as to whom I should appoint as my personal representative?

I do not recommend appointing anyone who may have a substantial conflict of interest. For example, there could be a conflict of interest if you appoint as your personal representative your partner in a business or the sole surviving stockholder of a corporation. The conflict could arise if there is an agreement that your partner, the corporation, or the surviving stockholder would have to compensate your estate for your interest in the partnership or corporation based on certain flexible and indefinite formulas provided in the agreement.

In this case, there would likely be a conflict of interest because it would be to the financial interest of your partner or the surviving stockholder to interpret the agreement so that the smallest possible amount is paid to your estate for your interest. Since it is the job of your personal representative to stand in your shoes and to negotiate for the best possible price, placing your partner in this position creates the potential for a conflict between his personal financial interest and his duty as your personal representative.

I wish to appoint my attorney instead of my spouse as executor (or personal representative) of my estate. Since either party would be entitled to commissions for serving as executor, what difference does it make to my family?

There would obviously be more money left for your family if your spouse served as executor. On the other hand, an executor who is an attorney can relieve the family of many burdensome administrative details and by appropriate after-death tax planning can save the estate money. Only you, the testator, can determine whether the expense of having a non-member serve is worthwhile.

Assume you left a (probate) estate of $200,000 and you lived in Maryland where the maximum executor's commissions (and those usually allowed) are 10% of the first $20,000 of the estate and 4% of the balance. The commissions would be:

10% of $20,000 =	$2,000
4% of $180,000 =	7,200
	$9,200

If your husband inherits the entire estate and your attorney serves as executor, your husband would receive:

Estate	$200,000
Less the commissions paid the attorney	9,200
	$190,800

If your husband serves as executor, your husband would receive:

Estate	$200,000
Less the commissions	0
	$200,000

If your husband serves as executor and accepts the commissions, he would receive:

Estate after deducting commissions	$190,800
Plus the commissions	9,200
	$200,000

Two things should be noted about the previous examples:

1. If an attorney serves as executor, in most cases he will also perform all legal services as part of the services as executor. Thus, if your husband serves as executor and the services of an attorney are used (which is usually required as a practical matter), the amount eventually received by him will be reduced by the attorney's fees. Such fees are usually a minimum of one-half the commissions allowed by law. If the services of the attorney are in fulfillment of the executor's work, then the fee can equal the commissions.

2. It is usually inadvisable for a spouse who serves as executor to claim and receive commissions. If commissions are paid they become taxable income to the recipient. If the executor will inherit the entire estate, why pay income taxes on property that will be received anyway?

Am I restricted in my choice of executor or trustee?

Generally not. However, in some states a non-resident of that state may not serve as executor unless he or she is closely related to the decedent. For example, in Florida a non-resident of Florida at the time of the decedent's death is disqualified from serving unless the person is a close relative; however, this prohibition against non-residents has been questioned by at least one Florida court as a violation of U.S. Constitutional provisions. I am of the opinion that any such prohibition should be eliminated.

You should consult with your attorney about necessary qualifications in your state.

How are the duties of a personal representative or executor carried out?

When the will is probated, the court will issue to the executor *letters of administration,* or as they are called in some states, *letters testamentary.* These letters are evidence of the executor's legal authority to represent the estate.

What are my duties as personal representative or executor?

Your duties are to have the will probated, collect the assets, give notice to the public at large of your appointment so that creditors may notify you of their claims, pay whatever taxes are due, and as soon as possible distribute the remaining assets to the persons who are legally entitled thereto.

Assets that are held for any length of time should be invested to ensure their safety and to secure adequate income from them.

A good broad statement of the duties of a personal representative follows:

A personal representative is a fiduciary who is under a general duty to settle and distribute the estate of the decedent in accordance with the terms of the will and with as little sacrifice of value as is reasonable under all the circumstances. He shall use his authority while fairly considering the interests of all interested persons and creditors.

How do I go about my duties?

The answer given here is based on the assumption that you are going to do the work yourself. Usually, you hire a lawyer to take care of the administration of the estate. In some states, a bank will perform the ministerial function for you even though it is not named as personal representative.

Whether a lawyer does the work or you do the work, the following are the steps that are necessary to accomplish the first part of your job, collection of assets. (I have assumed that the closest member of the family will have arranged for the funeral and the burial of the body. If there is no member of the family, then the personal representative usually undertakes this responsibility.)

1. Some states require that an estate receive a tax waiver issued by the state taxing authority before assets are turned over to the personal representative. New York is one such state. (By requiring a waiver, a state is notified of the possibility of a tax liability. This enables the state to be sure that its taxes are paid.) In New York, the personal representative fills out forms supplied by the state tax commission. The

waivers are usually issued promptly. A separate waiver is required for each asset of the estate.

In addition to the other requirements discussed below, the various banks, transfer agents, and others request tax waivers in the case of any decedent who resides in a state requiring same.

---

2. With respect to checking and savings accounts owned by the decedent in his own name at the time of death, the personal representative of the estate now becomes their owner. As the estate representative, you should collect the balance remaining in these accounts. To do this, the certificate or certified copy of the letters issued by the court must be submitted to the bank (hereafter we will refer to this certificate as *letters*). Some banks may require a death certificate in addition, but this is not the usual case.

As personal representative, you are the short-term manager of the estate and therefore you have a choice whether to leave the money on deposit with the institution or institutions or to withdraw it and place it in another bank or banks. If you decide to remain with the original bank, you should have the bank account titled in your name as personal representative. If you decide to move a savings account to another bank, be careful that the estate does not lose interest by reason of premature withdrawal.

A death certificate is a certificate issued by a state or local health department which certifies the death of the decedent. The certificate will usually be required by insurance companies, the Social Security Administration, and others. The funeral director customarily orders copies as an accommodation to the family. They usually cost $1–$2 each.

---

3. If there are certificates of deposit, the same procedure should be followed as for the checking and savings accounts.

---

4. It is important to note that the estate should have its own checking account. This enables you to keep a record of whatever is received and paid out. Therefore, all receipts should be deposited in this account and all payments should be made by check from this account.

---

5. With respect to stocks, bonds, and mutual fund shares, each institution has its own requirements. The illustration that follows, dealing with stocks, generally applies to bonds and mutual fund shares as well.

On the right-hand side of every stock certificate is the name of a transfer agent (usually a bank). The transfer agent's job is to have certificates properly issued to parties so entitled. When a person dies, ownership of his or her stock shifts to the personal representative as the representative of the estate (the representative is of course holding the stock in a form of trust fund for the benefit of those entitled to receive it).

The transfer agent will require letters dated within six months of the date you are asking them to make the transfer. Until rather recently the letters had to be dated within 60 days of the request for transfer. The transfer agent will ask for an affidavit of domicile, which is an affidavit that establishes the state in which the decedent resided at the time of death. Not every transfer agent requires this affidavit. Upon receipt of this document, the transfer agent will issue a new certificate showing you, the personal representative, as the owner. The transfer agent will also ask you to provide the federal identification number issued to the estate.

If a stock certificate is lost, the transfer agent will replace the certificate if you first submit to it a bond insuring the agent against claims by third parties for the value of the certificate. The premium cost of such a bond is usually 3% of the value of the certificate that is lost. It is therefore important when mailing certificates to send them by registered mail and to insure them for at least 3% of their value. If the certificates are hand-delivered to a local office of a brokerage house, and if the house is taking care of retitling the certificates, always get a receipt for the stock. The same procedure applies to bonds and mutual fund shares.

---

6. A federal identification number should be requested. This number is called a Federal Employer's Identification Number (even though the estate may not actually employ anyone) and is issued by the Internal Revenue Service (IRS). A request for this number is made on Form SS-4 which will be supplied to you by the local office of the Internal Revenue Service. The number is required on tax returns. Banks, transfer agents, and others will request this number and it is wise to obtain the number as soon as possible.

---

7. Federal law requires each personal representative acting for an estate to send a notice thereof to the IRS. This is done on Form 56 which can be secured from the local IRS office.

If the IRS is not notified, the personal representative may not receive timely notice of any change in the decedent's income tax returns that is made by the IRS. This is so because the IRS is authorized by law to mail the notice to the last known address of the decedent. The last known address would be the one shown on the decedent's last return. If the decedent left a spouse and the spouse remained in the old residence, notice would eventually be received by the spouse. However, the spouse may have moved or there may be no spouse.

Federal law provides that any taxpayer who receives a notice of a proposed assessment may contest the claimed tax before payment by going to the United States Tax Court. However, in order to go to the United States Tax Court, a petition must be filed with that court within 90 days of the mailing of any proposed assessment. If Form 56 is not filed, then you, as personal representative, may never receive the notice of the proposed assessment or the notice may arrive too late for you to do anything about it in the Tax Court.

If the estate is damaged by reason of your failure to send this notice, you personally may become liable to reimburse the estate for any damages sustained by it.

---

8. If the decedent lived in an apartment, you would have to consult local law and the lease, if any, to determine what is necessary to terminate the lease. Check the terms of the lease to see if there is a security deposit and if you are entitled to receive this as an asset of the estate. You must take possession and dispose of any household goods in the apartment. Before disposing of these contents, they should be appraised.

An appraisal establishes the value of the household goods for tax purposes. Sometimes, too, if the will does not bequeath the household goods to specified individuals, it would be advisable for you to get an appraisal before selling the goods at a private sale so that if a beneficiary contests the selling price as being too low, you can establish that you sold the goods for their appraised value. In this connection, bear in mind that in some states household goods are considered to belong to a surviving spouse, where there is one, and if none, to any surviving children.

The laws dealing with the selection of appraisers vary from state to state.

In Maryland, official court appraisers are available, but it is not necessary to use them. You may select your own appraiser. In other jurisdictions, you would seek outside help to choose an appraiser. The appraiser should be one who is qualified and is so recognized by the taxing and court officials.

If the will disposes of the household goods, you should arrange with the beneficiaries to have the merchandise picked up or delivered to them. It may be necessary for you to store the household goods until you can dispose of them at an appropriate time.

During the time when household goods are owned by the estate you should be sure that there is adequate insurance against fire, theft, etc.

If there are valuable paintings, jewelry, a coin or stamp collection, or valuable books, it is your job to take possession of these assets and dispose of them in accordance with the will. If the will has not provided for this, sell them at the highest possible price. In some states, the law encourages you to distribute the actual assets rather than to sell property. It is also your job as personal representative to distribute these assets as fairly as possible to those who are entitled to them.

As a practical matter, the personal representative should consult with the members of the family or others entitled to the property and see if an agreement can be reached as to who receives what. Unfortunately, in many families agreement cannot be reached and there have been bitter contests as to who is entitled to the favorite grandfather clock, tea service, china service, paintings of ancestors, favorite arm chair, etc. When this happens your state laws should be consulted as to what must be done. In some states, you must make the decision about who receives what assets. Usually, this can be done with the court's approval.

---

9. If the decedent owned a car, you should either transfer ownership in accordance with the terms of the will, re-register it in your name as personal representative (in some states it is not necessary to re-register it until the next license renewal date), or perhaps sell the car at the best obtainable price.

   If the decedent rented a car, it is your job to minimize the financial drain of the lease.

---

10. At the present time, most people are covered by Social Security. If the decedent was covered, the decedent's spouse would be entitled to a lump sum death benefit. If there is no spouse, any children may be entitled to the benefit and appropriate application should be made.

    If the decedent was a veteran or a railroad employee, there may be Veterans Administration or Railroad Retirement benefits. The personal representative should apply for any benefits due the estate.

11. The decedent may have had a safe deposit box. You should enter the safe deposit box as the estate representative to take possession of its contents. In some states, such as New York, the bank representatives will not allow you to enter the box until you receive a tax waiver from the appropriate tax agency and an official representative of the taxing agency is present. The official will inventory the box's contents. In some states, an officer of the bank must be present to inventory the contents of the box.

    Customs and laws vary throughout the United States as to the procedure necessary to gain entry and secure possession. Ease of entry may depend upon the name in which the box is rented. Rental may have been in the name of the decedent only, the decedent may have rented it jointly with a spouse, or the decedent may not have even been the one who leased the box but merely have had power of attorney granted by someone else.

---

12. The decedent may have owned brokerage accounts and the stockbroker may have held stock for the decedent as agent on behalf of the decedent.

    Stock could be held in the name of the decedent only and the certificates representing the stock could be lying in the vaults of the stock brokerage company. On the other hand, if the decedent actively traded in securities, the stock brokerage firm may just have registered whatever stock was purchased in the name of a "nominee." Registering the stock in the name of a nominee is merely a way to let the brokerage firm sell the stock quickly when called upon to do so.

In any event, where there is such an account, there would be monthly or perhaps quarterly statements showing the status of the account, what monies are owed to the brokerage company or to the decedent, and what stocks are being held for the account of the decedent.

Possession of these assets should be secured. Before turning over these assets to you, the stockbroker must be assured that you are legally entitled to them. The broker may therefore ask for letters and a death certificate.

13. The decedent may have owned life insurance on his life. If the life insurance is to be paid to a named beneficiary, the named beneficiary should apply for the benefits by direct application to the insurance company. Each company has its own forms for this purpose.

If no beneficiary is named, then you, as personal representative, should submit the application to the insurance company and receive the proceeds. If you receive the proceeds, they must be invested so that you receive the maximum return on the money consistent with safety and the terms of the will. Do not deposit the proceeds in a checking account and promptly forget about your duty to beneficiaries. Your duty is to safeguard the assets and make them productive until the time of distribution.

If the estate is required to file a federal estate tax return, bear in mind that you must annex to the return Form 712 which is issued by the insurance company. Request Form 712 when you make application for the insurance proceeds.

Even if insurance proceeds are not payable to the estate, there may be estate taxes due because of insurance. You may be required to collect a proportionate part of the taxes from the beneficiary. Consult with your lawyer about this rule.

14. If the decedent owned real estate, you should re-title the property in your name as personal representative, pay the taxes, and manage the property or hire somebody to manage the property. Be sure to collect any rents that are due.

See that the property is properly insured. It is your job to secure appropriate and proper insurance. Therefore, even if the decedent had insurance on the property as of the date of his death, you should review the insurance to see if it is adequate. Also, notify the insurance company to change the policy to show that you, as personal representative, are the owner.

The personal representative also has to decide whether to hold the property for eventual distribution to the beneficiaries of the estate or to sell the property. If a sale is made, the personal representative decides the terms of the sale. The terms of the will or state law may restrict or prohibit such a sale except for cash.

In some states, ownership of real estate passes directly to the beneficiaries on the death of the decedent. In these states, the personal representative need do nothing about securing possession of the real estate. However, the representative may be required to have it appraised for tax or other purposes.

---

15. If the decedent owned promissory notes, mortgages, royalties on oil or gas interests, or perhaps royalties for artistic endeavors such as books, movies, or paintings, it is the job of the personal representative to collect these assets. Sometimes it may become necessary for the personal representative to go to court to enforce his rights as any litigant might.

---

16. If the decedent was employed at the time of death, the personal representative should see to it that salaries or whatever other benefits are due are paid. If the decedent was a stockholder in a corporation and the stock is sold, the personal representative should try to get the highest price for the stock. It may be that the stock was held subject to the terms of the stockholder's agreement. If so, the terms of the agreement must be followed.

The decedent may have been the principal stockholder of a corporation, in which event the personal representative would have to determine whether the business should be continued or sold. The decision must be based solely on what is in the best interests of the beneficiaries of the estate. In the absence of any statement in the will, state law must be reviewed to see whether the business may be continued. The laws of most states prohibit the continuation of a business beyond a short period of time after the death of the owner, the idea being that it would be too risky to continue a business.

---

17. If the decedent was self-employed, the personal representative should collect whatever accounts receivable are due, perhaps try to sell the business, and sell assets owned by the business.

In most states, unless there are specific instructions or authority in the will, any unincorporated business may not be continued for any lengthy period of time. Some state laws provide that if it is advisable to continue to operate a business, the business must be incorporated.

---

18. The decedent may have been in the process of litigation when he died. In such a case, it is the duty of the personal representative to pursue such litigation. Usually, a personal representative has authority to settle such litigation or any claims.

19. If the decedent owned U.S. Savings Bonds, the bonds should either be cashed in or distributed in kind, depending on the terms of the will. Check on available tax options and consequences of various ways of handling the bonds.

20. The decedent may be entitled to union benefits or disability insurance claims. The facts should be reviewed to determine whether or not the estate is entitled to such benefits.

21. The estate may be entitled to proceeds from a qualified pension plan. In such an event, application must be made with the trustees of the plan.

    In this connection, investigate the several tax options available.

22. If the decedent was a partner in a partnership, the partnership interest must be disposed of as set forth in the partnership agreement. If there was no partnership agreement, the laws of most states provide that a partnership ends on the death of a partner. When the partnership ends (terminates), the remaining partner or partners must liquidate the partnership assets. After liquidation they must account to the deceased partner's estate for the decedent's interest in the partnership.

    Since the personal representative has a duty to the beneficiaries of the estate to collect all the assets to which the estate is entitled, the personal representative should carefully review the accounts submitted by the surviving partners.

23. The determination of other assets, aside from asking family members, is usually best made by looking at the checkbooks and income tax returns of the decedent for the past several years. Checkbooks would disclose what checks were issued in payment of assets, and tax returns would show sources of income which would enable the personal representative to trace these assets.

    Even such an ordinary item as payment of club dues by check may disclose that the decedent had loaned the club money many years earlier and that the estate is entitled to collect this loan.

After all the assets are collected, what should be done with them?

It is essential that every asset be safeguarded, invested (on a short-term basis) to secure the maximum return possible, and at the proper time distributed to those entitled thereto. Remember that the personal representative is a fiduciary, that is, one who is in a position of trust who is not acting on behalf of himself but on behalf of persons entitled to benefits. Accordingly, the law provides that the highest responsibilities are imposed upon a fiduciary.

A person should not undertake the duties of a personal representative without consideration of the responsibilities.

In discharging these duties, it is essential that a careful inventory be maintained of all assets belonging to the estate. Most courts will require that the personal representative make and, in most instances, file a document called an inventory as well as an accounting, which sets forth all of the assets collected by the personal representative. Most courts have forms that can be used for this purpose.

Unless this inventory is filed at the right time, the court can remove the personal representative, fine him, or impose other sanctions. Embarrassment will be avoided if the appropriate laws and rules are consulted shortly after appointment as personal representative to determine the duties of the position.

When may I distribute estate assets?

The laws of most states provide that creditors have a specific time period during which they may file claims to any debts owed them. If you make distribution before the time has elapsed for creditors to file claims with the estate, you may be personally liable to these creditors for any estate assets prematurely distributed to beneficiaries.

This is so because the laws of all states provide that creditors are entitled to be paid before any estate assets are distributed to beneficiaries.

Both federal and state laws are also very strict about death taxes being paid in full before any estate assets are distributed. Hence the personal representative should be certain that sufficient estate assets are retained to pay *all* tax claims.

In answer to the question then, estate assets may only be distributed when:

1. the time period for the filing of claims by creditors has expired, and

2. all taxes have been paid.

If the personal representative distributes estate assets to beneficiaries before the two events just mentioned and without withholding sufficient assets to satisfy all creditors and taxes, the personal representative will be personally liable for payment of these items.

Must I, as personal representative, pay every claim that is presented to me?

Certainly not. You need pay only valid and proper claims.

Your duty is to examine the claim to see that it is timely presented. Every state has a time limit (usually six months) during which time claims must be presented. If a claim is presented late, this would be a proper basis for denying the claim. Taxing authorities are not required to file claims and usually do not.

After you have examined the claim, you determine whether it should be paid in whole or in part, or rejected.

If a claim is rejected in whole or in part, or if you take no action on it, creditors will have rights to contest this action before the court that appointed you.

May a claim be paid even if no formal claim is filed?

Generally yes, but in a few states the filing of a formal claim, in the proper form and within the specified time period, is required.

The laws of your state should be consulted.

Give me some examples of problems that could arise if I distribute the assets of the estate too soon.

1. Assume a wife survives her husband and is entitled to his entire estate. I am the personal representative of the estate and you, the wife, ask me to make distribution to you of the entire estate sixty days after my appointment as personal representative. If I make the requested distribution and if creditors do file timely claims, I am personally responsible to them because I made premature distribution of the estate assets.

I can seek reimbursement of these amounts from you, of course, but you may have moved or you may have made some imprudent investments and lost all the money. At best, I would spend a lot of money to recover the distribution from you and at worst, I would never be able to recover anything. In any event, I could be personally liable for the premature distribution.

2. Assume similar facts but this time I made distribution to you ten months after date of death and after I have filed the federal and state estate tax returns.

The taxing authorities come in one year after I filed these returns and establish that there was an omission of assets from the return which neither you nor I knew about, or perhaps they say that the land we valued at $1,000 per acre was in reality worth $10,000 per acre. On this basis, the tax would be substantially higher than the tax we had paid when the returns were filed.

The assets from the estate have already been distributed to you and both the federal and state governments can properly sue me personally for these distributions which I made prematurely. The actual distribution should never have been made until the returns were accepted as filed. If there is any contest over the amount of tax claimed, this controversy should be resolved first. Accordingly, I may be personally liable for the tax.

Are there any other problems that I may be confronted with?

Yes. Despite all your efforts, the language of the will may not be clear enough to enable you as personal representative to distribute the property. You may require the assistance of the courts to interpret or to construe the will. This help is obtained by beginning a proceeding in court called a *construction proceeding*. These illustrations point out when construction problems may arise:

1. A $2,000 bequest is made under the will to cousin John. A problem may arise if the testator has two cousins who are named John. The question is which John was intended to be the beneficiary of the $2,000.

2. The testator leaves the remainder of his property, after the death of his wife, to his children in equal shares. At the time the testator made the will, and when he died, he had three children; by the time his wife died, one of the children was already dead. The question is whether the dead child's estate will inherit one-third of the estate since the will was not clear as to whether that child had to survive the wife in order to inherit the one-third share. This situation requires that the courts construe the will to determine the testator's intent.

3. The testator left a bequest of $5,000 to the First Memorial Methodist Church.

When the will was executed, there was a First Memorial Methodist Church in the community where the testator resided, and in the adjoining town there was a church with a similar name of which the testator was a member. The will was not clear as to which church was meant and you, the personal representative, may not distribute the bequest to one of the churches without seeking a construction of the will so that the court may determine the testator's intent.

A construction proceeding usually requires that a complaint be filed setting forth the facts about what is contained in the will and asking the court to construe the meaning of the language. This proceeding obviously requires the preparation of additional documents by an attorney, at extra cost to the estate, and will further delay any distribution to be made by the personal representative.

When a proceeding of this nature is begun, every possible person who is interested in the outcome of the proceeding must be notified of the proceeding. The problem becomes further complicated when persons who may be interested in the settlement of the estate are not yet born or perhaps are minors. In this event, the court, upon the request of the party seeking construction, would be duty-bound to appoint a guardian for the unborn persons or the minor or minors. This is so because of a basic rule of law that persons who have not appeared before the court, personally or represented by counsel, are not bound by the proceeding. Therefore, it is important that the personal representative bind everybody who could possibly have an interest in the outcome of the court proceeding.

The testator gave no instructions in his will concerning his burial wishes. The funeral home has now submitted a bill for $5,600. Am I, as personal representative, required to pay it?

The laws of the states vary on this matter. In general, funeral bills are to be paid before any other amounts are distributed. However, in many states, when a funeral bill exceeds a certain amount, the approval of the court must be secured before any funeral bill may be paid. Therefore, you should check your state's laws before paying any funeral bill.

The decedent signed a contract during his lifetime to purchase some property from another person. As personal representative, am I bound by this agreement?

Yes, to the same extent as the decedent was. However, since you are acting on behalf of the estate, only the assets of the estate, and not your personal assets, are subject to any financial responsibility.

I am the personal representative of my late brother's estate. He died in 1981. He left one-third of his property to his children, Mary and Harry, and two-thirds to his wife. In 1979, two years after my brother executed his will, his wife gave birth to another child, Charles. Is Charles entitled to any share of the children's one-third?

In most states, Charles would be entitled to take the same share that he would have received had your brother died without a will (*intestate*). In this case, Charles may even receive a greater share than the other children. For example, assume your brother lived in a state which provides that when a person dies intestate the wife is entitled to one-third of the estate and the children receive the other two-thirds. Assume also that your brother's estate is valued at $150,000. Charles, as one of three children, is entitled to one-third of two-thirds (two-thirds of $150,000 is $100,000), or $33,333.

Since the balance left for distribution is $116,667, your brother's wife will be entitled to the amount left to her under his will, or two-thirds of $116,667. This amounts to $77,778. The balance left for Mary and Harry is $38,889 and each will receive $19,444.50 (one-half of $38,889), even though Charles receives $33,333.

Many states now provide that an after-born child takes the same share that the other children do. In this case, each child would inherit $16,667 (one-third of $50,000).

A child born after a will is executed is known as a *pretermitted child*.

The testator died on July 1st. On June 15th he signed his will and left 90% of his property to a charity. He left a wife and one child. Am I, as personal representative, required to distribute the property as the will provides?

In many states, when a wife or children survive, no more than a certain percentage of a decedent's estate may be left to charity. In other states, if a will is executed within a certain number of days before death, the amount that may be left to charity is also limited. Check the laws of the state in which the will is being administered.

My late husband's will left to his sister some jewelry that he inherited from his mother. I am the estate's personal representative. What do I do with this jewelry?

This jewelry is specifically left (*bequeathed*) to his sister and therefore it is your job to hand it over to the sister. You should receive a receipt from her for the jewelry turned over to her.

The balance available for distribution from my husband's estate to our two sons is $50,000. I am the personal representative. After the appropriate waiting period, may I distribute $25,000 to each son?

Generally, yes. It is possible, however, that during your husband's lifetime, he gave one of your sons $10,000 or so and treated this amount as what the law calls *an advancement*. An advancement is essentially an advance against the inheritance that the beneficiary is entitled to where the decedent died without a will. It reduces the amount to be distributed upon death. Therefore, if there were indeed an advancement, this advancement must be taken into account before making distribution. The laws of most states require that if there is an advancement, written confirmation of this exists on the date of death. Note that the advancement rule applies only if the decedent died without a will.

One of my sons is a minor. As personal representative, may I distribute his share to him?

A minor is incapable of giving the personal representative a release for any distribution made to him. The personal representative should therefore never distribute estate property directly to a minor.

Until relatively recently, the laws of most states provided that when property was to be distributed to a minor, it was necessary to have a court-appointed guardian for such a minor. This was a time-consuming, costly procedure.

Many states now provide that when a minor is entitled to a distribution, the personal representative may make the distribution by giving the property to a custodian under the Uniform Gifts to Minors Act.

In most states, even those that have not simplified the procedure, provisions protect the personal representative from a later lawsuit for acting improperly in turning over to a minor, or perhaps to his or her parents, property that is valued either below a certain dollar amount or which consists of household furniture and goods.

My husband left to my son, Frank, his International Harvester tractor. About two months before my husband died, he sold the tractor to pay some of his hospital bills. Is it necessary for me to buy an equivalent tractor and turn it over to my son, Frank?

No. The bequest here was *adeemed*. Property is adeemed when the property is no longer in existence as of the date of death and therefore the bequest to Frank fails and you need do nothing about this matter.

As another example, let us assume that your husband left 100 shares of IBM stock to his mother if she survived him. Your husband's mother survived your husband but when your husband died, he no longer owned any IBM stock. This language is a classic illustration of a gift to someone which is intended to take effect only if the property is in existence as of the decedent's date of death. Therefore, the *bequest,* or the gift as it is sometimes called, is considered to be *adeemed*. This principle of law is also sometimes known as the *doctrine of ademption*.

When my husband died, our residence was titled as *tenants by the entireties*. I believe that at the moment of death, I became sole owner of the residence since I survived my husband. My question concerns a $40,000 mortgage that was left on the residence when my husband died. Am I now responsible for paying this mortgage?

Assuming that you signed the mortgage obligation, you are personally liable to the lending institution for this $40,000. If you did not sign the mortgage, you are not personally liable to pay it. However, the property is subject to the mortgage, and, unless you pay it, the property can be sold to pay the mortgage debt.

In some jurisdictions, including Maryland, there is a rule of law known as the *doctrine of exoneration*. This means that you are entitled to be exonerated, or made whole, from your husband's estate for one-half of this debt of $40,000. In other words, your husband left you with a debt of $40,000 and the entire burden of this $40,000 falls upon your shoulders. To the extent of one-half of the $40,000, you are entitled to be reimbursed by the other assets contained in your husband's estate. This right to exoneration, or to being relieved of part of the financial burden, is in reality treated as a debt owed to you by your husband's estate. Accordingly, as personal representative, you are entitled to pay yourself $20,000, which payment is treated like any other debt. This payment is due before you make distribution of any assets in the estate to any beneficiaries.

What is meant when a gift, or bequest, is considered to be *abated*?

Where there are insufficient assets to satisfy a bequest, then the bequest or gift is reduced proportionately. The laws of most states set forth the priorities as to who takes what first. An illustration will clarify this statement. Assume that the testator provided that from the monies on deposit with Maryland National Bank, he leaves $25,000 to your son Frank and $25,000 to your son John. At the date of your husband's death, there is only $40,000 in the Maryland National Bank account referred to. It is obvious that there is not enough money to satisfy this bequest from the source named and therefore the law provides that each bequest of $25,000 must be *abated*, or reduced, by the sum of $5,000.

I have heard the expression *family allowance*. What does it mean?

Virtually every state requires that some amount of money or property be set aside for the benefit of a surviving spouse and minor children. The intent is to provide for the family during the period when the estate is being administered. Essentially then a *family allowance* is an allowance from the estate to tide over the immediate family during the period of administration.

The family allowance takes many forms and it is therefore important that the personal representative learn what the allowance is in the state in which the estate is being administered.

In some states, the *homestead* (the principal residence) is set aside as the family allowance. In some states, it is a specific sum of money, household furnishings, tools, animals, etc. In yet other states, the allowance is a regular cash stipend for a fixed period of time.

I am the personal representative of my brother's estate. He left a bequest of $5,000 to a cousin, James, if James survived (my brother). James survived my brother by ten days. Am I now required to pay the $5,000 to James' estate?

In many states there are laws dealing with this subject. The answer to your question depends on the state in which your brother resided at the time of his death.

For example, in Maryland there is a law that says a *legatee* (a person who under the terms of a will would receive property) who fails to survive the testator by 30 full days shall be considered to have died before the testator. When someone dies before a testator, that person is not entitled to inherit under the will. These rules can be changed by the terms of the will. In this case, James will be considered to have died before your brother and is therefore not entitled to his legacy.

This rule (requiring someone to survive by a specified period) has an exception. This exception is known as the *lapse rule*. It says that when a bequest or gift is given to someone who is named or referred to, if that person dies after the will is executed but before the testator dies, the bequest or gift is still valid. That is, the bequest or gift does *not* lapse. Therefore, had your brother given $5,000 to James by will but not required that James survive him, the lapse rule would have been effective. This would have meant that James' estate would be entitled to the $5,000.

As interpreted under Maryland law, your brother's will requires that James actually survive by 30 full days. Since James died within 10 days, the lapse rule does not apply in this case.

As mentioned earlier, many states have similar rules (or laws), and the law of the state controlling your brother's will must be studied to see if James' estate would be entitled to the $5,000.

My brother died a resident of Maryland but had bank accounts and real estate in another state. How do I, as personal representative, get possession of these assets?

You were appointed the personal representative by a Maryland court. The estate is being administered under the laws of Maryland and therefore Maryland is considered to be the principal place of administration. Your authority as personal representative does not extend to property in another state.

It will be necessary for you, or someone who is qualified by the laws of the other state, to apply to the state in which the property is located for an appointment as the ancillary personal representative in that state. Maryland is the state in which you are the principal or domiciliary personal representative.

Whoever is appointed would then proceed with the ancillary administration of the estate in the state where the property was located at the time of death. This involves all the complications involved in the administration of an estate in the state where the decedent was domiciled at the time of death; that is, advertising notice of appointment (for the benefit of creditors), collecting the assets, paying debts, and paying taxes.

There is a measure of hope, however. In the last few years many states have liberalized their laws in this area. They have permitted personal representatives appointed by another state (called *foreign personal representatives*) to come into their state to administer assets located in their state without requiring the foreign personal representative to secure appointment as the ancillary personal representative.

For example, assume the domicile of a decedent is New York. His estate is being administered there. The personal representative there (called an *executor* in New York) learns of property located in Maryland. The letters issued by the New York court are sufficient authority for the New York executor to collect any Maryland assets belonging to the estate. Maryland requires only that the New York executor (the foreign personal representative) advertise a notice of his appointment and pay any applicable Maryland death taxes. The New York executor is not required to go through the probate process again nor is he required to secure letters issued by a Maryland court; his authority is already established by reason of having the New York letters.

Please review the rules with respect to distribution of estate assets.

All of the estate assets, including income from such assets, shall first be used to pay administration and funeral expenses, debts of the decedent, and any taxes for which the estate is liable.

What is left is then distributed in the following order:

1. Specific and demonstrative legacies. A *specific legacy* is a gift of some specific item that can be identified. For example, a gift of the decedent's oak rocking chair to John is a specific legacy.

   A *demonstrative legacy* is a gift of a dollar amount or a quantity of material, payable from a certain source. For example, a gift of $1,000 to be paid from decedent's account at the credit union is a demonstrative legacy.

2. A general legacy payable to a surviving spouse. A *general legacy* is one that does not specify the source from which it is to be paid. For example, a gift of one-half of the decedent's gross estate to his (or her) surviving spouse is a general legacy.

3. A general legacy payable to others.

4. Residuary legacies. A *residuary legacy* is what is left after all of the above, including expenses, debts and taxes, are paid.

If there are insufficient assets in an estate to pay all the legacies, the residuary legatees are the first affected and then the others shown here are affected in the reverse order of this listing. In other words, some of the legacies may be abated.

What happens if there are insufficient assets to pay all of a decedent's debts?

Each state sets forth, in its laws, what debts must be paid first.

As a guide, the laws of most states provide for payment of debts and expenses in the following order:

1. Court fees.

2. Funeral expenses.

3. Costs and expenses of administering the estate, including compensation of the personal representative, legal fees, and real estate brokerage commissions.

4. Family allowance.

5. Taxes due by decedent.

6. Reasonable medical, hospital, and nursing expenses for the last illness.

7. Rent for the last three months in arrears.

8. Wages, salaries, or commissions due for the prior three months in arrears.

9. All other claims.

Generally, too, the law prohibits preferring one claim in any of the above categories over another claim. For example, assume the assets were sufficient to pay in full all of the first eight items. There is a balance of $3,000 and the claims due, belonging in category 9, total $15,000. In this case, each of the creditors shall be entitled to only a portion of each claim. You may not pay 100% of the claim of one claimant leaving less for distribution to the other category 9 claimants.

What tax returns must be filed, when are they due, and where are they to be filed?

For citizens or residents of the United States they are:

1. The final federal income tax return of the decedent and payment of the tax are both due as though the decedent lived for the entire year. Thus, the return is due by the 15th day of the fourth month following the close of the taxable year in which the person died (April 15th for calendar year taxpayers).

   An automatic extension of time can be secured by filing Form 4868 and paying the tax that is estimated to be due.

   The place of filing is the appropriate office of the Internal Revenue Service based on the legal residence or place of business of the person making the return.

For the final state income tax return, consult your state tax authority.

2. A notice of qualification as personal representative should be filed as soon as possible. A federal Form 56 is available for this purpose. The form is filed in the office of the Internal Revenue Service where the decedent's return is filed.

3. A federal estate tax return is required when the gross estate (not taxable estate) plus adjusted taxable gifts exceed:
   $225,000 if death occurred in 1982,
   $275,000 if death occurred in 1983,
   $325,000 if death occurred in 1984,
   $400,000 if death occurred in 1985,
   $500,000 if death occurred in 1986,
   and $600,000 if death occurred in 1987 or thereafter. The return is filed on Form 706 which will be supplied, on request, by any Internal Revenue Service office. The return is due within nine months after the date of the decedent's death. The place of filing is set forth in the instructions to the return. Payment of the tax is due when the return is filed. (See the topic of Death Taxes on page 107 for a discussion of this topic.)

   The due date of the return and payment of the tax may be extended. Federal law and the regulations of the Treasury Department should be consulted to determine when an extension is available.

4. A federal gift tax return is required when a transfer in excess of $10,000 is made in any calendar year to any person. Prior to 1982 any transfer in excess of $3,000 required a gift tax return. (If

the gift is a *future interest*, then even if the transfer is less than $10,000, a gift tax return must be filed.) The return is on Form 709, supplied, on request, by any Internal Revenue Service office.

The return is due on or before the 15th day of April following the close of the calendar year. However, when death occurs in the year in which a gift is made, the return is due on the earlier to occur of the time when the estate tax return is due (usually nine months after date of death) or April 15. The place of filing is set forth in the instructions to the return. Payment of the tax is due when the return is filed.

The due date of the return and payment of the tax may be extended. Consult Federal law and Treasury Department regulations to determine when an extension is available.

Note: Forms 706 and 709 have separate instruction forms. Ask for them.

In addition to these tax returns, must any other returns be filed with taxing authorities?

Yes. The estate is a separate taxpayer. Accordingly, the personal representative must keep records of income and expenses of the estate to permit the preparation and filing of federal and, in some states, state income tax returns for the estate.

The estate federal income tax return is filed on Form 1041 and is known as a Fiduciary Income Tax Return. This return must be filed when the gross income of the estate for the taxable year is $600 or more, or when any beneficiary of the estate is a nonresident alien.

The form and instructions are secured from any office of the Internal Revenue Service. The place of filing is set forth in the instructions. You will find helpful a free publication, Publication 559, which is available at most Internal Revenue Service offices. It is entitled "Tax Information for Survivors, Executors, and Administrators." The return and the tax are due by the 15th day of the fourth month following the close of the taxable year. The taxable year begins on the date of death. For example, if the decedent died on March 15th, the taxable year of the estate begins on March 15th.

An extension of time may be granted upon application.

Is it necessary to keep any other types of records?

Yes. The value of the property owned by the estate as of the date of death must be determined in order to determine what death taxes must be paid. Estates also have the option of having the property owned by it valued as of another date. This other date is called the *alternate valuation date,* which for federal purposes is usually six months after date of death. The states that impose an estate tax usually follow the federal rule in this regard.

The personal representative should determine the value of all the assets of the estate as of date of death and as of the alternate valuation date. This is done to arrive at the values that would be most favorable to the estate and to the beneficiaries.

In terms of estate taxes, the lowest values should be used; however, higher income taxes might be levied at some time by reason of using the lowest values. (See the discussion concerning taxes on pages 148–150.)

Keep records accounting for every transaction affecting the estate. These would include, in addition to income received, amounts paid for expenses, taxes, repairs, payments made on sale of any property, and every other conceivable receipt or payment made by or to the estate.

A personal representative must account for all estate transactions either to the court or to the beneficiaries of the estate.

Where would I find a definition of income?

For federal income tax purposes, the rules are set forth in that part of the Internal Revenue Code known as Chapter 1, Subchapter J. While the deductions and exemptions of an estate are different from those available to an individual, gross income is determined in the same manner as for an individual.

For state income tax purposes, the laws of most states follow the federal rules concerning the definition of income.

Where can I find rules explaining the differences between income and principal from the non-tax point of view?

Most states have now adopted as part of their laws the (revised) Uniform Principal and Income Act. A national group of lawyers, appointed by the governor of each state, studied the matter for many years and recommended that each state incorporate the act in state laws. Most states have done so. The text of the act can be found among the laws of each state that enacted it into law. A copy of the act can be secured from the National Conference of Commissioners on Uniform State Laws, 645 North Michigan Avenue, Chicago, Illinois 60611.

In summary, the act provides that income is the return, in money or property, derived from the use of principal. *Principal* is the property that has been set aside by the owner or by the person legally empowered to do so.

The property that is set aside shall be held in trust and eventually delivered to the *remainderman* (the person entitled to principal, including income which has been accumulated and added to principal). While the principal is held in trust, the income from the principal shall be paid over to the *income beneficiary* (the person to whom income is presently payable or for whom it is accumulated for distribution as income) or accumulated, depending on the terms of the trust.

When a corporation distributes its own shares of stock, whether by a stock split or a stock dividend, this is considered principal unless the corporation declares that the distribution is being made instead of giving an ordinary cash dividend.

You must remember, however, that each state has its own laws on this entire suject. Therefore, it is important to consult the laws of your state to be sure of what is income and what is principal.

When does the right to income arise?

The following is reprinted from the revised Uniform Principal and Income Act:

1. *An income beneficiary is entitled to income from the date specified in the trust instrument or, if none is specified, from the date an asset becomes subject to the trust. In the case of an asset becoming subject to a trust by reason of a will, it becomes subject to the trust as of the testator's date of death even though there is an intervening period of administration of the testator's estate.*

2. *In the administration of a decedent's estate or if an asset becomes subject to a trust by reason of a will*

   a. *receipts due but not paid at the date of death of the testator are principal;*

   b. *receipts in the form of periodic payments (other than corporate distributions to stockholders), including rent, interest, or annuities, not due at the date of the death of the testator, shall be treated as accruing from day to day. That portion*

of the receipt accruing before the date of death is principal and the balance is income.

3. *In all other cases, any receipt from an income-producing asset is income even though the receipt was earned or accrued in whole or in part before the date when the asset became subject to the trust.*

4. *On termination of an income interest, either the income beneficiary whose interest is terminated or his estate is entitled to*

   a. *income undistributed on the date of termination;*

   b. *income due but not paid to the trustee on the date of termination;*

   c. *income in the form of periodic payments (other than corporate distributions to stockholders), including rent, interest, or annuities, not due on the date of termination, accrued from day to day.*

5. *Corporate distributions by stockholders shall be treated as due on the day fixed by the corporation for determination of stockholders of record entitled to distribution or, if no date is fixed, on the date of declaration of the distribution by the corporation.*

Please set forth, in general, the rules as to who is entitled to income earned by an estate.

As reprinted from the revised Uniform Principal and Income Act:

1. *Unless the will otherwise provides, and subject to subsection 2, below, all expenses incurred in connection with the settlement of a decedent's estate, including debts, funeral expenses, estate taxes, interest, and penalties concerning taxes, family allowances, fees of attorneys and personal representatives, and court costs shall be charged against the principal of the estate.*

2. *Unless the will otherwise provides, income from the assets of a decedent's estate after the death of the testator and before distribution, including income from property used to discharge liabilities, shall be determined in accordance with the rules applicable to a trustee under this Act and distributed as follows:*

   a. *To specific legatees and devisees, the income from the property bequeathed or devised to them respectively, less taxes, ordinary repairs, and other expenses of management and operation of the property, and an appropriate portion of interest accrued since the death of the testator and of taxes imposed on income (excluding taxes on capital gains) which accrue during the period of administration;*

   b. *To all other legatees and devisees, except legatees of pecuniary bequests not in trust, the balance of income, less the balance of taxes, ordinary repairs, and other expenses*
   of management and operation of all property from which the estate is entitled to income, interest accrued since the death of the testator, and taxes imposed on income (excluding taxes on capital gains) which accrue during the period of administration, in proportion to their respective interests in the undistributed assets of the estate computed at times of distribution on the basis of inventory value.

3. *Income received by a trustee under subsection 2 shall be treated as income of the trust.*

Is the personal representative entitled to compensation, and if so, in what amount?

Every state allows compensation, sometimes called a commission or fee. The amount of compensation varies from state to state and is based on the value of the probate estate. Commissions vary from 2 1/2% of receipts plus 2 1/2% of payments (Georgia) to 3% (and less, on a declining scale) of the value of the probate estate exceeding $300,000 and higher percentages for values below $300,000 (New York).

It is important to remember that compensation can be—and frequently should be—waived. Why? Compensation, when received, constitutes income and is subject to income tax. Many times the personal representative is the surviving spouse of the decedent. As surviving spouse, he or she will inherit all or most of the estate. Perhaps the children will inherit part of the estate. If the surviving spouse takes compensation, it will be subject to income tax. When no amount is taken as compensation, the surviving spouse will receive the same, or practically the same, inheritance but it will not be subject to income tax.

For example, the decedent dies a resident of Maryland and leaves a probate estate of $100,000. This estate consists of stocks, bonds, and cash. The wife is appointed personal representative under her husband's will. The will leaves everything to her outright.

Under Maryland law, she would be entitled to commissions of $5,200, subject to the approval of the court. (For purposes of this illustration, assume there are no debts, taxes, or expenses of any kind.) If she takes the commissions, she would receive the following from the estate:

Commissions	$ 5,200
Balance of estate	94,800
	$100,000

The commissions are subject to federal and Maryland income taxes, at the applicable rate.

If she waived her commissions, the spouse would receive the following from the estate:

| Entire estate | $100,000 |

In both cases she receives $100,000, but if she applied to the court for commissions and accepted them, $5,200 will be needlessly subject to income tax.

What legal fees can I, as personal representative, expect to pay?

Whatever the fees, they may be subject to the approval of the court.

Fees are based on several factors. The most important factor is the time devoted to the matter and this depends upon the attorney's work. Variable factors are: Is there a caveat to the will, is there litigation, is the estate involved in running a business, is a federal estate tax return required, are there complex legal problems requiring extensive legal research, are there contests with the taxing authorities, are there problems determining the price to be realized by the estate when closely-held stock is required to be redeemed, will contracts be required in connection with selling estate assets, will extensive work be involved in disposing of a professional practice?

Fees vary from attorney to attorney and from region to region.

As a general rule, an estate can expect to pay a fee of at least one-half the statutory commission rate payable to a personal representative plus something extra to handle assets that are not part of the probate estate. For example, a probate estate may consist of $50,000 in assets but property subject to taxation may involve hundreds of thousands of dollars. Dealing with these non-probate assets may require many hours of work for which legal fees are necessarily incurred.

Any legal fees paid are an expense of the estate.

My father died and his bank was appointed personal representative. Last month I received $38,000 from the bank as a final distribution from father's estate. What may I do with this money?

Anything you wish. This sum now belongs to you. You may buy a new car, take a world cruise, invest in a business, make a loan to your friends, deposit the money in a savings account, or pay off a mortgage.

If you deposit the money in a bank account and are entitled to interest income, the income will be subject to income taxes.

What does a spouse's *right of election* mean?

Under the laws of most states, a surviving spouse is entitled to a certain minimum portion of a decedent's estate. In some states, no matter what amount of property is left to a surviving spouse, the spouse has a right to take a share equal to the share that the spouse would have received had the decedent died without a will.

Thus, a surviving spouse can file a document with the court that has supervision over the estate electing to take the following:

1. In those states giving that person a minimum amount, the spouse can take an additional amount so that the surviving spouse does indeed receive the minimum.

For example, assume that the husband leaves to the wife $20,000 under his will and that under that state's laws, the wife is entitled to one-third of the estate, or $50,000. The surviving spouse could then demand and be entitled to receive the difference between $20,000 and $50,000, or $30,000. If, in this example, the husband left the wife nothing under his will, then by exercising the right of election the wife, who is the surviving spouse, would be entitled to $50,000.

2. In those states in which the surviving spouse has a right of election regardless of what is left under the will, the spouse can take the amount that the laws of such states allow to surviving spouses.

For example, if the minimum amount to which the surviving spouse is entitled is one-half the estate and the estate amounts to $150,000, then by filing the right of election the surviving spouse would be entitled to $75,000.

States that give a surviving spouse this right of election require that the election be made within a certain stated period of time. This varies from state to state. It is essential that the election be filed within the mandatory period set forth by the laws of the state administering the estate.

I have heard of *small estates*. What are they?

They are estates that consist of property of no more than a certain sum. This sum may be $5,000 or $10,000, or it may be smaller or greater than either of these figures. When this occurs, the estate may be administered under the so-called "small estates act" enacted by many states.

When an estate is administered under such an act, administration is simplified: the forms are less complicated, court fees are considerably reduced, there may be no death taxes to pay, and the waiting period necessary before assets can be distributed is waived or substantially reduced.

What is *independent administration*?

In some states, when a will is probated and the property is being administered, periodic reports in the form of accountings must be filed with the court. In other words, there is active court supervision of the administration of the estate. Maryland is an example of this type of state. In some states (New York is an example of the other extreme), after a will is admitted to probate, except for the procedure for fixing the tax, there is virtually no court supervision of the administration of the estate unless an interested party requests such intervention. In some states, such as Illinois, a great degree of independent administration is allowed, usually when the estate is below a certain dollar amount, so that virtually no documents need be filed with the court unless, of course, an interested person requests court intervention; otherwise, full court supervision of the estate is required.

The idea behind independent administration is to help reduce the costs of administering estate property.

TRUSTS

TRUSTS

What is a *testamentary trust*?

A trust that is created by the terms of a will. This type of trust is distinguished from a trust created during lifetime. A trust created during lifetime is called an *inter vivos* or "living" trust.

Why create a testamentary trust?

Some of the non-tax reasons to have a trust are:

1. To have professional management of property for the benefit of your loved ones. For example, assume you die, your husband is already dead, and you leave two children, aged 10 and 12. If you live in a state where the children attain their majority (legally become adults) at age 18, you have to ask yourself if you wish them to have control of their inherited property at age 18. If the answer is no, you may consider creating a trust under your will to let them inherit your property in various stages, such as one-third at age 21, another one-third at age 25 (actually one-half of the balance), and the balance at age 30.

2. To protect your loved ones from their own unwise acts. For example, you die and leave all your money outright to your wife. She remarries. Her new husband convinces her to invest most of the money in a very speculative business and all is lost. If the money had been left in a trust, your wife would have had to request the money from the trustee. Depending on the language you used in your will when you created the trust, the trustee could say yes or no to a request for additional funds from your wife. But even if she had the right to demand all the funds (that is, the trustee would have no choice but to pay the money over to her when she requested it), at the very least this would give the trustee an opportunity to talk with your wife and to give her the benefit of the trustee's advice.

3. To give someone the benefit of the use of the income from the trust but have it pass eventually to another party.

An example of this is a provision for your parents, leaving $100,000 in trust for their benefit during their lifetimes. On their deaths, the trust property is then paid over to your wife, if living, and if not living, to your children.

Would you advise creating a trust which is not part of the will?

There are tax and non-tax reasons for creating a trust. The tax reasons are discussed in the section on taxes. The principal non-tax reasons follow.

1. To avoid probate.

    a. The probate process can cause delay in transferring assets from a decedent to the trustee, especially when minors have an interest in the property. In New York State, for example, if a minor has an interest in the estate property, the surrogate's court will appoint an attorney to represent the minor's interests before it will probate the will. The New York lawmakers perceived that the parent of a minor may have an interest in the will that could be opposed to the best interests of a minor child. The job of an attorney appointed to represent a minor is therefore to investigate the facts in performing his or her duty to best represent the minor's interests. Essentially, the attorney is to consider whether or not there is any legal basis for opposing probate of

the will. Naturally, this takes time and adds extra fees and costs to the probate process.

If a trust is created during lifetime, the delay and costs noted above are avoided because there is already a trustee or a successor trustee appointed by the creator of the trust. (The creator of the trust may be called the *grantor, settlor, donor,* or *trustor.*) Shortly after a trust is created, all the property is titled in the name of the trustee. Thus, when the creator of the trust dies, there is no reason to go through the probate process for the trust property.

    b. If real estate in another state is owned by you, it will be necessary on your death to have your will probated in that other state. Why is this necessary? Assume you are unmarried and have a daughter to whom you wish to leave your possessions. Assume that you own real estate in Florida. On your death, this real estate is titled in your name. In order to transfer ownership to your daughter, it will be necessary to probate the will in Florida. When the will is probated in Florida, ownership or title to the property will pass to the administrator. The process whereby this is done is called *ancillary administration.*

    The Florida administrator could be your daughter or someone else, such as a bank or an attorney. The administrator would eventually be required to distribute the property to your daughter. This process of ancillary administration will be responsible for additional costs and will delay your daughter's inheritance of the property.

A living (*inter vivos*) trust would save the costs and delay since at the moment of your death the trustee would already own the property and the trustee could distribute the property to your daughter without court approval.

c. Probate documents are a matter of public record. Accordingly, anyone may examine these records to determine what assets are owned by the decedent at the time of death.

On the other hand, a living trust is usually not a matter of public record. If secrecy is desired, a living trust would usually achieve this goal.

---

2. To protect your property in the event of incompetence.

a. There are many reported instances in which a trusted employee or relative takes advantage of one's incompetence. The other person has the incompetent sign over property to him. If it can be proven that such an act took place when a person was incompetent, the court will require that the property be returned.

It is difficult and costly to prove incompetence. If someone creates a living trust and appoints another person as trustee, the trustee will protect the property from being transferred.

b. An incompetent individual sometimes does foolish things with his or her property. One may make unwise investments or uncalled-for gifts. For example, assume I am the trustee of a trust created by you. You, of course, have the right to revoke the trust. However, should you suddenly decide to give your housekeeper the gift of a substantial portion of your property, owned by me as trustee, I would investigate any such transfer that you wished to make.

If I felt that someone was trying to take advantage of you, I would present all the facts to an appropriate court before I would make any transfer. This would have the effect of protecting your assets. As trustee, I could even decline to make the requested transfer and put the burden of establishing entitlement to your property on the third person. Before any transfer is made, you would have the protection of the trustee and the courts.

---

3. To dispose of your property as you initially direct, thereby lessening the right of members of your family to claim that undue influence was exercised or that you were incompetent at the time you made your will.

Here is an example of the use of undue influence. Assume I am single and have two children named John and Mary. I am estranged from John. I have not seen or heard from him for the past ten years. During these ten years I have lived happily in Mary's home, baby-sat for her children (my grandchildren), and gone on many trips with Mary and her family. It is my wish that Mary shall inherit all my property to the exclusion of John.

If I leave all my property to Mary by will, John (who must be given notice of the probate of my will) can claim that the will was executed in favor of Mary because Mary exercised undue influence on me. The legal theory of "undue influence" in this case is that Mary exercised duress on me to leave all my property to her. Stated another way, the wishes expressed in my will do not in reality express *my* wishes but are Mary's wishes, imposed on me by Mary as a result of her wrongful influence. If Mary did exercise such wrongful influence on me, then the contents of my will are not due to my voluntary act and should be declared invalid.

The reader should here remember that when my will is offered for probate (that is, for acceptance by the court) I am no longer alive and therefore am unable to testify as to all the facts. The burden is placed on Mary to disprove something of which she was not guilty: namely, of taking advantage of her close relationship with me to substitute her wishes or judgment for mine.

While no one can prevent one person from bringing a frivolous lawsuit against another, having a living trust in this situation would strengthen Mary's defense against John's unfounded claims. Assume that you were on the jury hearing this case and learned that I had created the trust five years ago. I had approved or signed income tax returns for the trust all these years, made bank deposits and withdrawals, communicated periodically with my attorney about the disposition of my property, and perhaps made periodic modest gifts to Mary from the trust funds; in other words, over a period of several years I showed my involvement in trust affairs. Because of this history, it is likely that you, the jury, would more readily reject John's claim that Mary exercised undue influence on me to prefer her to John.

This example should not be interpreted by the reader to mean that if I left all my property to Mary by will, without creating a living trust, my wishes would not be respected. All I am suggesting is that based on this example, a living trust would make a stronger case for Mary's position.

The reader should also be aware that when a will is offered for probate, all persons who would inherit from the decedent if there were no will must be given notice of the attempt to have the will probated. This is not necessary in the case of trusts. In the case just discussed, if I had created a living trust, John might never have learned of the disposition of my property to Mary whereas, with a will, he would certainly have done so.

What are the duties of a trustee named in a will?

After your will is probated (remember, *probate* refers to the court procedure involved in the acceptance of the will as representing your last wishes), the estate goes through the process of being *administered*. When this process is completed, the amount due the trustee is paid over to him or her. The trustee's duties are then to:

1. See to it that the cash or property (which is commonly referred to as trust *corpus* or *principal*) received from the estate representative is what the trustee is entitled to.

2. Arrange to have the trust principal titled to show that the owner is the trustee. In other words, it is necessary to separate registration of ownership to clearly show that the trust property belongs to the trust rather than to the trustee as an individual.

3. Carry out the intentions of the testator as expressed by the terms of the will. What this normally means is that the trustee must:

   a. Invest the funds wisely and solely in the best interest of the beneficiary, so that the maximum amount of income is earned.

      Trusts frequently provide that on the death of the one who is entitled to the income for life or for a certain period of time, someone else is entitled to the trust property thereafter. The one who is later entitled to the property is referred to as the *remainderman*. Therefore, the trustee must, in these cases, not only invest the trust property to secure maximum income, but also must protect the remainderman. This entails meeting the needs of those entitled to income and also those eventually entitled to the trust property. This calls for making investments that produce income but also that have (hopefully) some growth potential to enhance the trust property that will eventually be distributed.

   b. Run the business efficiently and solely in the best interest of the beneficiaries if the trust property consists of a business which the testator requires to be maintained as a going business.

   c. Deal with each beneficiary fairly and advise the person of all the facts in connection with the trust assets.

   d. Carry out his duties and, as needed, insure the property, hire personnel to do whatever is required to run the business, prepare the necessary income tax returns, hire accountants and lawyers, and in general take whatever steps are necessary to carry out the duties set out in paragraph c above.

A trust that is created by the terms of a will is called a *testamentary trust*. A trust created during someone's lifetime is called a *living trust* or an *inter vivos trust*. (*Inter vivos* is a Latin phrase meaning "among the living.") A *Clifford trust* and an *insurance trust* are specialized types of living trusts.

When reading those portions of the will dealing with the trust, you or your lawyer must answer these questions: Whom did the testator intend to benefit by creating the trust and how is this to be accomplished?

Let us assume that the trust was created to provide the decedent's sister, Mary, with income for her lifetime. Upon her death the trust was to be divided among your two sons. Perhaps the testator (your husband) provided that part or all of the principal of the trust may be used for his sister's benefit if needed for her health or support. (Another word for "principal" is "corpus." Most wills that give the trustee authority to use principal will use the phrase "invade principal.")

So far, the important participants are as follows: There is a testator (your husband) who was the creator, or grantor, of the trust. You (the wife) are the trustee. Mary (your sister-in-law) is a beneficiary. Your children are also beneficiaries, but they will first derive benefit from the trust after Mary's death. Since your children will only be entitled to benefits from the trust after Mary's death, they are known as *remaindermen beneficiaries* or just *remaindermen*.

Your sister-in-law's interest as a beneficiary is as an income beneficiary. Since the terms of the trust require that income is to be paid over to her, it is your required or mandatory duty as trustee to see that income is actually paid over to her.

If Mary is in need of further funds from principal for her health or support, it is within your discretionary power to pay these to her. This would be your second specific duty. As trustee, the more principal

you pay to Mary, the less will be left for your children. As a mother, you would naturally prefer your children to your sister-in-law. Yet, despite this, you were trusted to be sole trustee. Finally, when Mary dies you have a specific duty to pay over whatever is remaining in the trust to your two sons.

Let us now assume that your husband gave you no further instructions in the will. We must then look to general legal principles as to your duties. They are as follows:

---

1. Once you accept appointment as trustee, you are under a duty to administer the trust (as long as you are a trustee).

---

2. You have a duty to administer the trust solely in the interest of the beneficiaries. As an obvious example of this rule, assume you are a customer's representative in a stock brokerage firm and the sole trustee. You should not use your brokerage firm to buy or sell securities for the trust with the motive of generating more commissions for the firm and yourself.

---

3. You have a duty not to delegate to others the administration of the trust or the performance of acts which you ought to perform yourself. As an example of this rule, let's say you are a lawyer in general practice and the sole trustee. If the trust is running a busi-

ness and gets involved in litigation which you normally handle, you should not refer the lawsuit to another lawyer.

This does not mean that you must personally perform every act which may be necessary or proper. You can permit others to perform acts which you cannot reasonably be required to perform personally.

4. You are under a duty to beneficiaries to keep clear and accurate accounts. These accounts should show what you received and what you spent; they should also show gains and losses. Further, the records should show what amounts are assigned to income and to principal.

5. You have a duty to the beneficiaries to give them complete and accurate information about the administration of the trust upon reasonable request.

6. You have a duty to administer the trust with the same care and skill as any person of caution would exercise in dealing with his own property; if you have unusual skills you should use them on behalf of the trust. As an example of this rule, assume you are a Certified Public Accountant with substantial tax experience. You should analyze the trust's affairs with the view to reducing taxes.

7. You have a duty to take reasonable steps to take and keep control of the trust property.

8. You have a duty to use reasonable care and skill to preserve the trust property, to collect on claims, and to defend actions when appropriate.

9. You have a duty to keep the trust property separate from your own individual property and to see to it that the property is designated as property of the trust.

10. When making bank deposits, you should use care in selecting a bank. A bank deposit is considered a loan to a bank and therefore such deposits should be insured.

11. You have a duty to make the trust property productive. For example, you should not leave large sums in a checking account that does not pay interest unless you will be needing the money to pay current bills.

12. When a beneficiary is entitled to receive the income, you have a duty to pay it over at reasonable intervals.

13. When there are two or more beneficiaries, you are obligated to deal with them impartially.

14. If there are several trustees, each trustee must participate in the administration of the trust.

15. When another party (not a trustee) is given certain powers, for example, the power to decide where to invest funds, you are under a duty to act in accordance with instructions received unless this would violate the trust terms or violate your fiduciary duty.

My lawyer has recommended a marital deduction trust for my will. I did not understand his hurried explanation. Would you please explain what it means?

If your taxable estate exceeds a certain amount, it will be subject to federal estate taxes. The taxes can be substantial. However, when property is left to one's spouse, federal estate tax law allows the estate a deduction, with certain requirements, for the amount of the property that passes to the spouse. This deduction, called a *marital deduction*, is obviously desirable because it reduces or completely eliminates your taxable estate and therefore the federal estate taxes.

In order to get the benefit of the marital deduction, you need not leave the property to your spouse outright. The property may be left in a trust that meets certain technical requirements of the federal estate tax law. There are two types of trusts that meet these technical requirements. One of these trusts is commonly referred to as a *marital deduction trust* and the other type as a *Q-Tip*. A more detailed explanation of this subject is found in this book on page 146.

I have heard of *sprinkling trusts*. What are they and when are they used?

A *sprinkling trust* allows the trustee to use his discretion to distribute the income of the trust equally or unequally among a certain class of beneficiaries. (Remember, a trustee is the one who holds property for the benefit of another; the one for whose benefit the property is held is called the beneficiary.)

This type of trust is usually used in two situations. First, when one or more of your loved ones have a greater need; second, when there may be an income tax saving.

Here is an example of the first situation. You have three children aged 26, 18, and 12. You have already paid for the education of the oldest child and there may be greater need for income for the two younger children. Instead of distributing all your property equally among your three children on the death of you and your spouse, you provide that the property shall be held in trust until the youngest child reaches 22. While the property is held in trust, the trustee has discretion to favor one child over another, based on need and your hopes for the educational achievements of each. Then, much like a parent, the trustee could spend more of the income on the two younger children since the older child has already received his or her education during your lifetime. The trustee would therefore "sprinkle" more of the income toward the younger children.

Here is an example of the second situation. Your three children are aged 35, 33, and 29. The oldest child is now happily employed as a schoolteacher. He has a wife, who is a homemaker, and three young children aged five, two, and one. Your middle child is an unmarried rock concert promoter earning aproximately $130,000 every year, and your youngest child is also unmarried, a gifted physician who has a private practice and is on the faculty of a major medical school. The physician is earning approximately $80,000 per year. If the income of the trust were equally divided among the three children, income taxes would take away more than half of the income distributed to the two younger children. And they do not need the extra trust income. By being able to "sprinkle" the income, the trustee could benefit the oldest child at least until his children are older and his wife begins to work. The trustee would then treat the income as you would: its distribution would be based on the needs of your children without your showing less affection for any of them.

What is meant by an *accumulation trust* and when should it be used?

When property is left in trust under your will, you may provide that income shall be accumulated and not paid out until a certain date or event occurs.

For example, your spouse may be in a very high income tax bracket. If income is paid to your spouse following your death, most of the income may very well be reduced by high income taxes imposed on all your spouse's income. You could then provide that all trust income be "accumulated" until your spouse's income falls below a certain amount. Or if it never falls below this level, the accumulated income can then be paid to your children who, we assume, are in lower income tax brackets.

What is a *power of appointment* and when should it be used?

A *power of appointment* is giving someone the legal authority to determine who shall own property. Tax reasons for giving or withholding a power of appointment are explained under the topic of "Death Taxes." However, there are also non-tax reasons for giving someone a power of appointment, as follows.

Let us say that by will you leave all your property in trust for the benefit of your wife during her lifetime and thereafter for your children. Your wife is ten years younger than you are and you have three children. While you wish your wife to benefit from your property during her lifetime, you do not wish to direct that the trust property shall be left on your wife's death to your children in equal shares. You realize that your wife may survive you by ten, twenty, or thirty years. During that time, the financial situation of your children may change. One child may become wealthy and have no need for your funds, another child may be physically disabled and require the extra assistance that your funds can provide, and another child may be incapable of handling money.

Who, then, is in the best position to make the determination twenty years after your death? Obviously, your wife is. In such a case you can give your wife a power of appointment, which grants her the authority (gives her the power) to appoint the property, that is, to designate who shall be the owner of the trust property after her death.

There are several types of power of appointment. You may give this power so that it may be used (exercised) only on the death of the one who has the power. (This is known as a *testamentary power of appointment*.) In this case the one who has the power can only exercise it by will. You may give this power so that it can be used during the lifetime of the person who is given the power. (This is known as an *inter vivos power of appointment*.)

You may grant the power so that the one to whom it is given may appoint the property only among a limited group of persons, such as your children. This type of power is known as a *special* or *limited power of appointment*. If the power is such that the one who has the power can appoint the property to anyone in the world, including the one who has the appointing power or

authority, then this type of power is known as a *general power of appointment*.

The one who gives the power to another is called the *donor*. The one who receives the power is called the *donee*. The person who is favored by an appointment of the property by the donee is called the *appointee*. If the donee does not choose to exercise the power, the person who takes the property is called the *taker in default*.

What authority do I, as trustee, have? For example, can I sell stock of a closely-held corporation that the testator bequeathed to me as trustee?

You must look to the trust instrument to see its instructions.

The instructions contained in the trust instrument must be followed unless they violate some law or public policy. If the trust instrument does not contain any instructions, then you must look at state law to see what authority you have.

In general, you have broad powers to do whatever is necessary or appropriate to carry out the purposes of the trust. This would include incurring expenses; selling, leasing, and mortgaging property; voting shares of stock; and compromising, arbitrating, abandoning, and pursuing claims.

What investments may I, as trustee, make?

Once again, study the trust instrument to see what it says, if anything. Any instructions that are contained therein must be followed unless an instruction violates some law or public policy.

In the absence of specific instructions in the trust instrument, in most states the trustee is given a free hand as to what investments may be made. While the trustee has broad discretion, the trustee does have a duty to invest as a prudent person would. This standard of investment was set forth many years ago in a Massachusetts court decision which most states now follow. The court stated that a trustee must observe how people of prudence, discretion, and intelligence manage their own affairs, not in regard to speculation but in regard to the permanent disposition of their funds, considering the probable income as well as the probable safety of the capital to be invested.

The laws of your state may contain a list of the types of authorized investments or have other requirements. You should consult the laws of your state, preferably with your lawyer, for guidance.

I am the income beneficiary. The trustee has invested all of the trust assets in non-income producing land which has excellent prospects for future growth. The remaindermen are happy with this investment but I am not. What can I do about this?

The trustee has a duty to deal impartially with the respective beneficiaries and there-fore the trustee is under a duty to administer the trust to preserve a fair balance between them. In this case, the trustee is apparently sacrificing income while attempting to increase the value of the principal.

While the trustee has discretion in administering the trust, his discretion is subject to the supervisory authority of the courts.

As income beneficiary you can file suit asking the court for an order to compel the trustee to invest the trust principal in an appropriate manner so that you will receive income from the property.

Will I, as trustee, be required to file any tax returns during the administration of the trust?

A trust is considered to be a separate taxpayer and federal law requires the trustee to file an income tax return when the trust has any taxable income, has gross income of $600 or more, or when any beneficiary of the trust is a nonresident alien.

You should also check your state's laws to determine when a state income tax return must be filed for the trust.

Do the rules just mentioned apply to living trusts as well as to testamentary trusts?

Yes.

When does a trust end?

The terms of the trust provide for this. The trust may end on a certain date or it may end on the happening or non-happening of a certain event.

For example, the trust instrument may provide that the trust ends (terminates is the word usually used) on October 1, 1990, or it may provide that it terminates on the death or remarriage of the income beneficiary.

When the trust is a living (*inter vivos*) trust, the settlor may have reserved the right to terminate the trust at any time merely by notifying the trustee of his desire. In such a case, the trust would terminate when the settlor so notifies the trustee.

In many states, if the settlor and all the beneficiaries desire to terminate a living trust, that desire will be sufficient to terminate the trust.

When the trust terminates, what am I to do with the trust property?

Turn the trust property over to the person or persons entitled to it. You should account for all assets and receive a receipt and release from the person or persons entitled to the property.

I am concerned about proper management of my property in the event of my having a stroke or sustaining other physical or mental disability. I am aware of the benefits of creating a trust to take care of this problem. Nonetheless, I am uncomfortable with the idea of a trust and do not wish to create one. Do you have any other suggestions?

Yes. The laws of most, if not all, states permit you to give someone a power of attorney. This enables the person who holds the power to act for you, on your behalf, as your legal representative.

Several years ago, if a person became incompetent, the power of attorney given to someone else was automatically revoked. This rule caused any such power to have limited practical value. Today, the laws of virtually every state provide that a power of attorney may contain appropriate language so that, even in the event of one's disability, the holder of the power may continue to act on behalf of the person who granted the power. A power of attorney that contains this language is known as a *durable power of attorney*.

A power of attorney may be revoked by the grantor of the power so long as that person is competent to act. On the death of the grantor of the power, the power is automatically revoked.

DEATH TAXES

Estate Taxes

Inheritance Taxes

Gift Taxes

DEATH TAXES
(ESTATE AND INHERITANCE) INCLUDING GIFT TAXES

Tell me what you mean by death taxes.

Death taxes are those taxes imposed on the property that is transferred to another upon the death of an individual. The federal estate tax and state inheritance and estate taxes are referred to as "death taxes."

There are three basic death taxes, one federal and two state. In addition there is a federal gift tax on the transfer of property by gift during lifetime. (Some states also impose a gift tax.)

1. The most important death tax is the federal estate tax.

   This tax is imposed on the *transfer* of property by reason of the death of a decedent who was a citizen or a resident of the United States at the time of his or her death. The tax is imposed on the total value of (a) property owned by the decedent at the time of death, (b) "other property" which the decedent either owned at one time or over which the decedent retained or

had certain rights, and (c) taxable gifts made *after* December 31, 1976. (The technical name given to such gifts is "adjusted taxable gifts.")

2. An inheritance tax is another form of death tax. Most states impose this tax. The inheritance tax is imposed upon the privilege of *receiving* property from a decedent at death. An inheritance tax is not imposed by federal law.

   There is a difference between an estate tax and an inheritance tax. The estate tax is imposed on the privilege of transferring property at death whereas the inheritance tax is imposed on the privilege of *receiving* property. For example, I die in 1983 with a taxable estate of $350,000. The federal estate tax, after the unified credit, is $25,500 and is imposed on the privilege of transferring the $350,000 (which will be reduced by the $25,000 tax). Since I live in Maryland, if I leave $50,000 of that $350,000 to my cousin, Maryland would impose an inheritance tax on my cousin's privilege of receiving the $50,000 at the rate of 10% or $5,000.

3. Most states also impose an estate tax on the taxable estates of their residents or on real and tangible personal property located within their borders whether the real or tangible personal property is owned by a resident or a nonresident.

The states that impose the estate tax may do so in addition to the state inheritance tax.

Please give me an overview of how the federal estate tax is calculated.

Individually owned property plus other types of property	= Gross estate
Minus: Expenses, debts and income taxes	(subtract)
Losses from fires, casualties, thefts, storms, shipwrecks	(subtract)
Bequests to or for charities and public uses	(subtract)
Bequests to, or for the benefit of, the surviving spouse (the marital deduction)	(subtract)
	= Taxable estate

Federal estate tax (using the rate schedule) applied to:

Taxable estate plus adjusted taxable gifts minus credit for gift taxes paid for gifts made after 1976 (except for gifts made within three years of death)	= Tentative estate tax
Minus: Unified credit	(subtract)
Credit for state death taxes paid	(subtract)
Other credits	(subtract)
	= Amount of federal estate tax due

What is the *unified credit*?

The unified credit represents a dollar-for-dollar offset or credit against the estate tax. Between 1981 and 1987 it increases each year from $47,000 (in 1981) as follows:

Year of death or transfer	Amount of credit
1982	$ 62,800
1983	79,300
1984	96,300
1985	121,800
1986	155,800
1987 and thereafter	192,800

What is the amount of the federal estate tax?

The amount is determined by the rate schedule set forth in Table 1 at the back of this book.

You should know though that, in general, if your taxable estate plus adjusted taxable gifts are not more than the amounts that are shown below, there will be no federal estate tax.

The amounts are:

Year of death	Amount transferred without any tax
1982	$225,000
1983	275,000
1984	325,000
1985	400,000
1986	500,000
1987 and thereafter	600,000

There will not be a federal estate tax on the amount shown, for the years shown, because the credit eliminates the tax. For example, in 1982 the tax on $225,000 is exactly $62,800. Since the amount of the credit in 1982 is $62,800, the tax will be completely eliminated if death occurs in 1982. The credit is increased each year, and therefore the amount that can be transferred without a tax can be similarly increased.

What are the amounts of the estate and inheritance taxes for each state?

This information is also set forth in tables at the back of the book.

In general, the amounts vary from zero (in Nevada only) and 1% to a spouse (in Maryland) to as high as 32% for property passing to a non-relative (in Montana).

Who or what determines what my federal taxable estate consists of?

The Internal Revenue Code of 1954 does so. This is a compilation of all currently applicable tax laws enacted by Congress.

The Internal Revenue Service, which is a division of the U.S. Treasury Department, is charged with the duty of applying, interpreting, and enforcing the tax laws.

State laws usually follow federal law as to what assets are includible in a taxable estate and their value.

What does my taxable estate consist of?

Under federal law it is your gross estate minus certain deductions.

What does my gross estate consist of?

Your gross estate for tax purposes includes property which you own in your own name at the time of your death, and "other property."

You will recall that property individually-owned by you at the time of your death is the kind of property that you transfer by will at the time of your death. This property is known as part of your probate estate. Individually-owned property could include the following: cash on hand; an automobile; stocks and bonds; real estate; jewelry; a stamp, coin, or rifle collection; and debts owed to you. This is not a complete list, but is given by way of illustration.

Would rights to income be considered individually-owned?

They could. For example, assume you are an insurance agent and are entitled to commissions on renewals of insurance you originally sold. Your rights to these renewals are considered property. Had you lived when you received them, they would have been income. These renewals are rights to income. The value of these commissions would be part of your gross estate. While the value of the commissions is certainly difficult to estimate, the commissions must nevertheless be included in your gross estate.

If you were in an individually-owned business or were a professional and had accounts receivable, these, too, would be included in your gross estate. Also, you would have to include in your estate any accrued rents, interest on savings, or debts due to you.

As another example, assume your father left some property in trust for your mother for her lifetime and provided that on your mother's death the property would belong to you as outright owner, whether or not you were then living. If you die at age 55 but before your mother who is then age 75, is any part of the property part of your gross estate? Yes.

Why? Because while you are not there to receive the property when your mother dies, your estate will eventually receive it. Even though you are then dead, your interest in the property is fixed. Your will can dispose of it. Even though the one you leave it to may have to wait some years (for your mother's death) before enjoying the property, the interest is yours and is a property right just like any individually-owned property. (Technically, when someone has fixed property interests, these rights are referred to as being "vested.")

The value of your interest in your mother's property is not 100% of the value of the entire property. After all, your mother has a right to use and enjoy the property during her lifetime before you or your estate receive it. Apart from valuing your interest in the property at something less than 100% of the whole, the law is clear that since you have a vested interest in the property, this interest is part of your gross estate too.

(Where someone has a vested or fixed property interest which will come into possession after someone else's interest lapses, this interest is known as a "remainder" interest.)

Instead of your father giving your mother an interest in the property before you, let us reverse the situation. Your father died in 1970 and by his will left an office building in a trust, from which you receive the income for *your* lifetime. His will then provides that if your mother is still alive when you die, she will receive the income for *her* lifetime. On the death of the last one of you and your mother, the building will then be paid over to your father's then surviving issue, *per stirpes*. (Remember, *issue* means descendants—children, grandchildren, great-grandchildren, and so on; *per stirpes* means "by the root" and a parent takes the property to the exclusion of the succeeding generation; the phrase *his then surviving issue* refers to the persons living at some particular point of time.)

By stating that the property will eventually belong to your father's then surviving issue, the property will go to your children (and perhaps grandchildren), if any, and to your brothers and sisters, if any. In this case, at the moment of your death, you have no property interest in the office building. Your will cannot direct who shall inherit it after your death. The income interest you had in the office building ceased at your death. Therefore, no part of the building's value would be included in your gross estate.

If, at the time of your death, the ground floor tenant owes $4,000 for past due rent, and this amount is paid over to the trustees who then pay it to your estate after your death, the $4,000 will be included in your gross estate.

What about Social Security benefits? Are they part of your gross estate? No, they are not.

You have loaned your daughter $10,000 to enable her to buy a house. She gave you a note to evidence the loan. When you die, you provide in your will that the debt is forgiven and cancelled. Is the $10,000 included in your gross estate? Of course. The debt is a property right owned by you at the time of your death.

Are taxable gifts made after December 31, 1976, part of the gross estate?

Technically the answer is no. However, even though they are not part of the gross estate (and therefore cannot be part of the taxable estate), the amount of such gifts is subject to the federal estate tax. The reason for this is that federal law unifies taxable gifts (made after December 31, 1976—called "adjusted taxable gifts"), with the taxable estate. The federal estate tax is imposed on the total of these two amounts. This is known as the unified system of taxation.

How does the *unified system* work?

The unified system imposes the estate tax on the total of the lifetime transfers made after December 31, 1976 (gifts), and death-time transfers. Thus the rate of tax, just as for income taxes, becomes progressively higher for the value of property or cash transferred—whether transferred by gift or by death.

A simple example will clarify this. Let us say that you are a widow, and you make a cash gift of $235,000 to your son in 1982 and die in 1985 owning another $225,000. You will not have to pay any gift tax on the 1982 gift of $235,000 because the law allows a transfer of this amount before a tax is imposed. However, when you die, the tax that will be imposed will be calculated *as though you died owning $450,000;* the $235,000 you gave away (less $10,000—which will be explained in the next question and answer) and the $225,000 you own on the date of your death. The rate of tax will be based on $450,000 and not on the total of two lower rates imposed on $225,000 each. Before 1977, a gift tax would have been imposed on the gift, and an estate tax would have been imposed on the $225,000 estate; each tax bracket would have been lower.

Based on these facts, the following is a comparison of what happens when gifts are made during lifetime and when gifts are not made in advance, but are owned until the date of death. Because the tax rates changed January 1, 1977, the comparison is shown under the old law (which applied when death occurred before 1977) as well as under the new law. In both cases we will assume that you never made any gifts before those shown.

Old law (before 1977)		
	Gifts made	*No gifts made*
Gift made in 1972	$235,000	0
Less: Annual exclusion	3,000	0
Lifetime exemption	30,000	0
Amount subject to gift tax	$202,000	0
Gift tax	$38,475	0
Taxable estate (before the $60,000 exemption)	$225,000	$460,000
Estate tax	$40,200	$113,700
Total Taxes	$78,675	$113,700

New law (after 1981)		
	Gifts made	*No gifts made*
Gift made in 1982	$235,000	—
Less: Annual exclusion	10,000	—
Amount subject to gift tax	$225,000	0
Gift tax	0	0
Taxable estate (1982)	$225,000	$460,000
Plus: Taxable gifts	$225,000	
Amount subject to estate tax	$450,000	$460,000
Estate tax (Less the unified credit of $62,800)	$76,000	$79,400
Total Taxes	$76,000	$79,400

Under the old law (before 1977) the tax savings would have been $35,025, whereas under the new law there is only a saving of $3,400. Under the old law the taxpayer not only received the benefit of the annual gift exclusion (of $3,000) and the lifetime exemption (of $30,000) but also the benefit of having the gift tax and the estate tax split into two lower brackets.

Under the new law the only benefit is the exclusion from taxation of the first $10,000 of the gift from being taxed. The next question and answer will explain why this $10,000 is not taxed.

You previously mentioned exceptions in regard to gifts. What are they? Also please explain the phrase *taxable gift*.

Taxable gift means the total gifts made in any year less the annual $10,000 exclusion and deductions for property gifted to charity and a spouse. Property that is transferred to one's spouse qualifies for a marital deduction. The rules for the marital deduction are similar to those for estates. (See page 145.) In general, all property, without limit, that one transfers to his or her spouse receives a marital deduction which reduces the amount of gifts subject to taxable gifts.

The most important exception states that when you make a gift, the first $10,000 of such gifts made to any person in any calendar year is excluded from the amount of taxable gifts. Stated differently, a taxable gift is that part of a gift greater than $10,000 made in any calendar year to any person. (The person who receives these gifts is called the *donee*. The one who makes the gifts is called the *donor*.)

For example, I make a gift to you of $8,500 this year, and this is my only gift to you. Since the first $10,000 of gifts made this year is excluded for federal purposes, I have not made any taxable gift to you. If the gift is $10,500, then I have made a taxable gift of $500 ($10,500 less the $10,000 exclusion).

You can make gifts of $10,000 to each of your ten grandchildren every year, and the total of $100,000 given each year will *not* be taxable. There will be zero taxable gifts. Also, the amount given away will not be subject to estate tax. (Why won't this amount be subject to an estate tax? Because the estate tax is levied on the total of the taxable estate *and* taxable gifts. Here the taxable gifts are zero because of the $10,000 exclusion. In the previous question and answer you will note that the taxable gift to your son was reduced by $10,000.)

Another example: You make gifts of $12,000 to each of your ten grandchildren in 1982. The first $10,000 of each gift will be excluded and only the balance of $2,000 to each grandchild will be considered taxable gifts. This totals $20,000. Therefore you gave away a total of $120,000, and, because of the annual exclusion of $10,000 for each grandchild, you will be considered to have made taxable gifts of only $20,000. In connection with this exception:

1. The $10,000 per year exclusion applies to anyone as the donee. The donee does not have to be related to the giver of the gift (the donor), but can be.

You can make $10,000 gifts each and every year of your life to each of your five closest friends without any part of

the gifts being considered taxable. These amounts will not be subject to federal gift tax nor will they increase your federal estate tax.

Clearly then, if you have enough money and income, you can make such gifts to each of your children, grandchildren, cousins, etc., without any gift or estate tax whatsoever.

2. In order to exclude the first $10,000 of gifts made each year to each donee, the gift may not be one that is a "future interest." An example of a future interest would be when I make a cash gift to you but instead of turning it over to you now, I give it to your banker with the condition that no part of the money may be spent for one year. Then at the end of a year the cash would be turned over to you. This gift is a completed one but in the eyes of the tax law it is a gift of a future interest because its use, possession, or enjoyment will begin at some future time.

The second exception can arise if you are married when you make a gift. If your spouse agrees to split the gift with you, then one-half of the amount of the gift will be considered as made by you and one-half by your spouse.

The practical effect of this exception is that it reduces or can eliminate the total tax. As an example, assume you gave $20,000 to each of your three children in 1982 and only you filed a gift tax return. Were you to die in 1986, $30,000 would be added to your taxable estate. Therefore, the federal estate tax would be figured on your total taxable estate plus the $30,000. The $30,000 is arrived at as follows:

A gift of $20,000 to each of three children	= $60,000
Three $10,000 exclusions	= 30,000
Taxable gifts	$30,000

On the other hand if the split gift treatment were elected, the result would be as follows:

Gifts considered made by you		Gifts considered made by your spouse	
Gift of $10,000 to each of 3 children	= $30,000	Gift of $10,000 to each of 3 children	= $30,000
Three $10,000 exclusions	= $30,000	Three $10,000 exclusions	= $30,000
Taxable gifts	$ 0		$ 0

In connection with this second exception the following should be noted:

1. To take advantage of the split gift treatment both you and your husband or wife must be citizens or residents of the United States at the time of the gift.

2. In order to have benefited from a tax reduction or elimination for split gifts before the 1981 tax law change, you would have had to live more than three years from the date you made the gift. Now it is immaterial how much longer you live after the date of the gift.

3. You may take advantage of the split gift treatment (but are not required to do so), even if all of the funds or property came from the individually-owned assets of one of you.

The third exception states that the value of all taxable gifts made by you (after December 31, 1976) is the value on the dates when you made the gifts. For example, you can make a gift of 50 acres of land to your son in 1982 when the value is $50,000. For gift tax purposes the value is $50,000 (less the $10,000 annual exclusion). If the value of this land is $350,000 when you die, only the gift tax value (the $50,000 gift minus the $10,000 annual exclusion) will be used in figuring the estate tax. Therefore, for estate tax purposes your estate will escape being taxed on the $300,000 increase in value of the land (plus the $10,000 that represents the annual exclusion).

The fourth exception provides that when a gift tax is paid for gifts made more than three years before death, the amount of the tax is not included in either your taxable estate or as part of your taxable gifts. You will therefore reduce the amount of estate taxes eventually paid by your estate to the extent of the gift tax paid.

In view of what you said I will now begin making yearly $10,000 gifts to each of my children and grandchildren. Do you approve?

From the tax point of view, yes. But remember that you may need the money for yourself. Once given away, you may never see it again—even if needed. Also, children and grandchildren may become spoiled with too much money. Be sure that they have learned how to handle finances before making regular substantial gifts.

You explained what a *taxable gift* is but you never explained what a *gift* is. Please do so.

A gift is any transfer of property that exceeds the value in money or money's worth of the consideration given by the recipient of the gift to the donor of the gift.

Here are some examples:

1. I give my son $20,000 toward a down payment on a house based on his promise that he will stop smoking for one full year. He does so. What my son gave me in return was pleasure and satisfaction. While pleasure and satisfaction are valuable to me, they are not consideration in money or money's worth. Therefore the gift tax law states that I have made a gift to my son. (The amount of the taxable gift is $10,000— the first $10,000 is excluded.)

2. I give my lady friend an engagement present of a $15,000 ring. In return I receive her promise to marry me and she does. Have I made a gift to her? Of course—what I received in return was not consideration in money or money's worth. For gift tax purposes I have made a taxable gift of $5,000 ($15,000 minus the $10,000 exclusion).

3. I perform legal services worth $15,000 for my brother and receive nothing in exchange. There is no gift subject to the gift tax law, because I did not transfer property to him. The giving of services is not considered the transfer of property.

You will note that the word *gift* is used. But if you sell something to someone the general rule does not apply. Why? Because you have not made a gift. Instead you have made a sale and substituted one type of property for another which is, in theory, of equal value.

For example, I sell you my house for $75,000. You pay me this sum in cash. If I die still owning the $75,000, my estate will include the $75,000 cash. If I own the house on my death, my estate will still include $75,000, only it would be represented by a house. From the point of view of estate taxation it does not matter what the item is; all items are "translated" into U.S. dollar values.

Sometimes a transfer is both a gift and a sale. For example, if you sell your business to your son at any time after 1976 for $50,000 when it is really worth $100,000, what have you done? You have partly made a $50,000 gift and partly made a $50,000 sale. The $50,000 sale price is included in your gross estate because you received it and presumably own it on your death. The balance of the $100,000, the $50,000 gift (less the annual exclusion of $10,000), is also included in your estate for tax purposes because of the rule that gifts made after 1976 to the extent they exceed the annual exclusion ($3,000 for years 1977 to 1981 and $10,000 thereafter) are part of your adjusted taxable gifts.

What are the principal changes in the law affecting taxation of gifts?

Increasing the tax rates and "unifying" transfers made by gift during lifetime and transfers made at death. In addition, between 1977 and 1982 the general rule was that if a transfer was made by gift within three years of death and at the time of the gift the value of such property exceeded $3,000, the value of all the property as of the date of death was included in the gross estate.

The new law, effective 1982, specifies that the only time property transferred by gift within three years of death is included in a decedent's gross estate is when the transfer is with respect to a life insurance policy, or the transfer represents gift taxes paid for gifts made in 1977 or thereafter. Certain technical exceptions still apply.

While it is now clear that the gross estate includes property individually-owned on date of death, please explain what is meant by "other property" which you advise is also required to be included in the gross estate?

There are eight categories of such property:

1. Lifetime transfers where an interest is retained for life. (See Part A, page 116, and Part B, page 123.)

2. Lifetime transfers where the beneficiary can receive his interest only if he survives you and you retain certain rights to get the property back. (See pages 117 and 125.)

3. Lifetime transfers where you have the power at the time of your death to alter, amend, revoke, or terminate the enjoyment of the property transferred. (See pages 117 and 126.)

4. Annuities (under certain circumstances). (See page 128.)

5. Joint interests (under certain circumstances). (See page 129.)

6. Property over which you have a general power of appointment at the time of death. (See page 131.)

7. Life insurance (under certain circumstances). (See page 134.)

8. Under very limited circumstances, certain property transferred within three years of death. (See page 142.)

The first three categories are known as property which you have transferred but over which there are "strings" attached. Some readers of this book may not be interested in reading a detailed discussion of the first three categories.

I have therefore divided a discussion of the first three categories into two parts, called Part A and Part B. Part A will give a broad overview and Part B will explain the subject in greater detail and with more illustrations. The reader who reads Part A only will, it is hoped, still be able to acquire a basic understanding of the law.

PART A—OVERVIEW

1. Lifetime transfers where an interest is retained for life.

You know, of course, that if you wish to make a gift of your house to your son, all that is necessary is for you to sign a deed and record the deed with the clerk of the court having supervision over land records. The ownership interest transferred by a deed is known as the *fee simple* interest.

Let us suppose that it is your desire to leave your house to your son but as long as you live you wish to live in the house. You then prepare a deed giving the house to your son on your death but reserving the right for you to live in it until your death. This is known as *reserving a life estate.*

You will note that in reality you gave away all of the property except for the value of what you kept. You will also note that the life interest you kept ends on the date of your death. Despite this, is the value of the entire property included in your gross estate? Yes. This is so because the law says that when you give something away but keep the right to the income or the right to the use and enjoyment of the property, you have kept a "string" on the property. Therefore, all of the property is included in your estate, even the part that you gave away.

Change the facts somewhat. Assume you create a trust and transfer all of your property to the trustee. You may make no changes in the terms of the trust, and it is irrevocable. On your death all of the property will be transferred to your son. During your lifetime, you will receive all of the income from the trust. Is any part of the trust included in your gross estate? Yes, all of it. Since you retained the right to the income from the property during your lifetime, all of the property is included in your estate even though you gave away the remainder interest (the part that remained after your death).

2. Lifetime transfers where the beneficiary can receive his interest only if he survives you and you retain certain rights to get the property back.

Let us say you create an irrevocable trust, and transfer to the trustee property worth $50,000. You provide that your mother shall receive the income for her lifetime and on her death the trust property will be paid to your daughter if then living, and, if she is not then living, it will be paid to you if living.

No part of this property will be included in your gross estate because the income to be paid to your mother is not dependent on surviving you. That is, your mother is entitled to the income regardless of whether or not you are then living. Also, your daughter's interest is not dependent on surviving you. But if you provide that the trust income shall be paid to your mother only *during your lifetime,* then you will notice that here she has to survive you to enjoy the income. If the value of what you retained (the "string") is more than 5% of the value of the property, the law requires that the value of all of the property be included in your gross estate.

3. Lifetime transfers where you have the power at the time of your death to alter, amend, revoke, or terminate the enjoyment of the property transferred.

When a gift is made directly to a minor, the minor has no legal capacity to sell the property. The Uniform Gifts to Minors Act is a law that was passed as a means of permitting someone else, the custodian, to legally act for the minor.

When you make a gift under this act, you transfer the property to an adult, usually the parent, who acts as custodian of the property for the minor. The custodian can pay out the income or accumulate it, sell the property, exchange it for other property, and in general act with respect to the property as though the custodian were the owner of the property. The only limitation is that everything must be for the benefit of the minor.

When you make a gift under the act, the income from the property is not taxed to you even though you are the custodian. This is because the owner of the property is the minor.

However, if you are the custodian of property at the time of your death and you made the gift of the property you are holding as custodian, even though you are no longer the owner of the property, the property will be included in your gross estate. Why? Because the law says that although you originally made the transfer, as custodian you have the authority to affect the time when the income is paid out. This authority amounts to a power to alter the enjoyment of the property. When you have this power (a "string"), the law says the property is includible in your estate.

It does not matter that you may have first made your wife the custodian when you made the gifts. If she resigns as custodian, or dies, and you are the custodian at the time you die, all the property over which you are custodian and which you had transferred would be included in your gross estate.

In this connection, consider the following circumstances. You have five children, each one year apart in age. The oldest is now 17. From the date each child was born and until 1982, you made yearly gifts of $3,000 worth of Exxon stock to yourself as custodian for each child. When you die, the value of the property owned by each child, with yourself as custodian, ranges from $60,000 to $120,000.

If you die when you are custodian, close to $500,000 (the total value of all these custodial accounts) will be included as part of your gross estate. If someone else is the custodian, no part of these accounts will be included in your gross estate.

When you made a $3,000 gift to a donee in any year before 1982, no part of it was includible in your gross estate even though you died within three years of the date of the gift. But if at the time of your death you were the custodian of property which you gifted, the old three-year rule and the old $3,000-per-year-per-donee exclusion (now $10,000-per-year-per-donee) are immaterial. The only material fact is that at the time of your death you had the power to alter the enjoyment of property (the prohibited "string") which you had transferred. Under this rule, the amount that is included in your gross estate is the value of all the property of which you are custodian.

PART B-DETAILS

What follows in this Part B is a more detailed analysis of the law dealing with property you have transferred and over which you have "strings" attached (the first three categories). The law states that when you transfer property during lifetime as a gift and retain *or* have certain rights at the time of your death, all or part of the property will be included in your gross estate.

Most transfers of this type require the creation or use of trusts. You will recall that a trust created under a will is called a *testamentary trust*. A trust that is created during lifetime is called a *living trust* or an *inter vivos* trust. Living trusts are either revocable or irrevocable. However, a trust that is created by will takes effect only some time after death. Therefore, such a trust is always irrevocable after the death of the creator of the trust (in this case, the testator).

If a trust is revocable, the one who creates the trust (who is usually called either the *settlor* or the *grantor*) may revoke the trust. Usually when a trust is created as a revocable trust all that is necessary for the settlor to revoke the trust is to send a written notice saying so. For example, you have just retired from business and have decided to travel around the world. If you own stocks, someone should be able to collect the dividends, exercise stock options, sell the stock, and vote the stock. You create a trust with perhaps either a child, your attorney, or a bank as trustee. You transfer all the stock to the trustee who collects the income and mails it to you periodically and watches the corporations' status. When you return from your trip, you might wish to revoke the trust and receive back all of the stock. Or you might like the arrangement so much that you decide to do nothing about the stock in the trust and let it continue.

A revocable trust does not have any income or estate tax advantages.

An irrevocable trust is one that the settlor (the one who creates the trust) may not revoke. He has given away his property either absolutely or for the period of time specified in the trust instrument.

An irrevocable trust frequently does have tax advantages, both in terms of income and estate tax.

An example of an irrevocable trust is a *Clifford Trust* (this name originates with a case entitled *Helvering v. Clifford*—the taxpayer was named Clifford).

Tax Saving Suggestion:
What is a *Clifford Trust*?

When a trust is revocable all of the income is taxed to the settlor even though someone else receives the income. For example, you (as settlor) hire a lawyer who prepares a written instrument called a revocable trust. You turn over to the trustee some cash. The terms of the trust instrument, which you and the trustee sign, provide that during your mother's lifetime she will receive all of the income from the trust property (in this case, as cash). Despite the fact that the income is in fact paid over to her as a gift, you are taxed on the income. She will pay no tax on the income.

If you create an irrevocable trust, this trust may be irrevocable during your lifetime or irrevocable for only one year or any number of years. An irrevocable trust that is created for ten years or more is commonly called a

Clifford Trust. A Clifford Trust is frequently used by a parent for the benefit of one or more children to help build up assets for their college education. If a trust is irrevocable for at least ten years, then during the time when it is irrevocable, the income is *not* taxed to the settlor. This will save income taxes and leave more money available for the benefit of the children.

How does this work? A trust instrument is written by your attorney and provides that for at least ten years and one month, the trust is irrevocable and that at the end of the ten years and one month, or a longer period, the trust ends. At the end of the period, whatever property you placed in the trust is returned to you. (The phrase that is used when property is placed into a trust is *funding the trust*.) During the time the property is held in trust, the income is paid over to your children if over 18 years (21 years could be substituted) and, if younger, to a custodian under the Uniform Gifts to Minors Act of your state.

The income will be taxed to each child at his or her low income tax bracket. Had you not created the trust, the income from the property would have been taxed to you at your highest income tax bracket. For example, let us say you place $150,000 in cash in the trust for your five children. The $150,000 earns $15,000 per year. If you held the money in an account in your name, you would pay an income tax of $7,500 (assuming you are in the 50% bracket). The children pay virtually no tax on the first year's income in view of the $1,000 exemption available to each. Regardless of the income each child has, as long as they are students and you supply more than one-half of their

support, you may claim them as dependents on your income tax return and also get the $1,000 exemption for each. The income of $15,000 per year that is invested will itself generate additional income.

At the conclusion of the ten-year period the $150,000 is returned to you. However, the accumulated income belongs to the children. This will amount to approximately $30,000 for each child (after taxes) or a total of $150,000. Had you continued to own the $150,000 throughout the ten-year period, the accumulated income, after taxes, would only amount to approximately $65,000.

You should be aware that a transfer of property to a Clifford Trust could constitute a taxable gift. But based on the facts just given, there would be no gift tax due, which is explained in the next question and answer.

Please explain why in the previous example, involving a Clifford Trust you stated that there would be no taxable gift. Also, in view of the fact that no gift tax will be due anyway, what difference would it make to my estate plans?

Let's say that you placed $150,000 in the trust and you have five children. When a gift is made of the use of the property for a ten-year period, the law states that the value of this gift is 61% of the property so transferred. Since you transferred to the trust $150,000 for a period of ten years, the gift tax law provides that the gift amounts to 61% of $150,000, or $91,500.

If you transfer $75,000 in December of any year, the value of this will be $45,750 (61% of $75,000). Since you will be entitled to exclude $10,000 of any gift made to a child in any year, you will be entitled to exclude the entire $45,750 ($10,000 × 5 children = $50,000; because this is higher than $45,750, the entire $45,750 is excluded). Immediately after the first of January in the succeeding year, when the trust still has at least ten years before it terminates, you should transfer the other $75,000. The value of this gift is $45,750 (61% of $75,000). Because of the $10,000 exclusion rule, no part of this gift will be considered part of your taxable gifts.

If you have a wife and agree to file split gift tax returns, these figures could be doubled without having any taxable gifts.

The answer to the rest of your question will enable us to review the broad rules as to how the new law (since 1977) has "unified" the estate and gift tax laws.

Let us assume you are single and own a total of $475,625. In 1979 you make a gift of $175,625 to one child. (Assume that the annual gift tax exclusion [then $3,000, now $10,000] is not available because the gift is of a future interest.) The tentative gift tax on a gift of $175,625 in 1979 is $47,000. However, since you are entitled to the unified credit of $47,000, the gift tax will be zero.

Although you have paid no tax, the entire $175,625 is added to your taxable estate for purposes of computing the estate tax due. If we assume that your taxable estate in 1983 is $300,000 (the balance remaining after the gift of $175,625), the estate tax will be calculated on the *total* of the $300,000 plus

$175,625. The $175,625 represents your taxable gifts made since January 1, 1977 (the law calls this "adjusted taxable gifts"). The tentative tax on $475,625 ($300,000 plus $175,625) is $147,513. From this tentative tax is subtracted the unified credit available in 1983 of $79,300 (the credit is higher in later years) to arrive at the net tax of $68,213.

Had you not made the gift of $175,625, the estate tax would be calculated on your taxable estate of $475,625 plus adjusted taxable gifts of zero, or a total of $475,625. This will produce the same taxes as those shown above where the gift was made.

Changing the above figures will produce a slight variation in the results shown.

Assume that the 1979 gift is increased by $50,000 and that what is left is reduced by this $50,000. The gift will therefore be $225,625 and the tentative gift tax is $63,000. After the unified credit available in 1979 of $47,000 (the credit is higher in later years), the net tax is $16,000. When you die (assume this occurred in 1983) your taxable estate will be $234,000, which is the original $475,625 minus the $225,625 gift and the $16,000 gift tax.

The estate tax will now be calculated on the taxable estate of $234,000 plus the adjusted taxable gifts of $225,625. The tentative tax on $459,625 ($234,000 plus $225,625) is $142,073. From this tentative tax is subtracted the unified credit of $79,300 *plus* the gift tax of $16,000 that was paid, to arrive at the net tax of $46,773.

Had you not made the gift of $225,625, the estate tax would have been calculated on your taxable estate of $475,625 plus adjusted taxable gifts of zero, or a total of $475,625. The difference between $459,625 and $475,625 is represented by the gift tax of $16,000. This $16,000 will not be subject to estate tax if the gift is made more than three years before death.

The specific answer to the second question would therefore be that there is no tax difference where no gift tax is due. However, when a gift tax is paid and the decedent lives more than three years after the gift is made, the gift tax paid will *not* be subject to estate tax. (The significance of living more than three years after the gift is made is that if death occurs within the three-year period, the gift tax will be included in the taxable estate.)

Tax Saving Suggestion:

I wish to be able to have my daughter taxed on the income from some of my savings without the expense of creating a Clifford Trust. Also, I do not wish to make taxable gifts. Do you have any comments?

Yes. Several years ago, a taxpayer named Crown loaned millions of dollars to several trusts which benefited several relatives. The loans bore no interest and were demand loans. The United States Tax Court held that the lender was not subject to gift tax on the value of the use of this money. On appeal, this decision was affirmed.

While the only question to be decided by the court was whether or not this type of loan was subject to gift tax, the court noted that prior court decisions "have uniformly rejected every attempt by the Internal Revenue Service to subject the making of non-interest bearing loans to income or gift taxes." The Internal Revenue Service, as expected, announced its disagreement with the decision.

The law was changed so that, with limited exceptions, the device of making interest-free loans is no longer desirable. This has been accomplished by treating such a loan, in general, as though interest were charged. Such interest belongs to the donor and is taxed to the donor.

However, where the loan between individuals does *not* exceed $10,000, if the loan proceeds are not invested in income-producing assets, there is no tax consequence to the lender. Where the loan exceeds $10,000 but does not exceed $100,000, if the donee has no investment income, there will still be no income tax consequence to you, but it will constitute a taxable gift.

The suggestion is either to make completed gifts of $10,000 per year, or to have the proceeds uninvested and used to pay the donee's expenses.

Other Trusts

When you create an irrevocable trust, unless there are "strings" attached to the trust, no part of the trust will be includible in your gross estate. (The Clifford Trust has a slightly different result because at the end of the ten-year period, the trust property is returned to you. The value of this property will therefore be included in your gross estate.)

Before we review the "strings," you might ask about the advantages of an irrevocable trust. The principal ones are:

1. The property in the trust is no longer yours and therefore, on your death, would be transferred to your loved ones rapidly without the delays and administrative costs of probate.

2. If the property that is placed in trust is located in several states, then on your death the property can be transferred to your loved ones by the trustee without the necessity of going through some form of probate proceeding in each state. Accomplishing the transfer by using a trust can save substantial sums in comparison to the state-by-state probate method.

3. From the estate tax point of view, there would be savings because:

   a. If the property increases in value after you transfer it to the trust, the increase in value will not be subject to any estate tax.

   b. Any tax you pay when you transfer the property will reduce the amount of your gross estate that will be subject to estate tax.

   c. The amount of the taxable gift made to the trust will be reduced by the $10,000 annual exclusion for each donee and can be greater if the "split-gift" treatment is elected. (We are assuming that the gift is not one of a future interest.) Therefore, the $10,000 that is excluded from taxable gifts will not be subject to either a gift or an estate tax.

4. From the income tax point of view there is usually a savings. When property is transferred it is usually for the benefit of a member of the family whose income tax bracket is lower than yours. The difference between the tax brackets represents the savings.

There are some disadvantages in transferring property to an irrevocable trust. The principal ones are:

1. If a bank, attorney, or third party is appointed the trustee, there will be trust commissions or fees to be paid every year.

2. If the property is sold after your death at a profit, income taxes will be higher than if you continued to own the property until death.

3. You will lose control of the asset. You may need the asset for your support or for investment in another business. When it is transferred to an irrevocable trust, the asset is forever lost to you.

4. A legal fee is incurred in preparing the trust instrument (also called a *trust agreement*).

The technical explanations that follow are patterned after the headings in Part A.

1. Lifetime transfers where an interest is retained for life.

An earlier illustration concerned creating an irrevocable trust whose income was to be paid to you for life. It was pointed out that even though you gave away the remainder interest (the balance remaining after your death), the value of the entire property was included in your gross estate. Why? Because by keeping the right to receive the income for your lifetime from all the property that you transferred to the trust, you have kept a prohibited "string" which causes all the trust property to be included in your gross estate.

What if you provide that for your lifetime you shall receive one-half the income from the trust property? In this case the law provides that one-half of the value of the trust property will be included in your gross estate.

Let us change the facts slightly and provide that while you are entitled to the income from the trust property for your lifetime, income shall be paid to you four times a year. You will receive the income on March 31, June 30, September 30, and December 31 of each year, but if you die on any date other than these dates, the income for the period from the last payment date shall not be paid to your estate. For example, you die September 15. Since the pay date for income is September 30, the income from July 1 to September 15 will not be paid to your estate. Your estate representative could then argue that since you have not retained the income for your lifetime (remember—the last payment you received was on June 30), the property should not be included in your gross estate.

However, the law also says that property will be included in one's gross estate not only when income is retained for life but also when income is retained for a period that cannot be determined except by reference to one's death. (The actual language of the law is "for a period not ascertainable without reference to his death.") In the example just given, the period for which you retained the income could be determined only by reference to your death and

therefore the trust property must be included in your gross estate.

Let us change the facts once again. You now provide that the trust income will be paid to you for 20 years and you die after 15 years. The rule just stated (retaining income for life or for a period that cannot be determined except by reference to your death) does not apply here. However, once again, the law covers this situation. It provides that if income is retained from property that is transferred for a period which does not actually end before the settlor's death, all of the trust property from which the income is derived is included in the gross estate. Here it is clear that since you retained the right to receive the income from the trust property for a period which did not actually end before your death, the trust property is included in your gross estate.

The technical requirement of the law goes one step further. It says that where the settlor of a trust reserves the right (either alone or with another) to determine who shall possess or enjoy the trust property or the income from the trust property, and he dies having this right, the trust property will be included in the gross estate. It does not matter that the settlor personally cannot enjoy the property or the income. The prohibited "string" is the power to determine who may enjoy the trust property or the income from the trust property.

Some examples will help to understand this rule.

a. You create a trust during your lifetime in which the income from the trust property is to be paid to your wife for life, and on her death the trust will terminate and be paid over to your children. When you create the trust, you retain the right to have principal of the trust paid over to your mother, but only if needed. Because of this right, you are considered to have a prohibited "string" to the property transferred. The trust property will therefore be included in your gross estate.

b. You create a trust during your lifetime in which the income from the trust property is to be paid to your children, Ann and Robert, in equal shares, during their lifetimes, or all to the survivor of Ann and Robert. On the death of both, the trust will terminate and be paid over to your daughter, Susan. When you create the trust, you retain the right to give more income to one of the children and less to the other, but Ann and Robert must *consent* to any such unequal distribution. Even though you must receive someone's consent, the law says that you have retained the right to determine who shall possess or enjoy the property. This retained right is a prohibited "string" to the property transferred. Therefore the trust property will be included in your gross estate.

c. You create a trust in which the trust income is to be paid to your sister for life, and on her death the trust will terminate and be paid over to your nieces and nephews. You retain the right to accumulate income and add it to the principal of the trust. Because of this power, you have really retained the right to determine who shall enjoy the

income. This retained right is a prohibited "string" to the property transferred. Thus, the trust property will be included in your gross estate.

Each of these examples illustrates a situation in which you have retained the right to determine who shall enjoy the property. This right is, in each case, a prohibited "string." The law seems to say that this is the equivalent of your enjoying the property yourself, and it therefore causes the property over which you have this power to be included in your gross estate.

2. **Lifetime transfers where the beneficiary can receive his interest only if he survives you and you retain certain rights to get the property back.**

Review of some definitions: The one who transfers property is called the *donor* or *transferor*. The one who receives the property is called the *donee* or *transferee*. The settlor of a trust is also usually the *transferor*. Why "usually"? Because you may create a trust and transfer to it $1,000. Later your son may add property to the trust and he becomes the transferor of such (added) property. The trustee of a trust is also the transferee. A *beneficiary* is the one who receives benefits from property.

If you, as transferor, provide that the property you gave be returned to you, this is known as retaining a *reversionary interest* (in other words, the property reverts, or is returned, to you). For example, you give certain property in trust for the benefit of your mother for her lifetime and provide that on her death the property be paid over to your children who survive her; however, if there are none, the property must be returned to you. This is known as retaining a reversionary interest. Of course, it is not certain whether you will actually outlive your mother and receive the return of the property.

The law says that if the value of your reversionary interest is greater than 5% of the value of the property the moment prior to your death, and when possession or enjoyment can be obtained *only* by surviving you, the property will be included in your gross estate.

In the prior example, you left property in trust, and your mother was to receive the income for her lifetime. She was entitled to receive the income regardless of whether or not you were then living. Since her possession or enjoyment of the income was not conditional upon surviving you, no part of the trust would be included in your estate by reason of this provision even though you retained a reversionary interest. However, suppose you provided in the trust that your mother was to receive income from the trust *only* if she survives you. You will note that here your mother's enjoyment of the trust property is dependent on her surviving you. In this case, if your reversionary interest was greater than 5% of the value of the property the moment prior to your death, the trust property would be included in your gross estate.

How is the 5% calculated? This is done by checking the tables prepared by the Internal Revenue Service, published as part of the Treasury Regulations issued in connection with the Internal Revenue Code of 1954.

The purpose of this rule is to tax property when there has not been a completed lifetime transfer. If the transfer is such that there is a prohibited "string" attached, then it is as though it is a transfer at death—and transfers at death are taxed as part of the gross estate.

3. Lifetime transfers where you have the power at the time of your death to alter, amend, revoke, or terminate the enjoyment of the property transferred.

In the two preceding categories, the property would be included in your gross estate only if you *retained* certain powers when you transferred the property. In this category, it is not necessary that you shall have retained the prohibited "string." It is only necessary that you have the prohibited power at the time of your death. In such a case the property involved will be included in your gross estate.

For example, suppose you transfer property to your cousin, Robert, as trustee and provide that the income from the property shall be paid to your daughters, Ann and Susan, in equal shares, during their lifetimes; on the death of one of them all the income shall be paid to the survivor for her lifetime. You also provide that the trustee may, at his discretion, use the principal of the trust for the benefit of any of your sons and any of your grandchildren. Five years later, Robert resigns as trustee and you are appointed trustee. You die while serving as trustee.

In this case, you have the power to alter or terminate Ann and Susan's enjoyment of the income. Why? Because you can distribute all of the principal to others, and this will either reduce or eliminate the amount of income available to Ann and Susan. Even if you can distribute only part of the principal to others, the amount of income available to Ann and Susan will also be reduced.

If the power you have to use principal could be exercised only with the consent of Ann, the property would still be included in your gross estate. The argument is that if Ann approved your proposed action, that would be contrary to her financial interests. In other words, she is an "adverse" party. The law makes no distinction in this situation. Since you have the power to invade principal, even though the power is available only with the approval of an "adverse" party, the property is includible in your gross estate.

The law further states that it does not matter that you cannot take back the property for your own benefit. As long as at the time of your death you have the power to alter, amend, revoke, or terminate the trust, any one of these powers will be sufficient to cause the property to be included in your estate.

Suppose you create a trust and retain some of the prohibited powers; however, four years before you die you are declared to be incompetent. By reason of this, you are legally incapable of exercising any of the powers. Is the property includible in your gross estate? Yes. The rule is that since you have the power, even though you could not do anything about it, the property is includible.

Exception to All Three Categories

It should now be reasonably clear that, if a person has certain "strings" to property he has given away, the situation is similar to his owning the property on the date of death.

That is, it is as though the decedent disposed of the property when he died rather than during lifetime. It is equally clear that when an individual disposes of property at death, this type of transfer is subject to the estate taxes that are imposed on property being transferred at death.

When property is transferred in exchange for a cash payment made to the transferor, the transferor's estate is not artificially reduced. If he receives cash of, say, $200,000 in exchange for property worth $200,000, the $200,000 cash is still part of his estate and will be subject to estate tax.

The law provides that if any of the transfers referred to in the prior three categories is made, the property that is included is only the amount, if any, that is greater than any cash or other property received in exchange for the transfer. The law refers to this important exception as a transfer made for an adequate and full consideration in money or money's worth.

For example, you transfer $200,000 to a trustee to be held in trust and you retain the income from the property so transferred for your life. On your death, the trust will terminate and will then be paid over to your son John, if then living, and if not then living, to his estate. When you made the transfer, your son paid you $150,000 to make the transfer.

Since you retained the income from the property for life, you have kept one of the prohibited "strings" which would cause the property to be included in your gross estate. If not for the exception that was just explained, your estate would include not only the $200,000 you transferred to the trust but also the $150,000 your son transferred to you in exchange. To include $350,000 in your gross estate is obviously unfair. Therefore, the law states that of the $200,000 you transferred to the trust, only $50,000 of it (the amount by which the transfer is greater than the amount that was transferred *to you*) will be included in your estate.

In this case your gross estate will include the $150,000 received by you from your son (assuming you still have it on the date of your death) plus the $50,000 of the trust property. This exactly equals the $200,000 you had originally.

We have now concluded the technical discussion of the first three categories (Part B) and what follows is a discussion of the remaining five categories.

---

4. Your gross estate includes annuities.

Simply stated, the word *annuity* as used in the law means the right to receive one or more payments extending over any period of time. The payments may be made on a regular basis, infrequently, or irregularly. Also, the payments do not have to be in equal sums.

The law includes an annuity in a decedent's gross estate, but only if (1) the decedent is entitled to receive payments and *in addition* a beneficiary is entitled to receive benefits under it *after* the decedent's death, and (2) the annuity is paid under any form of contract or agreement. The annuity is included in the gross estate only to the extent that its value is caused by contributions made by the decedent or his or her employer. For example, I buy an annuity

from an insurance company which entitles me to receive $1,000 a month for my lifetime. I die. Is any part of the annuity included in my estate? No. Why not? Because there is no beneficiary under this annuity contract after my death.

Assume, though, that I buy an annuity which entitles me to receive $1,000 a month for my lifetime and on my death my wife shall be entitled to receive $1,000 a month for *her* lifetime. If my wife outlives me, the value of her payments will be included in my gross estate for tax purposes.

When one thinks of an "annuity," one usually associates this with an insurance company. But annuities can be paid under other types of arrangements, too.

For example, you enter into a contract with your employer to pay you a retirement benefit of $1,000 a month for life and provide that if you are survived by your wife, Joan, she is to receive the benefit of $750 a month for her lifetime. It has been determined that this arrangement is really an annuity which is included in your gross estate.

The most important exception to these rules involves benefits paid under a *qualified* pension or profit sharing plan. (A qualified plan is one to which contributions made by an employer are deductible by the employer for income tax purposes. The contributions are not considered income to the employee when made.) This exception also applies to benefits paid under an Individual Retirement Annuity (I.R.A.) or H.R. 10 (Keogh) Plan.

This exception states that when the benefits are paid to a beneficiary other than the employee's estate, the benefits, limited to

$100,000, are not included in the gross estate. If the employee contributed to the plan, then the proportionate part of his or her contributions that was *not* deductible for income tax purposes would be included in the gross estate. For example, you are the employee and contributed $20 every pay period, but such contribution was *not* deductible for income tax purposes. Your employer contributed $80 every pay period. You die before retirement and your spouse is entitled to receive $1,000 per month for her lifetime. In this case, if at the time you die the "annuity" of $1,000 per month is worth $120,000, then only 20% of this amount would be included in your estate. The figure of 20% is chosen because you contributed $20 of the total of the $100 contributed each pay period (your employer contributed the other $80).

If your employer contributed the entire $100, then no part of the annuity to be received by your spouse (limited, however, to $100,000) would be included in your estate. Also, if the $20 you contributed every pay period was deductible for income tax purposes, it would be considered as an employer contribution.

However, if the benefits to be received by your spouse are paid in a lump sum, then another rule applies. This rule states that the entire lump sum is included in your gross estate *unless* the beneficiary agrees *not* to use, for these proceeds, the favorable ten-year averaging (or capital gain treatment) that would otherwise be available for income tax purposes.

5. Your gross estate includes joint interests.

If I died today and my name appeared as joint owner of any property with someone who is *not* my spouse, federal estate tax law provides that the value of the *entire* property must be included in my gross estate. However, if my personal representative or executor, or my joint owner can establish that part of the property originated with him or her, then *that* part will not be included in my gross estate. Tax law now provides that if the jointly-owned property is owned by husband and wife, then, regardless of who paid for the property, only one-half of the value of such property is included in the estate of the first one to die.

What is *jointly-owned property*?

It is property that is owned by joint owners, usually two persons, and on death of one the other one automatically becomes the owner of the entire property. (This is known as *right of survivorship*; that is, the survivor will own it all.)

What is **tenancy-by-the-entireties property**?

This is the name given to property jointly-owned by husband and wife. The tax rules applicable to jointly-owned property also apply to tenancy-by-the-entireties property.

Here are some examples of jointly-owned property: a bank account in your name and your wife's (or a child's) name as joint owners with right of survivorship; stock of General Electric Company registered in your name and your wife's (or a child's) name as joint owners with right of survivorship; the house you live in if the deed shows the owners to be you and your wife as tenants by the entireties (remember, tenancy-by-the-entireties property is treated as jointly-owned property).

What is the difference between property that is owned by two people as (a) joint owners (b) tenants by the entireties, and (c) tenants in common?

a. Joint owners
On the death of one, the survivor owns all the property. During lifetime, either joint owner can sever (break up) the joint ownership either by sale or deed. In such a case each party is entitled to receive one-half of the property. (If there are more than two joint owners, each joint owner is entitled to received the same proportion of the property as there are owners. That is, three owners—each is entitled to one-third; four owners—each is entitled to one-quarter; and so on.)

b. Tenants by the entireties
This is a joint ownership between husband and wife in which the survivor becomes the sole owner of the property on the death of the other. Neither party can break up the joint ownership without the other's consent. On divorce of the parties, the law provides that ownership changes from tenants by the entireties to tenants in common.

c. Tenants in common
Each party owns one-half of the property. On the death of one, that party's one-half interest passes as he or she provides by will or, if there is no will, as provided by state law.

When we celebrated our silver wedding anniversary, I gave my husband a gift of $10,000. He used the money to buy IBM stock. The stock is registered in our joint names. If I die first, will the stock be part of my gross estate?

No, only one-half will be part of your gross estate. Since the stock is jointly-owned, and you are one of the owners at the time of your death, the law provides that if you die in 1982 or thereafter, only one-half will be included in your gross estate. It is immaterial where the money came from or how the property was first registered or titled. What is important is how the property is owned (titled) at death.

My husband and I own the house we live in as joint tenants. The house was a gift to us both under the will of my Uncle George. If I die first and the house is then worth $90,000, what amount will be included in my gross estate?

Since it is owned jointly, the amount will be $45,000.

I have read that I can save taxes by titling property in joint names with my wife (or husband). Is this correct?

Generally, no. In a few situations, such as when the total value of the property owned by you and your spouse is worth less than $325,000 (in which case, because of the unified credit, there will be no federal estate tax if death occurs in 1984 or later), titling property in joint names may save a little money. The savings here would take place because in some states there is no state death tax for property inherited on the death of one spouse by a surviving spouse.

In the usual situation, titling property this way would cause substantially higher taxes because some property would be taxed twice, as shown by the following example.

Assume you own property worth $325,000, your wife owns property worth $525,000, and you title all *your* property (the $325,000) as joint tenants with your wife.

You die first. There will be no federal estate tax or state death tax (assuming you live in a state with laws similar to Maryland's). When your wife dies her *gross* estate will be $850,000. The federal estate tax, before the unified credit, will now be $287,300. If she dies after 1986, when the unified credit will be $192,800, the net tax will be $94,500. (If she dies earlier, the tax will be higher.) This amount ($94,500) *could* have been saved by your leaving $325,000 in trust for your wife.

When everything you own is in joint names with your spouse, at the moment of your death the spouse becomes the owner of all such property. Therefore, regardless of what your will says, you have no power to leave anything in trust for your wife.

It is, of course, appropriate to note that when property is titled in joint names, such property would not be subject to the jurisdiction of the courts; in other words, it would not be probate property. This may save commissions and legal fees to some extent. On the other hand, whatever legal fees are paid could be an income tax deduction to your spouse. (In any event, commissions can be saved by designating your spouse as the personal representative.)

---

6. Your gross estate includes property over which you have a general power of appointment at the time of death.

When one has a general power of appointment over property at the time of death or, under certain circumstances exercised or released this power, the value of the property is included in that person's gross estate (and is therefore subject to estate tax).

To understand this rule we must first understand what is meant by a *general power of appointment* as well as a *special power of appointment*.

A *power of appointment* (either *general* or *special*) is a right given to someone to dispose of property. The one who has this right does not own the property, but has control over it to a certain extent (that is, to the extent of determining who shall eventually own it). The one who has this right is called the *donee* of the power and sometimes the *holder* of the power. The one who gives the right to the donee is called the *donor* of the power. When the donee exercises the power, the law provides that the eventual owner acquires ownership from the original owner, the *donor* of the power, and *not* from the donee of the power.

For example, by your will you give your wife the power to designate who shall own your (former) house on her death. Under your will you did not leave her ownership of the house. She had a right to live in it for her lifetime. She does not own the house but she certainly has a lot of control over it—she has the right to determine who shall own it after her death. This right to give it away is called a *power of appointment.*

There are two kinds of powers—general and special. A *general* power is one in which the holder of the power (the donee) could give away (appoint) the property to anyone. "Anyone" includes even the holder of the power. Many years ago Congress decided that a general power of appointment should be included in the gross estate of the one who had this power, even though that person was not the owner. Congress felt that having this ability to give ownership of the property to anyone, including the holder of the power, was the equivalent of ownership.

A *special* power of appointment is one that limits the person or persons to whom property may be given. For example, by your will you give your wife the power to designate who shall own your (former) house on her death. However, you limit her power so that she may pick the owner from among only certain relatives of yours (normally children). Because of this limitation, this power is considered to be a special power. While the economic control over the property is a pretty broad one, it is not quite the same control as when someone has a general power. (A *special* power of appointment is sometimes called a *limited* power of appointment).

Congress decided that when someone has only a special power of appointment, the property over which the power is held should *not* be included as part of that person's estate for tax purposes.

When someone is given a power, what can he or she do with it? The person can exercise it, let it lapse, release it, or renounce or disclaim it.

To *exercise* the power means to act upon it. For example, if I give you the power to designate who among my children shall own my automobile next year and you give ownership to my daughter Jane, you have exercised the power. If you do nothing about the power you have let it *lapse*. On the other hand, if you give up the power, that is, you voluntarily waive any right to exercise the power, you have *released* it.

The law also permits you to refuse to accept the power I have given you. This is known as a *renunciation* or *disclaimer*. If you renounce or disclaim the power shortly after learning of the power I have given you, it is as though you never had it and it causes no tax problems.

The general rule is that when a person dies and has a general power of appointment over property at the time of his death, the value of the property over which he has the power is included in his gross estate. In addition, if the decedent had income rights in the property or kept certain "strings" and at any time during his life had a general power of appointment which he had exercised, let lapse, or released, the value of the property is included in the gross estate.

The two principal exceptions to the above rules are highlighted by the next two questions.

Exceptions to These Rules

In his will, my late father created a trust for the benefit of my mother for her lifetime. The trustee is a bank that is required to pay her all the income. On her death the property is to be paid over to me. My mother has the right to receive each year $5,000 or 5% of the trust if she requests it. The trust is now and has always been worth $350,000. My mother owns another $150,000. From what you have said, since my mother could have received most of the trust over all these years but did not, she had a general power of appointment which she let lapse. Do you mean that the $350,000 will be part of her taxable estate?

Your question illustrates an exception to the general rule.

The will permits your mother to request $5,000 or 5% of the trust, and this power on her part is a general power of appointment. In any year in which she does not take it she has let it lapse. When she lets it lapse she still enjoys the income from the $5,000 or 5% she could have received but which remains part of the trust. The general rule says that when a person has a general power of appointment and allows it to lapse and still enjoys the income from it, the property will be taxed as part of that person's estate.

The exception to this rule is that when there is a lapse, the first $5,000 or 5% of

property, whichever is greater, is exempt from death or gift taxes. In your mother's case, she could have taken either $5,000 or $17,500 (5% of $350,000) each year, neither of which she took. Any year in which she did not take the income there was a lapse. However, because of the exception, the property which she did not take (which lapsed) will not be included in her gross estate.

Assume the same facts as in the previous question except that the reader's mother was the trustee. The trustee could pay over to herself any amount of the principal of the trust if she deemed it necessary for her health, education, maintenance, or support. Am I to assume that since she can take whatever she needs for her support this is the equivalent of a general power of appointment and therefore the entire trust property will be included in her gross estate?

No. This question illustrates another exception to the general rule.

Here your mother's power is limited to satisfying her needs for her health, education, maintenance, or support. Because of these limitations, the law states that the power she has is *not* considered the equivalent of a *general* power of appointment. Therefore, the property over which she had this control will not be included in her gross estate.

7. Your gross estate includes proceeds of life insurance under certain circumstances.

Life insurance is a very important part of our lives. It provides people of even modest means with substantial funds at times of financial need. While the proceeds of life insurance are usually not subject to income tax, they can be the cause for substantial estate taxes.

Before I explain the basic rules, a simple example of how life insurance can cause high and unexpected estate taxes is appropriate. Assume that all my possessions (house, car, cash, and miscellaneous) are worth $225,000 and that when I die I have a wife. If I leave everything to my wife, there will be no federal estate taxes on my death. When my wife dies owning the $225,000 (assuming she has no other assets) there would be no federal estate tax in her estate either. But assume I also own term life insurance on my life which pays my wife $600,000 on my death. In this case, the federal estate tax could be substantial.

On my death there will be no estate tax but on my wife's death (if after 1986) the tax will be $84,750! If my wife dies in 1984, the tax will be $181,250! This tax can be saved, but before explaining how, let's discuss the basic rules.

Simply stated, they are:

a. When proceeds of life insurance are received by the estate of the insured, the amount received will be included in the gross estate of the decedent (and therefore subject to estate taxes) even if the insurance is not owned by the decedent.

b. When proceeds of life insurance are received by any beneficiary of the insured decedent, if the decedent owned any incidents of ownership in the insurance policy or policies on the date of death, then the proceeds of the life insurance insuring the decedent's life will be included in the gross estate of the decedent (and therefore subject to estate taxes) even if the insurance is not owned by the decedent.

If proceeds of life insurance on my life are not paid to my estate and I have no incidents of ownership in the policy, did I understand correctly that the proceeds will not be included in my estate for tax purposes?

Yes. However, if, when the proceeds are payable to another, that person is under a legally binding obligation to pay debts of the estate, it is *as though* the proceeds were paid to your estate. In the latter situation the proceeds of insurance would be included in your estate for tax purposes to the extent of such obligation.

Tell me what you mean by life insurance.

Life insurance is a contract in which there is a risk involving someone's life and the risk of a loss is shifted from an individual to a group. For example, you and I enter into a contract. You agree to pay me $100 per month for life. On your death, I agree to pay $10,000 to whomever you name. I am taking a risk that by the time you die the total amount paid over to me by you, together with the interest on the money, will be greater than the $10,000.

This type of arrangement is *not* considered life insurance for federal estate tax purposes because the risk I am taking involves only me, an individual.

However, if you enter into this same type of arrangement with the John Hancock Life Insurance Company, the risk is spread among a large group of people and this arrangement would be life insurance.

There are two broad types of life insurance policies: *term* and *ordinary*. (Ordinary is also called *whole life* or *universal life insurance*.) Term life insurance is the name given to that type of policy which never has any cash values. If the insured dies when the policy is in effect, then the company will pay over the face amount of the insurance. Ordinary life insurance is the name given to another type of policy which, with the passage of time, acquires cash values. With this type of policy (even before the death of the insured—when the face amount will become due) the owner can always ask the company to pay over to the owner the cash values.

An *annuity policy* is not life insurance. When you buy an annuity policy from a life insurance company, the company agrees to pay you a certain agreed-upon sum of money for a certain period of time. This amount is usually paid to you during your lifetime. The cost of the annuity is based on the amount that the insurance company believes it can earn with the money you pay less a reasonable amount for overhead and profit. Unlike life insurance, the amount of the annuity paid to you has no relationship to how many people of your age die at any particular time. In other words, the company undertakes no risk related to how many people live or die at any particular time.

What are some features of life insurance?

1. Life insurance is a contract, usually between you and an insurance company.

2. A policy may insure you and yet be owned by someone else. For example, I applied for a policy on my life many years ago. I transferred ownership of the policy to my daughter. The owner of the policy is my child.

   The one whose life is insured is called the *insured* and the owner of the policy is called the *owner*.

3. The one who receives the face amount of the policy on the death of the insured is called the *beneficiary*. The insured, the owner, and the beneficiary could be three separate people. A corporation could also be an owner or a beneficiary.

4. Sometimes someone other than the owner of the policy can have certain rights in the policy. For example, life insurance is issued on my life but my wife is the owner and beneficiary of the policy. If I have the right to either

borrow on the policy or change the beneficiary (even though I am not the owner), then I am the one who has certain rights in the policy. These rights are called *incidents of ownership*.

At the suggestion of my lawyer I transferred ownership of life insurance on my life to my wife. She died and all her property was left in trust for the benefit of our children. I am the trustee. Will the insurance be taxed as part of my estate?

If you have an incident of ownership in the policy, even though only as trustee, the answer is yes. If you as trustee can affect the time when your children will enjoy the policy proceeds, you have an incident of ownership.

Give me some examples of incidents of ownership.

a. The power to change the beneficiary.

b. The power to surrender or cancel the policy.

c. The power to transfer ownership of the policy.

d. The power to revoke an assignment of the policy.

e. The power to pledge the policy for a loan.

f. The power to obtain from the insurer a loan against the surrender value of the policy.

Why does the law treat life insurance differently from other property?

Because life insurance is by its nature property which benefits someone when there is a death. With other kinds of property, benefits are derived during lifetime. Although life insurance is singled out for special treatment, all the general rules for taxing property still apply to it.

Tell me how life insurance is taxed.

The way it is taxed is not widely understood and therefore many people are surprised that it is the cause of so much taxation.

While the premiums for term life insurance are initially lower than for other forms of life insurance, term insurance has no build-up in cash value. Its only value is when there is a death, when the face amount becomes payable. During lifetime, the cash value of term insurance is $0, but on death its value is the face amount.

Were you to own a term policy on your life with a face value of $100,000, you would not think that you have any substantial amount of wealth. But on your death your beneficiary would receive $100,000.

On receipt this sum does represent a substantial amount.

For federal estate tax purposes, the amount that is taxed is not the cash value during lifetime (which, in the case of term insurance, is zero), but the face amount which is payable on death.

Many readers may have heard or read that when insurance proceeds of a policy owned by a decedent-insured are paid to one's husband or wife there is no death tax. For state death tax purposes this may be the case (depending on the laws of your state), but this is not the case for federal death (or estate) tax purposes. For example, assume the insured is a woman who owns the policy and she designates her husband as beneficiary. If she is a Maryland resident at the time of her death, Maryland imposes no inheritance tax on the proceeds of this policy. However, for federal estate tax purposes, the policy proceeds are certainly subject to estate tax.

The ownership of a policy can be separated from the one who is the insured. The beneficiary can even be a third person. Thus, there is an opportunity to save estate tax.

Tax Saving Suggestion:

I am now 70 years of age and still happily married to my first wife. We have two lovely children who will eventually inherit everything we own. I own stock worth $600,000 and my wife owns stock worth $600,000. I also own life insurance with a face amount of $200,000 (after deducting its cash value). I wish to have my wife benefit from all this property. Is there any way I can arrange it so she can benefit from the property and yet minimize estate taxes?

Yes. We assume here that both you and your wife will die after 1986.

We should first look at what the taxes will be if you continue to own this property, you take advantage of planning so there is no tax on your death, and you die first. This will require you to leave part of your property in trust for the benefit of your wife.

On your death, the estate taxes will be as follows:

Gross estate (stock worth $600,000 plus life insurance of $200,000)	$800,000
Marital deduction for property transferred to wife	200,000
Taxable estate	$600,000

Tentative tax	$192,800	
Unified credit	192,800	
Net estate tax		$ 0

On your wife's later death, the estate taxes of her estate will be as follows:

Her own assets	$600,000
Received from your estate	200,000
Taxable estate	$800,000

Tentative tax	$267,800	
Unified credit	192,800	
Net estate tax		$ 75,000

Total taxes of both estates:	
Your estate	$ 0
Wife's estate	75,000
Total	$ 75,000

In this case, $600,000 of your property will be left in trust. Your wife will benefit from this $600,000 during her lifetime, but no part of it will be taxable in her estate.

Substantial taxes can be saved as follows:

Transfer the life insurance to an irrevocable living trust. If you live more than three years after the transfer, the life insurance will not be subject to estate tax in either your estate or your wife's estate.

On your death, the estate taxes of your estate will be as follows:

Gross state		$600,000
Marital deduction for property transferred to wife		0
Taxable estate		$600,000
Tentative tax	$192,800	
Unified credit	192,800	
Net estate tax		$ 0

All of your property, or $600,000, will be added to the irrevocable trust. Following your death, the trust will consist of the $200,000 of the life insurance proceeds plus your entire estate, or $600,000. The total will therefore be $800,000.

The terms of the trust shall provide that your wife will receive all of the income for life plus whatever principal she will need for her health, maintenance, or support to maintain the same standard of living she had when you died. You can also give her the privilege to withdraw from the principal of the trust, every year, $5,000 or 5% of the principal, whichever is greater. In other words, she will have full enjoyment of the property in the trust.

The trust will not be taxed in your wife's estate on her death after you.

On your wife's later death, the estate taxes of her estate will be as follows:

Her own assets	$600,000
Received from your estate	0
Taxable estate	$600,000

Tentative tax	$192,800	
Unified credit	192,800	
Net estate tax		$ 0

Total taxes of both estates:

Your estate	$ 0
Wife's estate	0
Total	$ 0

Total savings:

Total estate taxes when you keep ownership of the life insurance	$ 75,000
Total estate taxes when transferring ownership of the life insurance to an irrevocable trust	0
Total savings	$ 75,000

What will happen if my wife dies before I do and either (a) I still own life insurance on my death or (b) at least three years prior to my death I turn over the life insurance to an irrevocable trust?

Under (a), the estate taxes would be as follows: On your wife's earlier death, the estate taxes of her estate will be:

Her gross estate	$600,000
Marital deduction for property transferred to you	0
Taxable estate	$600,000

Tentative tax	$192,800	
Unified credit (1987 or later)	192,800	
Net estate tax		$ 0

On your later death, the estate taxes of your estate will be as follows:

Gross estate (stock worth $600,000 plus life insurance of $200,000)		$800,000
Received from wife's estate		0
Taxable estate		$800,000
Tentative tax	$267,800	
Unified credit	192,800	
Net estate tax		$ 75,000
Total taxes in both estates:		
Your wife's estate		$ 0
Your estate		$ 75,000
		$ 75,000

In this case, $600,000 of your wife's individually owned assets will be left in trust for your benefit. No part of these trust assets will be taxable in your estate.

Under (b) the total tax would be as follows:

On your wife's earlier death, the estate taxes of her estate will be:

Her gross estate		$600,000
Marital deduction for property transferred to you		0
Taxable estate		$600,000
Tentative tax	$192,800	
Unified credit	192,800	
Net estate tax		$ 0

On your later death, the estate taxes of your estate will be as follows:

Gross estate (stock only)		$600,000
Received from wife's estate		0
Taxable estate		$600,000
Tentative tax	$192,800	
Unified credit	192,800	
Net estate tax		$ 0

	(a)	(b)
Total taxes:		
Wife's estate	0	0
Husband's estate	$ 75,000	$ 0
	$ 75,000	$ 0

You will note that here, if your wife dies before you, you will save $75,000 (the difference between $75,000 and $0) when you transfer the life insurance to an irrevocable trust.

Transferring ownership of life insurance sounds too good to be true. What is the catch?

There are a few drawbacks, none of which is too serious. They are:

a. When you give ownership of your life insurance to a trustee of a trust, you cannot later change your mind and get it back if you so wish. The transfer is a final one. You can, of course, give your wife the right to return the insurance to you. Giving her this right will not be cause for any adverse tax consequence.

b. When the proceeds of the insurance are collected, your wife will not be the owner. While she will have virtually 100% of the economic benefits from the trust, she will not be the absolute owner of the property.

When I pay premiums on this life insurance, won't I be making taxable gifts?

No, provided there is a properly drafted *Crummey clause.*

What is a *Crummey clause* and why would this clause be necessary?

When you pay premiums on life insurance that you have given away, you make gifts of these premiums. When a gift is a *present interest,* the first $10,000 of gifts made to any person is excluded from federal gift tax. The law provides that when premiums are paid on life insurance in an irrevocable trust, the gift is usually one of a *future interest,* and that therefore the first dollar of the gift is taxable.

Since taxable gifts are included in the base against which the estate tax is calculated, it is obviously desirable to take advantage of the $10,000 exclusion if possible.

The Crummey clause is named after a court case. The court decided that when someone is given the right to withdraw from the trust each year the amount that is excluded from gift taxation (then $3,000 but now $10,000), since they can have the present use and enjoyment of amounts withdrawn, any premiums that are paid of $10,000 or less will indeed be gifts of a present interest.

Hence, if you use a Crummey clause, the premium payments (of $10,000, or less) will not be taxable gifts and will not be subject to estate tax.

Why bother with a trust? I can just transfer ownership of the policy to my wife. Is this okay?

No. If you do this, the insurance proceeds will be taxed in your wife's estate.

This can be demonstrated as follows, based on the last example given:

On your death, the estate taxes of your estate will be:

Gross estate	$600,000
Marital deduction for property transferred to wife	0
Taxable estate	$600,000
Tentative tax	$192,800
Unified credit	192,800
Net estate tax	$ 0

On your wife's later death, the estate taxes of her estate will be:

Her own assets	$600,000
Life insurance proceeds received	200,000
Received from your estate	0
Taxable estate	$800,000
Tentative tax	$267,800
Unified credit	192,800
Net estate tax	$ 75,000

You will note that, from the tax point of view, this result is not desirable.

Despite this, assuming you still do not choose to transfer ownership of the life insurance to an irrevocable trust but wish to transfer ownership to your wife, there will be a saving if your wife dies before you and if under her will she transfers ownership of the life insurance directly to your children. The saving will be accomplished because on your later death, the proceeds of the life insurance will not be part of your taxable estate.

I am a widower and am not in very good health. I have one living daughter who will inherit everything I own. I do not have much and therefore want to be sure that taxes are minimized. I own a $50,000 whole life insurance policy insuring my life. It now has a cash value of $19,000. If I transfer the policy to my daughter as a gift and I die within three years, I understand that the entire $50,000 will be subject to estate tax in my estate. Instead, I intend to sell my daughter the policy for the $19,000 cash value. Is this advisable?

Generally not. The law now provides that proceeds of a life insurance policy are not subject to income taxes. However, when you sell a policy to someone, the policy proceeds are then subject to income tax.

In this case, if you sell the policy to your daughter, she would have to report the amount she receives above her cost of $19,000 as ordinary income.

While it is conceivable that her income tax bracket is lower than your estate tax bracket, I would doubt this considering that you have what you describe to be a modest estate.

Let me demonstrate this by an example. Assume that in 1983 your taxable estate, including the life insurance, totals $300,000. If you give the entire policy to your daughter as a gift and survive more than three years thereafter, the estate tax of your estate will be zero. If you do nothing with the policy and die owning the policy, the estate tax will be approximately $8,000.

If you sell the policy to your daughter for $19,000, which is at least your cost, you would reduce your taxable estate by $31,000 (the $50,000 policy less the $19,000 you would receive for the policy). In this case the estate tax of your estate will be zero. But when your daughter receives the $50,000 life insurance proceeds, she will be required to report $31,000 as income (the $50,000 policy proceeds less the $19,000 she paid for it.)

Assume that your daughter has other income of $15,000 in the year in which she receives the $50,000 and that she is single. Her income tax without the life insurance proceeds will be approximately $1,900. Adding the $31,000 of income will cause the tax to be approximately $12,900 or an additional $11,000.

Thus, while you saved $8,000 in estate taxes, your daughter's income taxes were increased by $11,000 for a total tax dollar loss to your estate and your daughter of $3,000.

This result can, of course, vary depending upon whether we can use income averaging for calculating your daughter's income taxes, the additional state income tax, if any (offset by a federal deduction for state income tax), and the amount of her other income.

My husband died this year. I am the beneficiary of a $50,000 insurance policy on his life. I read somewhere that there are advantages to leaving this money with the insurance company which will pay it out to me over a period of years. Would you please tell me if this is true and the details?

With rare exceptions, proceeds of life insurance are not subject to income tax. Normally, you would take the $50,000 and—let's say—place it in a savings account paying 8 1/2% interest. You would be receiving $4,250 of interest plus such amounts of the principal as you care to withdraw. The interest of $4,250 is subject to federal income tax.

If you leave these funds on deposit with the insurance company, up to $1,000 of the interest that the company would pay would be excluded from being considered income for income tax purposes. For example, let us assume that you agree to leave the monies on deposit with the company for a ten-year period. Usually, you would have the right to withdraw the balance at any time. The company would then pay you $5,000 a year plus the interest on the balance they are holding. The rate of the interest they would agree to pay depends upon their rate of interest that they normally pay at that time. Thus, the excess above the $5,000 of principal will be con-

sidered interest income and the first $1,000 of this interest income will be excluded from being subject to federal income taxation.

This example is, of course, a simplification of how this works and it is important that you review this matter with your insurance agent and your own attorney to determine what is best for you.

---

8. Transfers within three years of death.

Earlier you stated that certain property transferred within three years of death was included in the gross estate. Please explain.

Before January 1, 1977, any gift made within three years of death was included in the gross estate only if it was made in "contemplation of death." The problem became one of having the Internal Revenue Service and sometimes the courts struggle with what was meant by the phrase "contemplation of death." Taxpayers tried to show that transfers were not made in contemplation of death. For example, taxpayers argued that motives included making a loved one financially independent, a desire to relieve oneself of responsibilities of managing assets, a desire to avoid possible claims of creditors, and similar motives.

Under the law effective from January 1, 1977, to December 31, 1981, the motive for making gifts is immaterial. The only question is whether the gift falls within the three-year period. If it does, and the gift exceeded the annual gift tax exclusion (then $3,000 but now $10,000), the entire gift (even the part that is otherwise excluded for gift tax purposes) may be included in the gross estate at its value on the date of death or its alternate value (discussed later), and if it does not, it may be excluded.

The new law, effective January 1, 1982, has eliminated even this three-year rule so that, with certain technical exceptions and with the exception of life insurance policies transferred and gift taxes paid within three years of death, *any* transfer will now be excluded from the gross estate.

(If the gift exceeds $10,000 to any person in any year, the excess above $10,000 will be considered a taxable gift and will be added to the taxable estate for purposes of calculating estate taxes.)

Apart from insurance, how is property valued for federal estate tax purposes?

The general rule is that for estate and gift tax purposes, the value of property is its fair market value. The date when the value is determined for state tax purposes is usually the date of death. However, the executor of the estate can choose to have the property valued on the alternate valuation date, which is usually six months after date of death. The date when the value is determined for gift tax purposes is the date of the gift.

Fair market value has been defined as, "the price at which the property would change hands between a willing buyer and a willing seller, neither being under any compulsion to buy or to sell and both having reasonable knowledge of relevant facts."

The value of property is essentially a factual one and has been the subject of much litigation. The reader should seek the advice and counsel of an attorney, accountant, or trust officer in connection with valuation of property.

Tax Saving Suggestion:

Under the new law, which increases the annual exclusion for gifts from $3,000 to $10,000, there is a unique opportunity to save substantial sums in estate and gift taxes! If a parent is close to death but legally competent, a gift of $10,000 could be made to each child and grandchild in one year. The separate $10,000 gifts would completely escape federal estate and gift taxes.

Recently a client of mine had her father make gifts of $10,000 to herself, her husband, her four children and each of their spouses, and two grandchildren. The total gifts in one year were $120,000. By eliminating $120,000 from the taxable estate, the estate tax was reduced by $44,400.

Please note that the new law does not apply to life insurance policies, regardless of value. For example, suppose that one year before death, you transfer the following:

1. A $100,000 group term life insurance policy to your son Frank.

2. A $20,000 whole life insurance policy to your son James.

3. A $20,000 whole life insurance policy to your daughter Karen.

4. A $2,000 whole life insurance policy to your daughter Anne.

When you transferred the group term policy, it had a cash value of $0, the $20,000 policy transferred to James had a cash value of $2,500, the $20,000 policy transferred to Karen had a cash value of $5,000, and the policy for Anne had a cash value of $800.

While at death a life insurance policy pays the beneficiary the face amount of the policy, before death the policy may have a *cash value.* That is, the policy could be cashed in at any time for its cash value. Will the $100,000 policy with a cash value of $0 be included in your gross estate? The answer is yes. The amount to be included in your estate will be the face amount of $100,000. While the cash value at the time of the gift is less than $10,000, the rule does not apply to life insurance. This same answer applies to the $20,000 policy with a cash value of $5,000.

What about the $2,000 policy with a cash value of $800? Even though the death value (the amount to be paid on death—in this case, $2,000) is under $10,000 (and even though the total of both the face value and cash value are under $10,000), the entire face amount of the policy, or $2,000, is still included in the gross estate. This same answer applies to the $20,000 policy with a cash value of $2,500.

Why is this so? Because the law says that the three-year rule does not apply to *any* transfer with respect to a life insurance policy.

What deductions are available to every estate?

As we pointed out earlier in this topic, the federal estate tax is based on the taxable estate plus adjusted taxable gifts.

The taxable estate consists of the gross estate minus certain deductions, as follows:

A. *Funeral expenses that are allowable by the laws of the state that has jurisdiction over the estate.* This item includes the expenses for a tombstone, monument, mausoleum, burial lot, perpetual care and maintenance, and even the cost of transportation of the person bringing the body to the place of burial. When a Social Security death benefit is paid to the decedent's surviving spouse or children, such benefit does *not* reduce the allowable funeral expense.

B. *Administration expenses that are allowable by the laws of the state that has jurisdiction over the estate.* Here the expenses are those related to the settlement of the estate and the transfer of the property of the estate to individual beneficiaries or to a trustee. This would include executor's commissions, attorney's and accountant's fees, court costs, and appraiser's fees. Also deductible would be expenses for selling property of the estate if the sale is necessary to pay the decedent's debts, and taxes and expenses of administration to preserve the estate or to effect distribution.

C. *Claims against the estate which represent personal obligations of the decedent existing at the time of his death and interest thereon to the time of death.* This would include income taxes on income received before death, mortgages on estate property, and alimony.

D. *Losses incurred during the settlement of the estate arising from fires, storms, shipwrecks, or other casualties, or from theft, if the losses have not been reimbursed by insurance or otherwise.*

E. *Transfers to or for the United States or any state and transfers for charitable and religious purposes.*

F. *Transfers to a surviving spouse.* This deduction is known as the *marital deduction.* While prior law limited the amount that could be deducted, present law allows an unlimited deduction (or 100%) for any property passing to a surviving spouse subject to the following conditions:

1. The decedent from whom the property is transferred must be a citizen or resident of the United States at the time of death. The surviving spouse does not.

2. The property interest that passes to the surviving spouse must be included in the decedent's gross estate, be outright and absolute, or be left in a fashion that meets the requirements of paragraphs 3 *or* 4 (following).

Except for interests in property passing on death of the spouse *and* meeting the requirements of paragraphs 3 or 4, the type of property must be such that *no* other interest in the same property can pass from the decedent to another person who can possess or enjoy the property. For example, assume the decedent leaves a house to his wife for life (called a life estate) with the house going to his children upon her death. Since the property interest will end on the wife's death and the children will possess or enjoy the property (the house) after her death, the value of the property will not qualify for the marital deduction. This type of property interest is called a "terminable interest," because it will terminate on the death of the wife.

A terminable interest in property is non-deductible only when someone other than the spouse may enjoy or possess the property.

3. The interest in the property may be left to the surviving spouse either for life or in trust and must meet *all* the following conditions:

   a. The surviving spouse must be entitled for life to all the income from the property or to a specific portion of the income.

   b. The income from the property must be payable to the surviving spouse annually or more often.

c. The surviving spouse must have the power to appoint the entire interest or the specific portion to either herself or her estate.

d. The power in the surviving spouse to appoint the property must be exercisable by him or her alone and must be exercisable in all events.

e. No person, other than the surviving spouse, may have a power to appoint any part of the interest in the property.

4. The interest in the property may be left to the surviving spouse either for life or in trust and must meet *all* the following conditions:

a. The surviving spouse must be entitled for life to all the income from the property or to a specific portion of the income.

b. There must be no power in any person (including the spouse) to appoint any part of the property to any person other than the spouse during the spouse's lifetime. In other words, the trustee may invade principal (corpus) of the trust for the benefit of the spouse.

c. The executor (personal representative) of the estate must elect, on the estate tax return, to treat the property as *qualified terminable interest property* (or *Q-Tip* as the profession now refers to it).

What is the importance of qualified terminable interest property (Q-Tip), and in what ways is it different from the traditional trust described in item 3 of the previous question?

In the traditional trust, the surviving spouse *must* be given the right to designate who shall own the property on his or her death. Thus, a second husband (or wife) of the surviving spouse can become the eventual owner of the trust property. With Q-Tip property the decedent can determine who shall own the property after the survivor's death.

For example, assume John and Mary are married. John has two children by a first marriage and Mary has one child by a previous marriage. If John dies in 1983, owns property worth $675,000, and leaves all this property to Mary outright, there will be no estate tax on his death. (Why? Because his estate receives a marital deduction for the $675,000 that Mary inherits.) However, the property can end up being owned by Mary's children and not by John's children.

Under the new law John can direct that the property be left in trust for Mary's benefit for her life and on her death that the ownership of the property pass to *his* children. In addition, John can direct his executor to elect that the property be treated as Q-Tip property. There will be no estate tax on John's death because of the marital deduction.

If the trust is properly structured and Mary dies in 1985 or thereafter, there will be no estate tax on Mary's death either (assuming she owns no other property).

What happens if the election is not made to treat such property as Q-Tip property?

The property will still be disposed of as John directs, but there will be no marital deduction in John's estate and the estate tax (in 1983) will be $141,250.

The Q-Tip device sounds great. Just think, my estate gets a marital deduction for property I eventually control and in addition, since I direct who owns the property, on my spouse's death the property will not be taxed as part of my spouse's estate.

While the Q-Tip is, in my opinion, a valuable estate planning tool, the property will be added to your spouse's gross estate, and taxed accordingly.

If what you say is accurate, where will the funds come from to pay the tax on my spouse's death since my spouse will have no control over the Q-Tip?

The new tax law provides that the additional taxes generated by the Q-Tip shall be paid for *from* the Q-Tip unless the surviving spouse directs otherwise.

For example, assume your spouse dies in 1988 (after you). She then owns $150,000 and you had created a Q-Tip worth $600,000. The Q-Tip is included in her gross estate. Adding the $600,000 to the $150,000 will cause her gross estate to be $750,000. Assuming no deductions (just to simplify this discussion), her taxable estate of $750,000 will create a tax liability of $55,500. If the Q-Tip were not added to her gross estate, her estate's tax liability would have been $0. Therefore, the $55,500 in tax will become a legal liability of those who will inherit the Q-Tip property worth $600,000; in other words, those beneficiaries must pay the $55,500.

The $150,000 can then be left by your wife to whomever she designates, unreduced by taxes.

Is there any advice you can give me concerning the tax caused by a Q-Tip?

Yes. While the law provides that the tax is to be paid from the Q-Tip itself, this provision of the law shall not apply "if the decedent otherwise directs by will."

In the past, wills traditionally have used "boiler-plate" language which directed that all death taxes shall be paid from the rest, residue, and remainder of one's estate. If this "boiler-plate" language is used, it may very well constitute the direction concerning the source for the payment of death taxes. Using the facts from the prior example, the tax of $55,500 may be required to be paid from the wife's own $150,000; undoubtedly an unintended result.

I have a joint will with my spouse. On the death of the last of us to die, all our property will go to our children. Will the property that my husband receives from me qualify for the marital deduction?

One of the conditions that must be fulfilled to qualify for the marital deduction for property left in trust (unless the trust is a Q-Tip) is that your husband *must* have the sole right to determine who shall receive the property on his death; that is, he must have the complete freedom to give it to anyone. In many states a joint will has been considered by the courts to be a contract to leave the property as agreed upon by the two parties to the will. In such a case your husband will not have the complete freedom to give it to anyone he wishes. Therefore, the property interest he receives will not qualify for the marital deduction.

I left all my property in trust. The trustee must give the income from this property to my wife for life. Upon her death she has the right to have the trustee give the property to whomever she specifies. To protect my wife and children, I have given my trustee the discretion to give whatever principal my trustee determines to be necessary to either my wife or children to meet their emergency needs for health or support. Since my trustee can give principal to my children only in emergency situations, the trust property will qualify for the marital deduction, correct?

Wrong. The law requires that your wife be entitled to and receive all of the income from the trust property you left to her at the tiime of your death. Here, since the trustee has the discretion to pay over principal to the children, even though the trustee may never actually exercise this power, your wife *may* not receive all of the income. Therefore, no part of the trust property will qualify for the marital deduction.

However, if the discretion were limited to paying out principal to your wife, this would be a permissible act since no one but your wife would be possessing or enjoying the property.

I would like the proceeds of life insurance on my life to be paid out by the insurance company to my wife on my death. Could this be done in such a way that my estate receives the marital deduction?

Yes. You should consult with your attorney and insurance agent to be sure that the terms of the contract with the insurance company comply with *all* the requirements of Section 2056(b)(6) of the Internal Revenue Code.

Tax Saving Suggestion:

I understand that the usual rule for valuing estates is to value the property as of the date of death. I understand that I may choose the *alternate valuation*. Please tell me what alternate valuation is, why I should choose it, how I choose it, and its details.

Alternate valuation permits the executor of an estate to value the estate at a date other than date of death.

1. Why is it important?

Selecting alternate valuation permits the estate to reduce its estate taxes. For example, on the decedent's date of death in 1982, all the assets are valued at $850,000. These assets consist of a house worth $100,000, life insurance of $100,000, and stock of a closely held corporation (which we will call X Corporation) worth $650,000. If the decedent dies without a surviving spouse and without ever having made any taxable gifts, the net estate tax in 1982 (after applying the unified credit of $62,800) will be approximately $225,000.

If, within six months of death, X Corporation goes into bankruptcy without any assets, then if there were no such thing as alternate valuation, the estate would still be valued as of date of death, namely, $850,000, and the estate tax will remain at $225,000. In this case all of the other assets will have to be paid over to the government, leaving nothing, after taxes, for members of the family.

With alternate valuation, the estate representatives could elect to have the estate valued at the "alternate valuation date," which would be six months after death. If they do so, the estate would have a value of only $200,000, and the estate tax would be zero.

The importance of alternate valuation, therefore, is to reduce estate taxes.

2. What is the alternate valuation date?

The alternate valuation date is as follows: With respect to property distributed, sold, exchanged or otherwise disposed of within six months after death, the property is valued as of the date of distribution, sale, exchange, or other disposition; with respect to property not so distributed, sold, etc., the property is valued as of six months after decedent's death.

3. How is alternate valuation elected?

By indicating this on the Federal Estate Tax return. While this election is available even if the return is filed late (not more than one year late, however) if the election is not made on the first filed return it is lost forever. Also, once the election is made it cannot be changed.

4. When would I not elect alternate valuation?

When to do so would cause the beneficiaries of the estate to have higher income taxes. To understand why this is so, we will now have to review some general income tax rules.

For income tax purposes, the general rule is that if you buy any property for $100 and during your lifetime you sell it for $1,000, you will have a profit of $900. This result is arrived at because the income tax law states that what you paid for the property is your *basis* in the property. When you sell it for $1,000, you subtract from the $1,000 your basis (or cost) to arrive at the gain realized (the profit).

Usually, this profit is taxed as a capital gain. This means that of the $900 profit you are able to deduct the capital gain deduction of 60%, and only the balance of $360 (40% of $900) is considered as income. This $360 is then added to the other income that the taxpayer has and that person must then pay income taxes on all his income, including the $360 gain.

When a person dies, the law states that the property owned by the decedent as of his date of death gets an artificial cost, or a new basis, equal to the value of the property as valued for estate tax purposes. Thus, when an estate owns stock which is valued on the decedent's date of death at $1,000, the law says that the one who inherits the stock may treat the stock as if it cost $1,000. In other words, the stock gets a stepped-up basis of $1,000 even though the decedent may have paid substantially less than this amount. Therefore, if the beneficiary sells the stock for $1,000, there will be no gain (or profit) because the basis of the stock, that is, its artificial cost, is equal to its selling price of $1,000.

Sometimes, it is advisable to elect alternate valuation even when it would increase estate taxes somewhat, if by so doing the income taxes are reduced. Consult your accountant or lawyer to determine which is best.

In this connection, it is important to remember that if you do choose to value estate property on the alternate valuation date, then *all* the property, not just one or two items of property, owned by the estate must be valued on the alternate valuation date.

---

5. Is alternate valuation available to every estate?

No, it is available only where both the total value of the gross estate *and* the amount of the estate tax liability are reduced as a result of the election.

In the past it was permissible to make the election to increase the gross estate. If the total estate and (eventual) income taxes were thereby reduced, it made sense to make this election. Now the election can be made only under the circumstances specified in the preceding paragraph.

Tax Saving Suggestion:
What are *flower bonds*?

This is the name given to certain United States Treasury bonds that now pay a low rate of interest but that can be purchased for approximately 90% of their face value.

The law now states that these so-called *flower bonds* may be used to pay federal estate taxes at the face value of the bonds. In other words, if you were to buy a $1,000 flower bond, you would pay approximately $900 for it. On death, this bond could be used to pay $1,000 of any estate tax liability and therefore there would be an economic gain of $100.

Your Federal Reserve Bank has a list of the bonds that can be used to pay estate taxes at the face value of the bonds. A knowledgeable stockbroker would also have this information. The law states also that to use these bonds the decedent must have owned the bonds on the date of his or her death. The effect of this rule is that the estate cannot, *after* the decedent's death, go out and purchase these bonds and use them to pay estate taxes due by the estate.

Tax Saving Suggestion:
When my widowed mother died, she owned approximately $5,000 of face value United States Series E Savings Bonds. The bonds have been accumulating for the past 30 years. I am the executor of my mother's estate as well as her only child and will be inheriting these bonds from her estate. My husband has a good income. What advice can you give me with respect to these bonds?

The increase in value of the bonds is usually not reported as income. If your mother held these bonds for the last 30 years, then the present value of the bonds will be approximately two-and-one-half times their original cost. If the total face amount of the bonds is $5,000, they cost $3,750 which means that their present value is approximately $9,375. The difference between these two figures is $5,625. The law states that this amount of $5,625 constitutes taxable income.

As executor, you have the choice as to which person shall report this amount as income. The income may be reported on your mother's final income tax return, on the estate's income tax return, or on your personal income tax return. If you choose the third option, you may report the income in the year in which you receive the bonds, any later year, or when you surrender or dispose of the bonds.

You should therefore compare the income tax brackets of your mother, the estate, and yourself (I assume you file a joint return with your husband) to see which result would be most favorable to you.

Why would we have to report the increase in value of the bonds as income? I thought you said that when a person dies all of the property owned by that person's estate gets a stepped-up basis equal to the estate tax value of the property in the estate (usually date of death values or alternate valuation values if so elected).

That is the usual rule but the exception involves property known as *income in respect of a decedent*. The increase in the value of the bonds is considered to be income in respect of a decedent and the law says that this type of property does not get a stepped-up basis but must be considered as ordinary income to the person eventually receiving it. Essentially, any income which the decedent had a right to receive, and could have received had death not occurred, is income in respect of a decedent.

For example, assume that at the time of my death I was a practicing lawyer and unpaid bills owed me for legal services totaled $10,000. Had I lived and received payment of these bills, they would have represented income to me. Thus, when these outstanding bills are received by my estate, the estate will have to pay an income tax on the money. This will be required even though the right to the $10,000 may be valued in my estate at $10,000 and even though it will also be subject to estate tax. U.S. Series E Bonds income falls into this income category.

The law gives those who receive or report this type of income a deduction for the estate tax generated by the income. This is known as a Section 691 deduction (named after Section 691 of the Internal Revenue Code of 1954). It is beyond the scope of this book to give the details of this provision but I wish to point out its existence to the reader.

Tax Saving Suggestion:

My wife and I own a house as joint tenants. It is worth $90,000. I own life insurance policies that will pay my wife $250,000 on my death. I also own stocks and bonds worth $410,000. I wish to save the costs of having my estate administered. Therefore, I will have the stocks and bonds re-titled to show my wife as joint owner with right of survivorship. On my death all this property will automatically be owned by my wife. Do you agree that this is a good idea?

No. You may have saved pennies on probate costs but you have just cost your wife's estate an extra $53,419 in estate taxes. When the estate is administered under court supervision, the personal representative is entitled to a fee. Since your wife will become the sole owner of all the assets, we will assume you will appoint her the personal representative. She will serve without a fee.

	Total value of assets	$750,000

	Costs and Fees	
	When no probate court supervision in view of all property being titled jointly	*When property is required to be administered under probate court supervision*
Additional costs to date as compared with joint ownership of all assets		$ 0
Approximate additional costs of filing fees of court, advertising, etc. (when there is probate) compared with joint ownership of all assets (when there is no probate)		$ 250
Additional legal fees by reason of work performed to probate will, file accountings in court, transfer title to stock to personal representative and eventually to wife (approximation) (Note: Federal and state estate tax returns will be required whether everything is disposed of as you suggest or by will. Therefore, the fee does not take this cost into account.)		$1,000
Cost of husband's simple will to dispose of assets, if any, that might		

	Costs and Fees	
	When no probate court supervision in view of all property being titled jointly	When property is required to be administered under probate court supervision
have been overlooked (approximation)	$ 75	
Cost of husband's complex will with residuary trust (approximation)	$350	
Additional legal fee by reason of probate		$ 275
Gift taxes when you, the husband, re-title stocks in joint names		0
Cost of re-titling stock, assuming you do this work yourself		0
Federal estate taxes on your death, whether leaving property as you suggested or by complex will		0
Stock ownership passing to wife on husband's death, after registration during lifetime as joint owners with right of survivorship. Maryland inheritance tax.		

Note:
(Because of the variation in state death tax laws, the author is arbitrarily using the Maryland tax rate and law.

	Costs and Fees	
	When no probate court supervision in view of all property being titled jointly	When property is required to be administered under probate court supervision
Under Maryland law, there is no inheritance tax in this situation.)	0	
State inheritance tax when transfer is under will	$4,100	
Additional state death tax		$ 4,100
Additional total expenses, fees and taxes when property is left to wife under will as compared with leaving all property outside of will		$ 5,625
When your wife dies (assuming death occurs after 1986 and there is no change in values of these assets—they could go up as well as down) her estate's federal estate taxes will be calculated as follows:		
Property acquired on husband's death		$750,000
Less expenses, fees, and taxes (approximate)		5,625
Taxable estate		$744,375
(I am assuming that there will be no legal fees,		

Costs and Fees		
	When no probate court supervision in view of all property being titled jointly	*When property is required to be administered under probate court supervision*
etc., on your wife's death. While there will obviously be some, which would reduce the amount subject to tax, I wish to simplify the illustration.)		
Tentative tax	$246,219	
Less unified credit	192,800	
Net tax		$ 53,419

This figure of $53,419 includes the state death taxes. A properly prepared will could save this $53,419. How can this be done? Your will should provide that $425,000 of your estate is left to your wife outright, including the house and insurance proceeds, and the balance (or $325,000) is left in trust for her benefit during her lifetime.

The $325,000 that your trustees hold in trust for your wife will *not* be subject to estate tax on her later death. However, in order to accomplish this, it is necessary that some of your assets not be jointly-owned with your wife. Remember that when a decedent owns jointly-owned property, on the death of the first joint owner he or she cannot dispose of it under his or her will. On such death, the surviving joint owner will automatically become the sole owner.

On your death, your wife will automatically become the sole owner of the house and the executor (or personal representative) of your estate will distribute to your wife $335,000 worth of stock. The trustees under your will shall receive the insurance proceeds plus $75,000 of the stock.

The terms of the trust will provide that your wife receive all of the income from the trust property (here, $325,000) for life, *plus* whatever she will need for her health, education, maintenance, or support, *plus* an additional $5,000 per year (or 5% of the value of the trust, if higher) if she so desires it. Your wife will have virtually 100% economic control of this trust.

This trust is known as a "residuary trust" ("residue" means what is left over). This trust will *not* be subject to federal or state estate taxes on your wife's death. Also, in this case, because of the value of property she individually owns, there will be no federal estate tax in your wife's estate.

A summary of all this is as follows:

	When all property is jointly-owned	When approximately one-half of your property is left in a residuary trust under your will
Expenses, fees, and taxes on husband's death	0	5,625
Estate taxes on wife's death	$53,419	0
	$53,419	$5,625

The total *loss* by having all your property owned jointly will therefore be $47,794 ($53,419 minus $5,625)!

Tax Saving Suggestion:

At the time of my husband's death last year, he was the sole owner of a 150-acre farm. My husband farmed the land for the last twenty years. Ten years ago, a shopping center was built next to this farm. The farm land is now worth $5,000 an acre, or $750,000. Both my children and I wish to continue to farm this land. To pay the estate taxes, we would be forced to sell the land to raise the cash to pay estate taxes. I am heartbroken about this. Can you suggest anything?

Yes, I can. Under present federal law, Congress has given every estate the option to value the land not on the basis of its fair market value, which would be in this case $5,000 an acre, but at its value as a farm for farming purposes. As farmland, the value of this 150-acre tract would be $1,000 per acre, or $150,000.

If this election is made, the farmland value would be reduced. The law provides that when reducing the value of farmland, the value may not be reduced by more than $750,000. While, if this farmland is left to you, there would be no estate tax to be paid on your husband's death, no matter what the value of the farmland is declared to be on your death there would be a substantial estate tax. By taking advantage of the provisions of this law, you can eliminate or substantially reduce all estate taxes on your death thereby enabling your children to farm the land without having to sell off any land to pay estate taxes.

This rule enabling one to secure a lower valuation of property is also available for any real property located in the United States which is used in a trade or business.

The provisions of this section are highly technical and require professional help in applying them.

Do all these rules apply to me? I am a nonresident who is not a citizen of the United States.

No. Special rules apply to you. A discussion of these special rules is beyond the scope of this book.

It should be noted, though, that the law applies to any decedent who, at the time of death, is either

1. a citizen or

2. a resident of the United States.

I am a citizen of Spain. My employer in Spain sent me to the United States to be a roving trouble-shooter. I now live in New York. If I die while living in New York, will my property be subject to the federal estate tax law?

It depends on whether or not you are really a resident of the United States. A person establishes a residence in a certain place by living there, even for a short period of time, with no present intention of moving therefrom.

In your case, you probably have a visa that permits you to remain in the United States for a short time. Considering this fact and the fact that you were sent to the United States by your employer as a trouble-shooter (which usually indicates a short-term assignment), I would be of the opinion that you are not a resident of New York or the United States.

Even if you are a resident of the United States, special rules apply to citizens of certain countries because of treaties entered into between the United States and these countries. The countries are Australia, Austria, Canada, Finland, France, Greece, Ireland, Italy, Japan, Netherlands, Norway, Switzerland, Union of South Africa, and the United Kingdom.

subject to estate tax; the estate subject to estate tax is called the taxable estate.) The tax on a taxable estate of $262,200 is $74,948 (without the credit).

If there were no deductions, the taxable estate would be $325,000. The estate tax on this amount, after the unified tax credit of $62,800, would be $33,500.

I have deliberately given an example where the deductions and credit are equal. You will also note two things. First, deductions are subtractions from the gross estate to arrive at the amount that is subject to the estate tax. Second, a credit is a dollar-for-dollar offset, or subtraction, of the tax that is due.

Comparing the estate tax of $74,948 (using deductions of $62,800) with the estate tax of $33,500 (using a credit of $62,800) demonstrates that a credit is far more valuable to a taxpayer than a deduction.

Please explain the difference between estate tax deductions and estate tax credits.

Assume you died in 1982 owning $325,000 in bank accounts, with your daughter named as the one who will receive the account balances on your death. The only expenses when you die are funeral expenses of $3,500, legal and accounting fees of $3,300, and debts you owed of $56,000. These items, totaling $62,800, are deductions from the $325,000, and your taxable estate will therefore be $262,200. (You will note that deductions are made from your gross estate to arrive at the estate which is

What are the most important estate tax credits?

1. The unified credit is $62,800 in 1982 and will increase every year thereafter until it reaches $192,800 in 1987 and thereafter. This credit is available to all estates of citizens or residents of the United States. The exact amount of the credit is shown in Table 1 at the end of this book.

2. A credit is given for death taxes paid to a state. In a few states, the state death taxes are higher than the amount of the

credit allowed under federal law. In such cases, the credit is limited by federal law to the amount allowed by federal law.

---

3. A credit is given for the federal estate tax paid with respect to the transfer of property as a result of the death of a decedent prior to the decedent whose estate is being taxed now. For example, John's sister Mary dies in 1984 with an estate of $500,000. She leaves John her entire estate. The estate tax on her death is $59,500. John dies in 1985 with an estate of $250,000. John's estate will receive a credit of $59,500, the amount of estate tax generated by Mary's estate, because of the property transferred to John. If Mary dies more than two but less than four years before John, the credit will be reduced by 20%; for every additional two-year period the credit will be reduced by an additional 20% until the credit disappears. If Mary dies more than ten years before John, the credit will be zero.

---

4. A credit is given for death taxes paid to other countries. When a U.S. citizen or resident dies owning property in a foreign country, the U.S. federal estate tax is applied to *all* the property owned by the decedent—even to property in a foreign country. Most foreign countries will tax the property found within their territory. In this situation, the property will be taxed twice: once by the U.S. and once by the foreign country.

To alleviate the problem of having the same property taxed twice, our federal tax law allows a credit to estates of U.S. citizens or residents for any foreign death taxes paid.

Please note that the foregoing rules contain certain restrictions, exceptions, and limitations which are beyond the scope of this book.

Please tell me about state death taxes.

In addition tc the federal estate tax, every state (except Nevada) imposes some form of death tax.

The death tax is either an inheritance tax or an estate tax, or both.

The inheritance tax is imposed on the privilege of receiving property from a decedent at death whereas an estate tax is imposed on the privilege of transferring property from a decedent at death.

There are practical differences between the two taxes.

1. For inheritance tax purposes, the property subject to the tax is reduced by the estate tax paid. Also, the rate of tax is based on the relationship of the heir to the decedent (a spouse or children pay the lowest rate).

2. For estate tax purposes, the property subject to the tax is reduced by neither the estate tax nor the inheritance tax paid. Also, the rate of tax is based on the total amount subject to the tax and is not dependent on who inherits the property.

There are variations among the states (for this purpose the District of Columbia is considered a state) as to what is taxed, the rate of tax, exemptions, and exclusions. What follows is therefore a general and broad overview of this subject.

The general rule is that a state imposes a death tax on all property, whether of a resident or nonresident, which is located in the state on the date of decedent's death, and which passes to another on the death of a decedent. The technical legal way to describe the status of such property is to say that it has a *taxable situs* in the state.

Clearly, real estate (also called *real property*) is located in the state where the real estate exists. Accordingly, the taxable situs of real estate is always the state where the real estate is located. The rule with respect to personal property is more complicated and needs some explanation.

Personal property means property that is movable. There are two kinds of personal property, *tangible* and *intangible*. Personal property that can be felt or touched is tangible personal property. Jewelry, clothing, a stamp collection, automobiles, and paintings are examples of tangible personal property.

Tangible personal property would generally be subject to the death taxes of the state in which it is located. This is so because the taxable situs of tangible personal property is the place where the property is physically located at the time of decedent's death. However, this

rule has some exceptions. For example, assume you were a Maryland resident and in connection with a six-week vacation trip abroad, you stayed at a Washington, D.C., hotel. You left all your jewelry with the hotel for safekeeping until your return—clearly a temporary agreement. Were you to die abroad, the jewelry should not be taxed by the D.C. authorities, even though it was physically in the District of Columbia at the time of your death.

Intangible personal property is property which cannot be felt or touched. Stock certificates, bonds, and promissory notes are considered to be intangible personal property. While each asset is usually represented by a piece of paper and the paper can, of course, be felt, the paper is only evidence of a property interest. In the case of the stock certificate, the certificate is evidence of an ownership interest in a corporation.

Intangible personal property is considered to be located—to have a taxable situs—in the state where the decedent was a resident at the time of death. If a decedent was a resident of Maryland and owned a promissory note which was held by the decedent's Connecticut attorney, the value of the promissory note would be subject to death tax in Maryland. This is because the taxable situs of the note is considered to be in Maryland.

What is meant by the term *residence*? For most legal purposes, including death taxes, a *residence* is that place where a person is domiciled, and *domicile* is that place where one resides with the intent to make a fixed and permanent home. A person can have several residences but only one domicile. For example, you may have a residence in Florida (for the winter), a residence in northern Michigan (for the summer), and a residence in Pennsylvania. If your fixed and permanent home is in Pennsylvania, then Pennsylvania is your domicile and for tax purposes that is your residence.

Sometimes it is not clear where a person's domicile is, and this is something the taxing authorities frequently have to determine. They may inquire where the decedent voted, where his automobiles were registered, where a safe deposit box was maintained, where his children go to school, where checking and savings accounts were maintained, what state the decedent declared to be his residence in his will, and so on. In other words, they will look to see where his "roots" are.

Some states maintain that certain intangible property has a taxable situs and therefore should be taxed in their states, even when the decedent was a resident of another state. This could happen where the nonresident of the taxing state owns stock of a corporation that is incorporated in the state. For example, Utah exercises the power of taxation in this situation on the theory that because the corporation has incorporated there, the state has extended the mantle of its legal protection over the corporation and therefore the property of the nonresident decedent has a taxable situs in Utah.

The same result occurs when a trust is created in state X by a nonresident with a trustee who is a state X resident. In this situation, state X claims that the intangible property of a nonresident decedent should be taxed by it because the property has acquired a taxable situs in its state.

Even when a state has legal authority to impose a death tax upon intangible property of nonresidents because such property has acquired a taxable situs in its jurisdiction, its laws may exempt intangible personal property from taxation. This happens when the laws of the state that can impose a tax on the nonresident decedent's intangible personal property has a reciprocal exemption with the other state. As an example, Maryland law states that it will not tax such property of a resident of another state if the laws of the other state similarly exempt intangible personal property of Maryland residents.

When the laws of another state do tax intangible personal property of a nonresident decedent, there is really nothing the decedent's estate can do about it. The reader should be aware of this possibility and be aware that if the tax laws of another state do apply, it may be necessary for the estate's local attorney to seek the assistance of an attorney in the other state. Certainly, extra tax returns will be required and there may be delays and increased costs before property is transferred to the decedent's loved ones.

What is a state inheritance tax?

This tax is imposed on the privilege of receiving property from a decedent. Property can be "received" from a decedent even though the decedent did not own it at the time of his or her death. There are two broad categories of property that can be "received" from a decedent and which therefore can be subject to inheritance tax:

1. Property owned by the decedent at the moment of death.

    For example, I own 100 shares of General Motors common stock (considered probate property) at the time of my death. I die and leave it to you by my will or I die without a will (intestate) and state law provides that you become the owner of this stock. In either of these cases, you will have received the stock from me (the decedent).

2. Property which is *not* owned by the decedent at the moment of death.

    In this second category, you will find the same type of property that is subject to the federal estate tax. This statement is of necessity a general one since there are variations among state laws. Property that falls into this category includes:

    a. Property in which the decedent had an interest as a joint tenant.

    b. Property which the decedent had transferred to someone in contemplation of death, or within two to three years before death.

    c. Property which the decedent owned at one time but whose ownership he transferred and whose control or income he kept during his lifetime.

    d. Property which the decedent transferred during lifetime but over which he retained the power to revoke the transfer.

    e. Property over which the decedent had a general power of appointment (whether or not he owned it at one time).

    The power of the states to tax property for inheritance tax purposes is limited to property which has acquired a taxable situs in the state. This usually means

    1.) real property (real estate) located in the state,

    2.) tangible personal property located in the state, and

    3.) intangible personal property of a resident of the state.

    With respect to intangible personal property, it does not matter where the property is located since the taxable situs of this type of property is the place where the decedent resides at the time of death. This does not mean that another state cannot tax such property when it finds that intangible personal property of a nonresident acquires a taxable situs in its state, too.

    Since inheritance taxes are imposed on the privilege of receiving property, the amount that is subject to tax is the net value of property actually received. Hence, there are subtracted from the gross value of such property any debts to which the property is subject, estate taxes, mortgages, and costs of administering the property such as commissions and legal and accounting fees.

Most states exempt from inheritance taxes proceeds of life insurance that are paid to a named beneficiary other than the estate. If a beneficiary of an insurance policy is not named, then with rare exceptions, on the insured's death, the insurance company will pay the proceeds to the estate of the insured. This will cause the insurance proceeds to be subject to an inheritance tax.

Some states also exempt from an inheritance tax any type of property jointly-owned by a husband and wife for which, on the death of the first one to die, the survivor becomes the sole owner.

Property received by charitable and religious institutions is usually exempt, as is property received by a government agency.

The rate of tax that is applied depends on the relationship of the person who receives the property to the decedent. Details of these variations are shown in the inheritance tax tables at the end of this book. In general, the lowest rate is applied to the net amount received by a surviving spouse (husband or wife) of the decedent as well as by parents, grandparents, children, grandchildren, and more remote descen-

dants. In some states, everyone else is taxed at the highest rates.

When a state imposes more than two rates, the next lowest rate is imposed on property received by brothers, sisters, nieces, nephews, and perhaps a spouse of any of them. The highest rate would be imposed on property received by all others.

What is a state estate tax?

The majority of states impose a state estate tax. This tax falls into two broad categories.

1. A state estate tax on "certain" property which also has a taxable situs in its state. Generally speaking, this "certain" property would be subject to state estate tax if federal law causes such property to be subject to federal estate tax.

2. Imposing a state estate tax only to the extent that any inheritance tax or state estate tax paid is less than the credit allowed by federal law for state death taxes paid. This type of tax is referred to as a *pickup tax*.

The first category needs no further comment. The second category can be explained by what follows. You will recall that under federal law the estate tax is imposed on the total of the taxable estate and adjusted taxable gifts. When this figure is arrived at, the unified credit is then deducted from the total tax due. When the property subject to federal estate tax is

$275,000 or less, the tax is $79,300 or less. Because of the unified credit of $79,300 (in 1983; higher in succeeding years), there will be no federal estate tax to pay.

However, where the federal estate tax is higher than $79,300, federal law gives each estate, in addition to the unified credit, an additional credit for death taxes paid to a state. The amount of the credit is set forth in a table provided by federal law. This table is reproduced at the end of this book.

In some states it is possible for the amount of the inheritance tax due the state to be less than the federal credit for death taxes paid to a state. When this occurs, 32 of the states impose a state estate tax to make up the difference between their inheritance tax and this federal credit. In other words, the state estate tax becomes a "pickup" of the difference.

A simple illustration will explain this. Assume I die in 1983 owning a life insurance policy which pays $350,000. The beneficiary is my daughter, who receives this amount from the insurance company. Assume also that I never made any taxable gifts, I own cash (in bank accounts) totaling $30,000, and my debts amount to $30,000. For federal estate purposes, my taxable estate is:

Life insurance		$350,000
Cash		30,000
		$380,000
Less debts		30,000
Taxable estate		$350,000
Federal estate tax:		
Tentative tax	$104,800	
Unified credit	79,300	
Federal estate tax		$ 25,500

My estate is also entitled to a credit for death taxes paid to Maryland. Federal law provides that this credit be $5,200. However, under Maryland law my daughter will pay no inheritance tax on the $350,000 of life insurance proceeds she receives. This is because Maryland exempts from inheritance tax the life insurance proceeds she receives as a named beneficiary.

Since Maryland is one of those 32 pickup states, my estate will be required to pay a Maryland estate tax which is equal to the federal credit allowed my estate, or $5,200.

Had Maryland not imposed its estate tax, my estate would have had to pay the federal government $25,500. Because Maryland imposes the estate pickup tax, my estate will still pay only a total of $25,500 but instead of paying it all to the federal government, the payment will be as follows:

To the federal government	$20,300
To the Maryland government	5,200
	$25,500

You will then ask, what difference does it make to you whether or not you save the inheritance tax since there will be an estate tax and the actual payment of tax dollars will be the same?

There *could* be a difference, as the following examples will show.

---

1. Assume you live in a state that has a death tax system similar to Maryland's, and the amount of your estate subject to federal estate tax is less than $350,000, say $250,000. Assume also that you die in 1983 and that the $250,000 represents proceeds of an insurance policy on your life.

If the policy proceeds are paid to your estate and your will leaves all your property to your niece, the $250,000 will be subject to inheritance tax. The inheritance tax on this property will be $25,000 (10% of $250,000). There will be no state estate tax since there is no federal estate tax and no federal credit for state death taxes.

If the life insurance proceeds are paid directly to your niece, there will still be no federal estate tax and no inheritance tax (because state law exempts life insurance proceeds paid directly to a named beneficiary). There will be no state pickup estate tax because when there is no federal estate tax, no federal credit for state death tax is allowed or necessary.

2. Assume once again that you live in a state with a death tax system similar to Maryland's and that the amount of your taxable estate is $350,000. Assume this $350,000 represents proceeds of a life insurance policy on your life.

If the policy proceeds are paid to your estate and your will leaves all your property to your husband, the $350,000 will be subject to inheritance tax. The inheritance tax on this property will be $3,500 (1% of $350,000). Assuming you die in 1983, under federal law your estate receives a marital deduction for the $346,500 ($350,000 minus $3,500) your husband inherits. There will be no federal estate tax and therefore no federal credit for state death taxes paid. In view of this, there will be no state pickup estate tax.

If the insurance proceeds are paid directly to your husband there will still be no federal estate tax and no inheritance tax (because state law exempts life insurance proceeds paid directly to a named beneficiary). There will be no state pickup estate tax because when there is no federal estate tax, no federal credit for state death tax is allowed or necessary.

You can therefore see that in the two examples just given, it is sometimes advisable to avoid, if possible, being liable for the inheritance tax. In neither case was there a federal estate tax. In one case there was a state inheritance tax of $25,000 that could have been saved, and in the other case there was a state inheritance tax of $3,500 that could have been saved.

Some states (New York is one of them) have a state estate tax which is patterned after federal law but which has lower rates. These states have an estate tax but not an inheritance tax. In 26 states the state estate tax is payable regardless of any other death taxes that are due. These states also have a pickup estate tax. They also provide that if the regular state estate tax is less than the federal credit for state death taxes, the difference between the state's regular estate tax and the amount of the credit allowed by federal law will still be imposed as a state pickup estate tax.

Finally, I wish to point out that 11 states impose a gift tax. The states that have a gift tax are shown in the state tax tables at the end of this book.

Tax Saving Suggestion:

My husband died and left all of his property to me outright. I have more than enough assets owned by me in my own name plus enough income to support myself comfortably for the rest of my life. I understand that if I receive all of my husband's assets, when I die his assets will be added to my assets and will be subject to a very high estate tax. Is it too late to do anything about this situation?

No. Under present federal law and the laws of most states, you have a right to renounce all or any part of your late husband's property (which is now owned by his estate). *Renounce* means that you forever give up an interest in this property. The act of renouncing is sometimes called *disclaiming*.

What does this do?

In the eyes of the law, renouncing property is the same as dying before the other person. In this case, it is as though you died before your husband. Assume that your late husband's will provided that everything was to be left to you if you survived him, but that if you failed to survive him the property would be left to such of your children as survived him. In this case, your children would inherit the property which you renounced since, by your renouncing, the situation is the same as if you did not survive your husband.

The advantages of renouncing can be demonstrated by the following. Let us assume you own $550,000 and when your husband dies he owns $150,000. For federal estate tax purposes, when your husband dies there will be no estate tax at all.

If you inherit the $150,000, then on your death your total estate would amount to $700,000. The estate tax of an estate totaling $700,000 will be approximately $37,000. (This assumes you die in 1987 or later. If you die earlier the tax will be significantly higher.) On the other hand, if you renounce the entire $150,000 that you could have inherited under your husband's will, the estate tax on your death would be zero. As you can see, this would result in a savings of $37,000.

When you renounce you are essentially giving up any interest in the property that you are renouncing. Therefore, you would lose the benefit of being able to use this money.

The law permitting you to renounce (or disclaim) an interest in property also allows you to enjoy the income from other property that you have not renounced. For example, assume that your husband's will left you an outright bequest of $125,000 and that he left the balance of his estate in trust. The trust provides that you are to receive the income from the trust for life. If you renounce the $125,000, that is *all* you renounce; you will still be entitled to the income from the trust. Also, the $125,000 may even be added to the trust property, depending, of course, on the language of the will. If the $125,000 is added to the trust property you will be entitled to the income, even from the $125,000.

When a person renounces an interest in another's property or estate, the law states that this act does not make the property or estate a gift because the one who renounces never had any ownership interest in the property and therefore had nothing to give away. For your renunciation to be effective without causing any tax problems, the law says that the renunciation must be timely and must comply with certain other requirements of state and federal law.

In your case, federal law requires you to file your renunciation within nine months of your husband's death. In addition, you must file the appropriate documents with the state court having jurisdiction over the estate. If these requirements are not strictly complied with, then the law says you acted as if you made a gift. If you make any taxable gifts after January 1, 1977, the amount of such gifts will be added to your taxable estate and thus be subject to federal estate tax as though you owned the property in your own name. This is why it is important that there be strict compliance with the renunciation rules. When, how, and why you should renounce are matters that should be discussed with your attorney.

At the time my husband died he was employed. Under his employer's pension plan, I am entitled to receive a lump sum payment of $150,000 or an annuity of $10,000 per year payable in monthly installments. I understand that the payments I receive will be made under what is known as a *qualified plan*. What is a *qualified plan*? Also, should I take the proceeds in a lump sum or in periodic payments?

A qualified plan is any retirement plan that meets certain technical requirements of the income tax law. The advantages of a plan being "qualified" are that the employer gets a deduction for its contributions to the plan on behalf of the employee and the employee pays no tax until benefits are distributed or made available to him. Also, prior to 1985, the law provided that under certain conditions, up to $100,000 of such proceeds would not be taxed as part of your husband's estate. The Tax Reform Act of 1984 provides that, with certain limited exceptions, the entire amount of payments due or made under a qualified plan is subject to taxation in the decedent's estate. (Obviously, if such amounts are paid to a surviving spouse, they will usually qualify for the unlimited marital deduction.)

As noted, the income from the contributions is not subject to any income tax until it is distributed. In addition, if a lump sum distribution is made to an employee when he retires, while the distribution is subject to income tax, the tax is calculated very favorably. This is known as ten-year averaging, and substantially reduces the income tax that must be paid on the distribution.

When a lump sum distribution is made on the death of an employee, the law states that the beneficiary has a choice of (1) having all the distribution subject to income tax at the normal tax rates payable by that beneficiary or (2) having the proceeds subject to the favorable income tax calculation based on the ten-year averaging rule.

You, as the beneficiary, have this choice. In order to make an informed decision, you should have your accountant or lawyer calculate for you the amount of tax that would have to be paid under each alternative. This means calculating and comparing the income taxes if option (1) is selected with the total amount of the extra estate tax plus the income taxes if option (2) is selected.

Consideration should also be given to receiving periodic payments, thereby enabling the principal of the fund to accumulate income tax-free until it is actually distributed.

Tax Saving Suggestion:

Because of the complexity and amount of the assets in my husband's estate, the legal, accounting, and appraisal fees and the other expenses of administering the estate amount to $15,000. Since these expenses are deductions from the gross estate, the estate should of course claim these deductions. This would have the effect of reducing estate taxes. Is this correct?

Administration expenses can certainly reduce the amount of the gross estate and thus reduce estate taxes. However, these expenses can be claimed as an income tax deduction instead of an estate tax deduction.

An estate is a separate taxpayer. You may be wiser to pay a higher estate tax by not claiming these expenses as a deduction on the estate tax return, and to claim these administration expenses as a deduction on the income tax return. These expenses may not be claimed on both the estate tax return and the income tax return.

To illustrate: If the taxable estate is $400,000 (assuming death occurs in 1983) and the administration expenses are claimed as an estate tax deduction, the estate taxes saved would be 34% of the $15,000. This amounts to $5,100.

If the estate has taxable income of $30,000, the income tax would amount to $8,755.

If the administraton expenses of $15,000 are deducted from the $30,000 of taxable income, then the taxable income would be $15,000. The income tax on $15,000 amounts to $3,042.

Therefore, by claiming these expenses as income tax deductions instead of estate tax deductions, the income tax is reduced by $5,713 at a higher estate tax cost of $5,100. By claiming these expenses as an income tax deduction, there would be a net savings of $613.

The following calculations demonstrate the previous example:

Claiming deductions on the estate tax return produces higher estate taxes of		$5,100
Estate income taxes on $30,000	$8,755	
Estate income taxes on $15,000 by claiming expenses as income tax deductions	3,042	
		5,713
Savings in taxes by claiming $15,000 of administration expenses as income tax deductions		$ 613

I have heard that Congress has imposed a new tax called the *generation-skipping tax*. What is it?

Before I explain the new tax, let me tell you what the law was before the law was changed in 1976.

Under the old law, a parent or grandparent could leave property in trust for a child and have the property eventually pass to that child's children. On the death of the child, this property would not be includible in the child's gross estate. Thus, there would be no death tax on this property in the child's estate. In other words, by so structuring the transfer of property by will or by a living trust, property could pass free from a later estate tax by skipping one or more generations.

To illustrate this, let us assume you are the parent, have no spouse, and own $1,000,000. On your death, the tax will be approximately $300,000. Under the law prior to 1977, you were able to leave the balance of $700,000 in trust for your son (or daughter), and to provide that the $700,000 would be inherited by your grandchildren upon the death of your son or daughter without there being any further tax on your child's estate by reason of the $700,000.

The *generation-skipping tax* has changed the prior result. The new law treats your child as the person who transferred the property. The law refers to your child as the *deemed transferor*. When this occurs, a generation-skipping tax will be imposed on the property that was held in trust and passed to your grandchildren. The estate will be taxed at the same estate tax rate as if your son or daughter had owned the property that originated with you.

An exception is provided in the law for the transfers of property through any child (the deemed transferor) from a set of parents of up to $250,000 received by grandchildren, collectively. Any such transfer to a grandchild or grandchildren would be free from the generation-skipping tax. In the example just given, $250,000 transferred to a grandchild would be deducted from the $700,000 that you left in trust. Thus, only the balance of $450,000 would be subject to the generation-skipping tax. The tax rate will be the equivalent of the tax that your son's (or daughter's) estate would have paid had your son (or daughter) owned this $450,000 in his or her name outright.

The law is imposed on any generation-skipping transfer and is therefore not limited to transfers to grandchildren only.

For planning purposes, as well as to satisfy any legal obligations, the reader should consult with an attorney. While the United States Senate voted to repeal the generation-skipping tax, the House of Representatives voted to retain it. The Tax Reform Act of 1984 contained no provision repealing same. Further efforts will undoubtedly be made to repeal or modify the tax (and deservedly so).

If death taxes are due when I die, who is required to pay these taxes and what will be the source of the payment?

The law permits you to specify in your will which of your assets shall bear the burden of the estate tax. If you do not specify this or if you die without a will, then state and federal laws specify what is required.

Whatever the source of the funds, existing federal and state laws require that the executor or personal representative pay all taxes that are due from your assets before a beneficiary can receive any property from the estate. If there is no executor or personal representative, then such taxes must be paid by any trustee holding property subject to death taxes from such property; if there is no trustee, then any person in possession of property subject to death taxes is required to pay such taxes from such property.

Unless you give specific directions, the rules are as follows:

1. When a state imposes an inheritance tax, the amount of this tax comes directly from the property to be received by the beneficiary or legatee.

   For example, if I leave my daughter a bequest of $30,000 and the inheritance tax rate on this bequest in my state is 1%, then the $300 tax must be deducted from my daughter's $30,000. She will therefore receive $29,700.

2. Any federal and state estate taxes must be apportioned among all property subject to such tax. There is an exception to this rule: when property is left to someone who would be entitled to a deduction by reason of such a bequest, then the property so left shall be exempt from having to share in paying the tax.

   An example of this exception would be when property is left to a surviving spouse. Assume that the property subject to tax totals $600,000 and that the spouse is left $300,000. This $300,000 qualifies for a marital deduction which will reduce the amount subject to estate tax to $300,000 ($600,000 minus $300,000). If death occurs in 1982, the net estate tax, after the unified credit, will be $25,000. But for this exception, the surviving spouse's share would have to pay one-half of the $25,000, or $12,500. Because of the exception the entire $25,000 tax will have to be paid from the one-half passing to others.

To illustrate the general rule, if the total amount subject to estate tax is $542,700, in 1982 the estate tax after the unified credit will be $108,800. Assume that the entire estate is left to three children, Abner, Bertha, and Charles. Abner and Bertha each are entitled to 40% and Charles to 20%. Then from each of Abner and Bertha's shares there shall be paid $43,520 (40% of $108,800) and from Charles' share $21,760 (20% of $108,800). The total tax will be paid as follows:

Share of Abner	$ 43,520
Share of Bertha	43,520
Share of Charles	21,760
Total tax	$108,800

After taxes, each child will then inherit the following:

Abner ($217,080 minus $43,520)	$173,560
Bertha ($217,080 minus $43,520)	173,560
Charles ($108,540 minus $21,760)	86,780
Total inherited	$433,900
Total taxes paid	108,800
Total estate	$542,700

If a decedent wishes to vary the rule illustrated above, appropriate language should be inserted in the will.

I have put $15,000 in a bank account in my name as custodian under the Uniform Gifts to Minors Act. Since I am the custodian as well as the donor I have not made a gift. Right?

Wrong. A gift under the Uniform Gifts to Minors Acts is a completed gift. The legal owner of the gifted property is the minor. The custodian is just that—a custodian.

The custodian manages the property for the benefit of the minor. If the donor dies while acting as custodian, the property will be included as part of the gross estate of the custodian.

To avoid having this property taxed as part of the gross estate, the spouse or other relative of the donor should serve as custodian.

When my son purchased a house I loaned him $20,000. He gave me a note due this year. I tore up the note and told him it was my Christmas gift to him. Have I made a gift subject to the gift tax?

Yes. Forgiveness of a debt is considered to be the making of a gift. The amount of the taxable gift will be $10,000 since the first $10,000 of a gift made to any person in any year is excluded.

The $10,000 of taxable gifts will be added to your taxable estate for purposes of figuring the estate tax eventually due from your estate.

Tax Saving Suggestion:

Is there something you can suggest to reduce the eventual estate tax in connection with the last transaction?

Yes. I am assuming that you are married. You can forgive one-half of the debt at Christmas or at any time during the year, and immediately after the first of the year can forgive the other half. Also, you and your spouse can file split-gift tax returns. In this case there will be no gift taxes to pay *and* no estate taxes to pay with respect to the $20,000 gift.

Why is this so? When you have forgiven one-half the debt this year you have made a gift of $10,000 (1/2 of $20,000). However, since there is an annual exclusion of $10,000 per donee, the taxable gift will be zero. Forgiving the balance of the debt next year will also produce a taxable gift of zero next year.

In addition, the law provides that a husband and wife can elect to treat any gift made by one of them to a third party as though each made a gift of one-half the gift. This election is entirely optional. However, in order to do this, each spouse must be a U.S. citizen or resident, and a gift tax return must be filed showing that the split-gift treatment is desired (elected).

In the latter case then, you and your husband should both file gift tax returns showing the split-gift treatment. When this is done the gift of $20,000 will be treated as two $10,000 gifts. Each one of you will now be able to exclude the first $10,000 of gifts made to your son this year. Therefore, the taxable gifts for each of you will be $0.

Next year you can repeat this procedure if you wish to transfer an additional $20,000.

My mother died in 1981. In her will she left my sister the family home, and

she left my brother and me the balance of her estate. The home was worth approximately $100,000, and at the time she signed her will the balance of her property was worth $200,000. About two years before my mother died she sold the home for $100,000 and used the proceeds to live in a nursing home. She never changed her will. At the time of Mother's death her estate was worth $240,000, which my brother and I are now legally entitled to. Our sister will receive nothing from Mother's estate. We feel this is unfair and we wish to share the estate with our sister. Can we do so? Also, will we have made any gifts if we do so?

Your wishes are quite understandable. Your mother's undoubted wishes were that each of you three children would receive approximately $100,000 before taxes. Because the house was sold, and the will left property to two children, only you and your brother will inherit anything from your mother. Your sister will receive nothing.

I estimate that taxes and administration expenses would be approximately $30,000. This would leave $210,000 to be divided.

You and your brother are each legally entitled to receive $105,000 (if we first deduct the estimated $30,000). If you choose to take less and divide the $210,000 three ways, thus providing $70,000 each, the law says that you and your brother will each have made a gift to your sister of $35,000.

What you are proposing to do is praiseworthy, but may cause problems for each of you. The problem is that when the money is transferred to your sister, the amount transferred (less the $10,000 annual exclusion) will be a taxable gift by each of you.

What tax consequences are there if a taxable gift is made?

There are two consequences: once during lifetime and once at death. The lifetime consequence is that there may be gift taxes due when the gift is made. Thus, you lose the benefit of the use of these taxes during your lifetime. However, at death the amount of the gift taxes as well as the taxable gifts usually reduce the eventual estate taxes. The reasons for this are explained in what follows.

You may remember that gift and estate taxes are unified. Even though you gave property away during lifetime, the grand total of all taxable gifts made after 1976 (called adjusted taxable gifts) will be added to the amount of your taxable estate in figuring the estate tax. (Your taxable estate is your gross estate less deductions.) In these inflationary times, the value of property usually rises. Therefore, if the gift were not made and the property were owned by the decedent as of date of death, the amount subject to tax would be the higher date of death value of the property still owned.

For example, assume I own a small parcel of land in New York City. I transfer it to my daughter as a gift at a time when the parcel is worth $100,000. Because of the $10,000 annual exclusion, I have therefore made a taxable gift of $90,000. If, on the date of my death, I own another $500,000, the unified rate schedule (the estate tax) will be applied to a total of $590,000. On the other hand, assume I continue to own the parcel of land and on the date of my death it is worth $300,000. By adding this $300,000 to my other property worth $500,000, the total estate subject to the unified rate schedule (the estate tax) will be $800,000. In addition, if the amount given away during lifetime causes gift taxes to be paid and if you live more than three years after making the gift, the amount of the gift taxes will reduce the amount of the gross estate and this will therefore reduce the estate tax. Also, while gifts made during lifetime will be added to your taxable estate and be subject to tax on death, the amount of each annual gift will be reduced by the $10,000 annual exclusion.

An illustration will demonstrate the savings due to the elimination of any gift tax as well as the annual exclusion from the gross estate.

Assume you are unmarried and have three children and one sister. In 1982 you make the following gifts:

To sister	$ 60,000
To each child, $80,000	240,000
	$300,000
Less four annual exclusions	40,000
Taxable gifts	260,000
Tentative tax	$ 74,200
Unified credit	62,800
Net gift tax	$ 11,400

Assume you die in 1986 and then own $488,600 ($500,000 less the gift tax of $11,400). On your death the estate tax will be as follows:

Taxable estate		$488,600
Adjusted taxable gifts		260,000
Total amount subject to estate tax		$748,600
Tentative tax	$247,982	
Unified credit	155,800	
		92,182
Less: Gift tax paid		11,400
Net estate tax		$ 80,782

Had you not made any gifts, the estate tax would be as follows:

Taxable estate		$800,000
Adjusted taxable gifts		0
Total amount subject to estate tax		$800,000
Tentative tax	$267,800	
Unified credit	155,800	
Net estate tax		$112,000

The total taxes paid are as follows:

	Where gifts made	Where no gifts made
Gift tax	$11,400	0
Estate tax	80,782	$112,000
	$92,182	$112,000

The net tax saved is therefore $19,818.

After 1976, I gave my son $250,000 as a taxable gift. If this amount is added to my taxable estate for purposes of calculating the estate tax due, this will have the effect of taxing this property twice. Is this correct?

No. When the estate tax is calculated, the amount due is reduced by any gift taxes that are paid. Therefore, there is no duplication of the gift and estate taxes.

This was demonstrated in the prior question.

I understand that when a person gives away a total of $335,000 or less to one person in 1984, and has never made previous taxable gifts, there will be no federal gift tax. Why is this so?

From $335,000 you are entitled to deduct $10,000, which is the amount of the annual exclusion. The balance of $325,000 is subject to the gift tax. The gift tax on $325,000 is $96,300. In 1984 the law allows every person a $96,300 credit against gift taxes. Since a tax credit is a dollar-for-dollar offset against the tax, when the tax is $96,300 and the credit is $96,300, the gift tax due will be $0. This credit became part of the law as of January 1, 1977. The amount of the credit has increased each year beginning in 1977, and will continue to increase as follows:

Year	Amount of Credit	Year	Amount of Credit
1977	$30,000	1983	$ 79,300
1978	34,000	1984	96,300
1979	38,000	1985	121,800
1980	42,500	1986	155,800
1981	47,000	1987 &	
1982	62,800	thereafter	192,800

Since several states impose a gift tax, you should consult with your accountant or lawyer as to the effect of such laws.

Is there a credit for estate tax purposes?

Yes, the credit is identical.

Since there are separate credits for gift and estate tax purposes, I gather that if I gave away, after 1976, gifts totaling $235,000 and I died in 1982 owning another $225,000, there would have been no gift or estate taxes to pay. Is this correct?

No. While there is a separate credit for each type of tax, the mechanics of the interchange between the two taxes prevent your getting the practical effect of both credits.

To illustrate: when a person dies in 1982 owning $225,000 (ignoring for this purpose any deductions) the taxable estate is $225,000

To this figure (the taxable estate of $225,000) we add taxable gifts and disregard the fact that because of the gift tax credit there was no gift tax paid ($235,000 less one $10,000 annual gift)		$225,000
Total of taxable estate *plus* adjusted taxable gifts		$450,000
Tax on $450,000	$138,800	
Estate tax credit (in 1982)	62,800	
Net tax		$ 76,000

You will note that the amount subject to tax at death (the taxable estate) is added to the amount of adjusted taxable gifts (those made after 1976); that is, they are "unified" to arrive at the total amount against which the estate tax is calculated.

A friend of mine told me that he and his wife gave away $106,000 to their son in July of 1976 and paid a total of $2,400 in gift taxes. He said that if he dies before his wife, still owning the $650,000 he owns now, there will be no estate taxes to pay either on his death or on the death of his wife. In view of what you have said, how can this be?

You will note that your friends made the gift in July of 1976. At that time, the unified system of estate and gift taxation was not the law.

At that time, if a couple made no prior taxable gifts and agreed to split the gift, then each one made a gift of one-half. In your friends' case, each made a gift of $53,000. The law excluded the first $3,000 of each gift. In addition, the law permitted each person a lifetime specific exemption of $30,000. When you subtract $33,000 from the gift of $53,000 each of your friends made, then each one has made a taxable gift of $20,000. The tax on $20,000 made by each person was then $1,200, or a total of $2,400.

The present estate tax law does not unify gifts made before January 1, 1977, and therefore when your friend dies owning $650,000, we look only to these assets to see what the tax will be.

If, on your friend's death in 1984 or later, he leaves $325,000 to his wife outright and leaves $325,000 in a trust whose assets will not be taxed on his wife's death, what happens? We start out with his gross estate which will be $650,000. Since he will leave $325,000 to his wife outright, his estate will receive a marital deduction of $325,000. His taxable estate will therefore be the $325,000 left in trust.

The estate tax is figured on the total of the taxable estate (here $325,000) plus adjusted taxable gifts. Since adjusted taxable gifts only include such gifts made after December 31, 1976, such gifts here would be zero. The tax on $325,000 is $96,300. In 1984, the estate receives a credit of $96,300. (Of course, if your friend or his wife dies after 1984 a greater amount can be transferred without tax.) Since the credit is equal to the tax of $96,300, there will be no estate tax on his death.

When your friend's wife dies, the amount she receives outright, $325,000, is the only amount that her estate will be taxed on. Once again, the credit available to her estate is equal to the tax. Hence, there will be no tax due on her death.

The fact that one leaves property in trust does not always mean that the survivor's estate will not be taxed on it. It is clear, though, that if the only control your friend's wife had over the trust was the right to receive income, no part of the trust property would be taxed in her estate.

Your friend is therefore correct that there will be no estate taxes to pay either by his estate or by his wife's estate. He has had the benefit of wise counsel.

When and where must estate and gift tax returns be filed?

The answer to this question is found on the instructions to the Estate Tax Return (Form 706) as well as on the instructions to the Gift Tax Return (Form 709).

In general, an Estate Tax Return must be filed when the gross estate (not taxable estate) plus adjusted taxable gifts exceeds the following:

Year of death	Amount
1982	$225,000
1983	275,000
1984	325,000
1985	400,000
1986	500,000
1987 and thereafter	600,000

Also, in general, the Gift Tax Return must be filed when the amount of the gift exceeds $10,000 in any year to any one person (even if no gift tax is due).

What are the advantages and disadvantages of making gifts?

The disadvantages are as follows:

1. The one who makes the gift loses the benefit of having the use of the property that is transferred.

2. When a gift tax is paid, there is also a loss of use of the money.

The advantages are as follows:

1. The first $10,000 of gifts made to a donee each year is excluded from being considered part of the adjusted taxable gifts. Therefore, this amount will be subject neither to estate tax nor to gift tax.

   For example, I make $10,000 gifts each year to each of my three children for ten years and similar $10,000 gifts to each of my six grandchildren. I have then disposed of $90,000 each year ($10,000 times nine individuals) for ten years, or a total of $900,000. If my wife agrees to split the gift, we have disposed of $1,800,000 which will not be subject to gift tax or to estate tax.

2. The income generated by these gifts will belong to each donee (my children and grandchildren in the above example). The income tax on this income will presumably be taxed at a lower rate since the income will be spread among a greater number of taxpayers. Also, since I can afford to make these gifts I am presumably in a higher income tax bracket than the donees. Therefore the total income tax impact on the family of the income generated by the gifted property will be less.

3. If I make a gift of land or stock, the value for gift tax purposes is the value of the property at the time I make the gift. If the property grows in value over the years, the growth in the property transferred by gift will not be subject to estate tax in my estate.

For example, I own ten acres of land now worth $12,000. If on the date of my death I still own the land and it is then worth $100,000, this $100,000 will be part of my taxable estate and taxed accordingly. However, if I have given the land to my son as a gift, even though the value of the land on the date of my death is $100,000, only the value of the land on the date of the gift, or $12,000, will be considered as an adjusted taxable gift. Therefore, only $12,000 will be added to my taxable estate for purposes of calculating the estate tax due on my death. (If I have made no other taxable gifts to my son that year, the $12,000 gift will, of course, be reduced by the annual $10,000 exclusion.)

I have heard that I can give away all my property during my lifetime and avoid the federal estate tax. Is this true?

No. Federal law states that if you make gifts of all your property, with certain exceptions, the value of the property will be subject to federal gift tax. The amount of the federal gift tax is equal to the federal estate tax. Therefore, with exceptions, as a practical matter the total tax will be the same whether one calls the tax an estate tax or a gift tax.

From the technical point of view, when you give away property during your lifetime (again with certain exceptions) the property is no longer part of your taxable estate.

However, in calculating the estate tax, the taxable gifts made after December 31, 1976, are *added* to the taxable estate.

If what you say is correct, why do I have the impression that I can save on taxes by giving away property as gifts during my lifetime?

The law was changed in 1976, effective for persons who died after December 31, 1976.

Before then, the law provided that the federal estate tax was imposed only on a taxable estate (plus some gifts made within three years of death). Therefore, if you lived more than three years after making a gift, your taxable estate was reduced. The gift tax that was imposed was three-quarters of the estate tax rate—and even this was reduced by exempting from the gift tax the first $30,000 in gifts made by any person. At that time, you were able to accomplish an overall lowering of the tax by having in effect two taxpayers (one paying estate taxes and one paying gift taxes) and each tax began at the lowest brackets.

Present law imposes the federal tax on the total of (1) your taxable estate and (2) taxable gifts made after December 31, 1976 (taxable gifts made after December 31, 1976, are called adjusted taxable gifts).

Note that even though you pay a gift tax now, you get credit towards the estate tax for the gift tax paid. The present system of taxation is known as the *unified system* of taxing estates and gifts.

I create an irrevocable trust. I retain the right to receive the income for life and provide that on my death the trust will be distributed to my two children. Have I made a gift?

Yes. Assuming I placed $100,000 in the trust, I have made a gift of what is left after my death. The value of the gift is based on tables published by the U.S. Treasury Department. Assuming I was age 50 when I transferred the money, the tables show the gift to be worth .32003 of the value of the property transferred. In this case it would be $32,003. (Because I have retained the income for life the entire property will also be includible in my gross estate.)

Important Note: The Internal Revenue Service has proposed a new regulation which changes the valuation of such transfers to reflect a 10% income factor (in place of the present 6% factor) and to eliminate any distinction between male and female mortality experiences. Your lawyer or accountant should be consulted to determine if this change affects you.

What if the trust provides that I may change the beneficiaries? Have I still made a gift?

No. The law states that when you reserve the right to change beneficiaries the transfer is an incomplete one and there is no gift.

With my own money I purchased 2,000 shares of common stock of Foster Wheeler Corporation. The stock cost $24,000. I have had the stock registered in my name and my son's name as joint tenants with right of survivorship. Have I made a gift?

Yes. Each joint tenant becomes the owner of one-half of the property. Therefore, as a joint tenant you are the owner of $12,000 worth of stock and have therefore made a gift of $12,000 (the cost of the stock—$24,000, less the amount retained by you—$12,000). The taxable gift is therefore $2,000; $12,000 less the annual exclusion of $10,000.

What if the stock is purchased in my name and my husband's name as joint tenants with right of survivorship? Is there still a gift?

Yes, but, as in the case of the estate tax law, the gift tax law allows a marital deduction for all property one spouse transfers to his or her spouse as a gift. The deduction is the entire value of the gift.

As in the case of the estate tax marital deduction, the donor must be a U.S. citizen or resident to get the benefit of the gift tax marital deduction. It is not necessary that the donee spouse (the one to whom the gift is made) be a U.S. citizen or resident.

Please summarize the rules about gifts made when title to property is taken as joint tenants (or tenants by the entirety).

A gift is made when any property is purchased and titled as joint tenants, when one party contributes more to the purchase price than his proportionate share of the ownership, except in the case of

1. property owned by husband and wife,

2. bank accounts, and

3. U.S. Savings Bonds.

In general, you should bear in mind that when property is registered in joint names, the percentage of ownership of each joint owner is divided by the number of joint owners. For example, if there are two joint owners, then, as soon as stock is bought in two names, each person will own one-half. If one of the new owners puts up $7,500 to buy stock and the other puts up $2,500 when the stock is registered in joint names, each will then end up owning $5,000 worth of stock. The one who put up the $7,500 made a gift of $2,500 to the other person.

In the case of joint bank accounts and bonds, there will be a gift, if at all, when the non-contributing joint owner withdraws any money or redeems the bonds without any obligation to the other owner for the amounts withdrawn or the money received.

I thought that when property, other than real property, was purchased by husband and wife and one of them supplied the purchase price, a gift was made for tax purposes.

The law was changed effective January 1, 1982. Since there is now an unlimited marital deduction for gifts for any property transferred outright from husband to wife, or wife to husband, no gift tax will be due and no gift tax return will be required.

Do you have an opinion about the present laws dealing with estates and taxes?

Yes, I do. I think that they are too complicated. Also, I think that the rate of tax imposed is too high and that too little is left for the support and comfort of the remaining family after taxes are paid.

I am of the opinion that any taxes imposed by Congress, usually at the urging of the United States Treasury Department should be geared to the cost of living index in a manner similar to the Social Security system.

At present, the laws are much too complicated. In view of the complexity, professional guidance should always be sought. This area of the law has pitfalls and perils even for the professional. If the reader tries to settle estate questions alone, such efforts are bound to create problems and delays and to be costly.

All of these complex rules convince me that I should seek professional assistance. You have not indicated what a lawyer would charge to plan an estate or to counsel with respect to some of the items you mentioned. Would you please discuss this?

In general, fees vary from lawyer to lawyer and from region to region. In the Baltimore, Maryland, area, hourly fees (as of October, 1983) were generally from $75 to $150 for the experienced lawyer. Obviously there are those who charge less and those who charge more. No lawyer I know of will resent your inquiring as to what that lawyer charges.

If a client wishes a complex will with trust clauses, the time necessary to plan and draft the instrument will be greater than for the simple will. The time necessary for the lawyer to learn all the financial facts, the family history, and the wishes of the client may vary from one hour to five or more hours. The time necessary to prepare the simple will would be one hour or less.

Time will necessarily be spent reviewing other documents such as corporate records, pension plan provisions, insurance policies, land records or deeds, income tax returns, and registration of passbooks. It may be important to learn who supplied the cash to purchase jointly-owned assets (a residence, land, a business, or stocks).

The lawyer may want to review prior gift tax returns. He or she will surely wish to consider making suggestions and research may be required.

Additional documents may be appropriate, such as a stockholder's agreement, partnership agreement, trust agreements, and memoranda of facts. It may be necessary to re-title property, among other steps.

At the first meeting, after learning some of the facts, the lawyer can be in a position to give his estimate about the total cost. Frequently, it will also be necessary for the lawyer to spend time conferring with one or more of the following: client's accountant, insurance agent, pension consultant, trust officer.

I am of the opinion that fees paid a professional are well worth the expenditure in terms of peace of mind so that your property is left to your loved ones as you would wish and at the least cost for administration expenses and taxes.

When a person has a potentially taxable estate, the portion of legal fees paid for estate planning that is allocable to tax advice and services is currently deductible for income tax purposes.

APPENDIX

Table 1

Unified Rate Schedule
Imposed by Federal Tax

Table 2

Credit for State Death Taxes

Table 3

Death Taxes Imposed by the States

Table 4

State-Required Disposition of Property
When Property Is Not Otherwise Disposed of
by Will or Otherwise

Table 5

Requirements for Wills, by State

Table 6

Compensation Allowed to
Executors and Trustees, by State

APPENDIX

TABLE 1

Unified Rate Schedule
Imposed by Federal Law
(For persons dying January 1, 1977, and thereafter
and for gifts made January 1, 1977, and thereafter)

Summary of Steps to Be Taken in Calculating
the Net Federal Estate Tax to Be Paid:

1. Figure total gross estate.

2. Deduct debts, expenses, and deductions.

3. Subtract item 2 from item 1 (the result is called the taxable estate).

4. Add adjusted taxable gifts (all taxable gifts made on or after January 1, 1977) to taxable estate.

5. Apply the Unified Rate Schedule to the sum total of item 4 (the taxable estate plus adjusted taxable gifts). The amount arrived at will be the tentative tax.

6. Subtract from the tentative tax any federal tax imposed by reason of gifts made after 1976 (using the current rate schedule). Then subtract:

   a. the unified credit,

    b. the credit for state death taxes paid (shown on Table 2), and

    c. other credits (such as for foreign death taxes paid).

7. The net amount, after subtracting item 6 from item 5, will be the federal estate tax due.

Summary of Steps to Be Taken in Calculating the Net Federal Gift Tax to Be Paid:

---

1. Figure total taxable gifts (gifts made since June 7, 1932) including gifts made this year. (Subtract from *gross* gifts (i) the annual exclusion (now $10,000) and (ii) the lifetime specific exemption where gifts were made prior to 1977, to arrive at taxable gifts.)

2. Apply the Unified Rate Schedule to the total amount shown in Item 1.

3. Apply the Unified Rate Schedule to total taxable gifts *except* exclude gifts made this year.

4. Subtract the amount shown in Item 3 from the amount shown in Item 2. This amount will be the tentative tax.

5. Subtract from the unified credit any such credit used in prior years (since 1977) plus 20% of any lifetime specific exemption used for gifts made after September 8, 1976, and before January 1, 1977.

6. Subtract the amount shown in Item 5 from the amount shown in Item 4. This amount is the net federal gift tax due for this year.

Unified Credit

Year of death or transfer	Amount of credit	Year of death or transfer	Amount of credit
1977	$30,000	1983	$79,300
1978	34,000	1984	96,300
1979	38,000	1985	121,800
1980	42,500	1986	155,800
1981	47,000	1987 and thereafter	192,800
1982	62,800		

Unified Rate Schedule

Column A	Column B	Column C	Column D
Taxable amount over	Taxable amount not over	Tax on amount in Column A	Rate of tax on excess over amount in Column A
0	$ 10,000	0	18%
$ 10,000	20,000	$ 1,800	20%
20,000	40,000	3,800	22%
40,000	60,000	8,200	24%
60,000	80,000	13,000	26%
80,000	100,000	18,200	28%
100,000	150,000	23,800	30%
150,000	250,000	38,800	32%
250,000	500,000	70,800	34%
500,000	750,000	155,800	37%
750,000	1,000,000	248,300	39%
1,000,000	1,250,000	345,800	41%
1,250,000	1,500,000	448,300	43%
1,500,000	2,000,000	555,800	45%
2,000,000	2,500,000	780,800	49%
2,500,000	3,000,000	1,025,800	50%

In the case of decedents dying, and gifts made, in 1981 the last item (over $2,500,000, etc.) is substituted by the following:

Over $2,500,000 but not over $3,000,000 .. $1,025,800, plus 53% of the excess over $2,500,000

Over $3,000,000 but not over $3,500,000 .. $1,290,800, plus 57% of the excess over $3,000,000

Over $3,500,000 but not over $4,000,000 .. $1,575,800, plus 61% of the excess over $3,500,000

Over $4,000,000 but not over $4,500,00 ... $1,880,800, plus 65% of the excess over $4,000,000

Over $4,500,000 but not over $5,000,000 .. $2,205,800, plus 69% of the excess over
$4,500,000

Over $5,000,000 .... $2,550,800, plus 70% of the excess over
$5,000,000

In the case of decedents dying, and gifts made, in 1982 the last item (over $2,500,000, etc.) is substituted by the following:

Over $2,500,000 but not over $3,000,000 .. $1,025,800, plus 53% of the excess over
$2,500,000

Over $3,000,000 but not over $3,500,000 .. $1,290,800, plus 57% of the excess over
$3,000,000

Over $3,500,000 but not over $4,000,000 .. $1,575,800, plus 61% of the excess over
$3,500,000

Over $4,000,000 .... $1,880,800, plus 65% of the excess over
$4,000,000

In the case of decedents dying, and gifts made, in 1983 the last item (over $2,500,000, etc.) is substituted by the following:

Over $2,500,000 but not over $3,000,000 .. $1,025,800, plus 53% of the excess over
$2,500,000

Over $3,000,000 but not over $3,500,000 .. $1,290,800, plus 57% of the excess over
$3,000,000

Over $3,500,000 .... $1,575,800, plus 60% of the excess over
$3,500,000

In the case of decedents dying, and gifts made, in 1984, 1985, 1986, and 1987 the last item (over $2,500,000, etc.) is substituted by the following:

Over $2,500,000 but not over $3,000,000 .. $1,025,800, plus 53% of the excess over
$2,500,000

Over $3,000,000 .... $1,290,800, plus 55% of the excess over
$3,000,000

TABLE 2

Credit for State Death Taxes

The credit is only available to the extent that state death taxes are actually paid to a state. Thus if the decedent died a resident of Nevada, where there is no state death tax, no credit will be available.

Column A	Column B	Column C	Column D
Taxable amount equal to or over	Taxable amount not over	Credit on amount in Column A	Rate of credit on excess over amount in Column A
$ 100,000	$ 150,000	0	0.8%
150,000	200,000	$ 400	1.6%
200,000	300,000	1,200	2.4%
300,000	500,000	3,600	3.2%
500,000	700,000	10,000	4.0%
700,000	900,000	18,000	4.8%
900,000	1,100,000	27,600	5.6%
1,100,000	1,600,000	38,800	6.4%
1,600,000	2,100,000	70,800	7.2%
2,100,000	2,600,000	106,800	8.0%
2,600,000	3,100,000	146,800	8.8%
3,100,000	3,600,000	190,800	9.6%
3,600,000	4,100,000	238,800	10.4%
4,100,000	5,100,000	290,800	11.2%
5,100,000	6,100,000	402,800	12.0%
6,100,000	7,100,000	522,800	12.8%
7,100,000	8,100,000	650,800	13.6%
8,100,000	9,100,000	786,800	14.4%
9,100,000	10,100,000	930,800	15.2%
10,100,000	amounts in excess of 10,100,000	1,082,800	16.0%

TABLE 3

Death Taxes Imposed
by the States

The listings that follow are intended to serve as a guide only and are not intended to be a complete statement of the applicable tax laws. For example, the listings do not reflect available deductions (for charities, marital deduction, orphans' deduction, gift taxes paid) nor do they reflect exclusions or exempt property such as life insurance proceeds, government benefits, benefits from qualified plans, or community property laws. Some states also impose a generation-skipping tax.

Not all states define "child" in the same way. Some include in the definition an adopted child, a stepchild, children of an adopted child, and so on. The applicability of the tax to property of a non-resident decedent is also not apparent from a reading of this table.

ALABAMA

Inheritance Tax: None.

Estate Tax: Equal to federal credit for state death taxes.

Gift Tax: None.

ALASKA

Inheritance Tax: None.

Estate Tax: Equal to federal credit for state death taxes.

Gift Tax: None.

ARIZONA

Inheritance Tax: None.

Estate Tax: Equal to federal credit for state death taxes.

Gift Tax: None.

ARKANSAS

Inheritance Tax: None.

Estate Tax: Equal to federal credit for state death taxes.

Gift Tax: None.

CALIFORNIA

Inheritance Tax: None.

Estate Tax: Equal to federal credit for state death taxes.

Gift Tax: None.

COLORADO

Inheritance Tax: None.

Estate Tax: Equal to federal credit for state death taxes.

Gift Tax: None.

CONNECTICUT

Inheritance Tax (called successor and transfer tax):
    Class AA beneficiary: Spouse.
    Class A beneficiaries: Parent, grandparent, descendant.
    Class B beneficiaries: Spouse or surviving spouse of child, stepchild, brother and sister or their descendants.
    Class C beneficiaries: All others.

Amount received by each	Class AA	Class A
To $20,000	0	0
From $20,000 to $25,000	0	2.6%
From $25,000 to $100,000	0	3.9%
From $100,000 to $150,000	3.9%	3.9%
From $150,000 to $250,000	5.2%	5.2%
From $250,000 to $400,000	6.5%	6.5%
From $400,000 to $600,000	7.8%	7.8%
From $600,000 to $1,000,000	9.1%	9.1%
From $1,000,000 and over	10.4%	10.4%

Amount received by each	Class B	Class C
To $1,000	0	0
From $1,000 to $6,000	0	10.4%
From $6,000 to $25,000	5.2%	10.4%
From $25,000 to $50,000	6.5%	11.7%
From $50,000 to $150,000	6.5%	11.7%
From $150,000 to $250,000	7.8%	13.0%
From $250,000 to $400,000	9.1%	14.3%
From $400,000 to $600,000	10.4%	15.6%
From $600,000 to $1,000,000	11.7%	16.9%
From $1,000,000 and over	13.0%	18.2%

(Exemptions are reflected in the tables and are available to the entire class and not to each beneficiary in each class.)

Estate Tax: Equal to federal credit for state death taxes. Thus, if an inheritance tax amounts to less than the maximum credit allowable under federal estate tax law, an additional tax is imposed by the state to make total death taxes collected by the state equal to the maximum allowable credit under federal estate tax law.

Gift Tax: None.

DELAWARE

Inheritance Tax:
   Class A beneficiary: Spouse.
   Class B beneficiaries: Grandparent, parent, descendants, spouse, or surviving spouse of child.
   Class C beneficiaries: Brother or sister or their descendants, aunt or uncle or their descendants.
   Class D beneficiaries: All others.

Amount received by each	Class A	Class B
To $3,000	0	0
From $3,000 to $25,000	0	1%
From $25,000 to $50,000	0	2%
From $50,000 to $70,000	0	3%
From $70,000 to $75,000	2%	3%
From $75,000 to $100,000	2%	4%
From $100,000 to $200,000	3%	5%
From $200,000 and over	4%	6%

Amount received by each	Class C	Class D
To $1,000	0	10%
From $1,000 to $25,000	5%	10%
From $25,000 to $50,000	6%	12%
From $50,000 to $100,000	7%	14%
From $100,000 to $150,000	8%	16%
From $150,000 to $200,000	9%	16%
From $200,000 and over	10%	16%

Estate Tax: Equal to federal credit for state death taxes. Thus, if an inheritance tax amounts to less than the maximum credit allowable under federal estate tax law, an additional tax is imposed by the state to make total death taxes collected by the state equal to the maximum allowable credit under federal estate tax law.

Gift Tax: Tax imposed.

DISTRICT OF COLUMBIA

Inheritance Tax:
Class A beneficiaries: Spouse, ancestor, and descendant.
Class B beneficiaries: All others.

Amount received by each	Class A	Class B
To $1,000	0	0
From $1,000 to $5,000	0	5%
From $5,000 to $25,000	1%	5%
From $25,000 to $50,000	2%	10%
From $50,000 to $100,000	3%	14%
From $100,000 to $500,000	5%	18%
From $500,000 to $1,000,000	6%	22%
From $1,000,000 and over	8%	23%

Estate Tax: Equal to federal credit for state death taxes. Thus, if an inheritance tax amounts to less than the maximum credit allowable under federal estate tax law, an additional tax is imposed by the District to make total death taxes collected by the District equal to the maximum allowable credit under federal estate tax law.

Gift Tax: None.

FLORIDA

Inheritance Tax: None.

Estate Tax: Equal to federal credit for state death taxes.

Gift Tax: None.

GEORGIA

Inheritance Tax: None.

Estate Tax: Equal to federal credit for state death taxes.

Gift Tax: None.

HAWAII

Inheritance Tax:

Class 1 beneficiary: Spouse.
Class 2 beneficiaries: Parent, child, and grandchild.
Class 3 beneficiaries: All others.

Amount received by each	*Class 1*
To $25,000	2%
From $25,000 to $100,000	3%
From $100,000 to $200,000	5%
From $200,000 and over	7%

Amount received by each	*Class 2*
To $25,000	3%
From $25,000 to $75,000	5%
From $75,000 to $150,000	7%
From $150,000 and over	8%

Amount received by each	*Class 3*
To $20,000	3%
From $20,000 to $70,000	6%
From $70,000 to $145,000	8%
From $145,000 and over	10%

(Exemptions: Class 1, $300,000; Class 2, $150,000; Class 3, $5,000. The rates shown are for amounts in excess of the exemptions.)

Estate Tax: Equal to federal credit for state death taxes. Thus, if an inheritance tax amounts to less than the maximum credit allowable under federal estate tax law, an additional tax is imposed by the state to make total death taxes collected by the state equal to the maximum allowable credit under federal estate tax law.

Gift Tax: None.

IDAHO

Inheritance Tax:

Class 1 beneficiaries: Spouse, descendant, and ancestor.

Class 2 beneficiaries: Brother and sister and their issue, spouse or surviving spouse of son, spouse of daughter.

Class 3 beneficiaries: Uncle, aunt, and their issue.

Class 4 beneficiaries: All others.

Amount received by each	Class 1	Class 2	Class 3	Class 4
To $25,000	2%	4%	6%	8%
From $25,000 to $50,000	4%	6%	9%	14%
From $50,000 to $100,000	6%	8%	12%	20%
From $100,000 to $200,000	8%	12%	15%	30%
From $200,000 to $500,000	10%	16%	20%	30%
From $500,000 and over	15%	20%	25%	30%

(Exemptions: Spouse, all property; minor child, $50,000; other Class 1 beneficiaries, $30,000; Class 2, 3, and 4 beneficiaries, $10,000. The rates shown are for amounts in excess of the exemptions.)

Estate Tax: Equal to federal credit for state death taxes. Thus, if an inheritance tax amounts to less than the maximum credit allowable under federal estate tax law, an additional tax is imposed by the state to make total death taxes collected by the state equal to the maximum allowable credit under federal estate tax law.

Gift Tax: None.

ILLINOIS

Inheritance Tax: None.

Estate Tax: Equal to federal credit for state death taxes.

Gift Tax: None.

INDIANA

Inheritance Tax:

Class A beneficiaries: Spouse, child.

Class B beneficiaries: Brother and sister or their descendants; spouse or surviving spouse of child.

Class C beneficiaries: All others.

Amount received by each	Class A
To $25,000	1%
From $25,000 to $50,000	2%
From $50,000 to $200,000	3%
From $200,000 to $300,000	4%
From $300,000 to $500,000	5%
From $500,000 to $700,000	6%
From $700,000 to $1,000,000	7%
From $1,000,000 to $1,500,000	8%
From $1,500,00 and over	10%

Amount received by each	Class B
To $100,000	7%
From $100,000 to $500,000	10%
From $500,000 to $1,000,000	12%
From $1,000,000 and over	15%

Amount received by each	Class C
To $100,000	10%
From $100,000 to $1,000,000	15%
From $1,000,000 and over	20%

(Exemptions: Spouse, all property; child, $5,000 or $5,000 times number of years under 21; Class B beneficiaries, $500; Class C beneficiaries, $100. The rates shown are for amounts in excess of the exemptions.)

Estate Tax: Equal to federal credit for state death taxes. Thus, if an inheritance tax amounts to less than the maximum credit allowable under federal estate tax law, an additional tax is imposed by the state to make total death taxes collected by the state equal to the maximum allowable credit under federal estate tax law.

Gift Tax: None.

IOWA

Inheritance Tax:

Class 1 beneficiaries: Spouse, parent, descendant.

Class 2 beneficiaries: Brother and sister, spouse of child, stepchild.

Class 3 beneficiaries: All others except those in Classes 4–6.

Class 4 beneficiaries: Societies, institutions, or associations of other states or countries for charitable, educational, religious, cemetery, or humane purposes, or resident trustees for uses outside the state.

Class 5 beneficiaries: Firm, corporation, or society organized for profit.

Class 6 beneficiaries: Aliens or nonresidents of U.S.

Amount received by each	*Class 1*	*Class 2*	*Class 3*
To $5,000	1%	5%	10%
From $5,000 to $12,500	2%	5%	10%
From $12,500 to $25,000	3%	6%	10%
From $25,000 to $50,000	4%	7%	10%
From $50,000 to $75,000	5%	7%	12%
From $75,000 to $100,000	6%	8%	12%
From $100,000 to $150,000	7%	9%	15%
From $150,000 and over	8%	10%	15%

The tax on Class 4 beneficiaries is 10%; on Class 5 beneficiaries, 15%; on Class 6 beneficiaries, 20%, except if any are brothers and sisters or are within Class 1 (in which event the rate is 10%).

(Exemptions: Spouse, $120,000 when death occurs on or after January 1, 1982, $150,000 beginning January 1, 1983, $180,000 beginning January 1, 1984, one-third of tax beginning January 1, 1986, two-thirds of tax beginning January 1, 1987, and thereafter, none; child, $50,000; each parent, $15,000; lineal descendants other than child, $15,000. The rates shown are for amounts in excess of the exemptions.)

Estate Tax: Equal to federal credit for state death taxes. Thus, if an inheritance tax amounts to less than the maximum credit allowable under federal estate tax law, an additional tax is imposed by the state to make total death taxes collected by the state equal to the maximum allowable credit under federal estate tax law.

Gift Tax: None.

KANSAS

Inheritance Tax:

Class (b) beneficiary: Ancestor, descendant, stepparent and stepchild, surviving spouse of child.

Class (c) beneficiary: Brother and sister.

Class (d) beneficiary: All others.

(Note: The spouse was formerly the Class (a) beneficiary. There is no longer a Class (a) beneficiary since all property passing to a spouse is exempt.)

Amount received by each	Class (b)
To $30,000	0
From $30,000 to $55,000	1.0%
From $55,000 to $80,000	2.0%
From $80,000 to $130,000	3.0%
From $130,000 to $530,000	4.0%
From $530,000 and over	5.0%

Amount received by each	Class (c)
To $5,000	0
From $5,000 to $30,000	3%
From $30,000 to $55,000	5%
From $55,000 to $105,000	7 1/2%
From $105,000 to $505,000	10%
From $505,000 and over	12 1/3%

Amount received by each	Class (d)
To $100,000	10.0%
From $100,000 to $200,000	12.0%
From $200,000 and over	15.0%

(Exemptions: Spouse, all property.)

Estate Tax: Equal to federal credit for state death taxes. Thus, if an inheritance tax amounts to less than the maximum credit allowable under federal estate tax law, an additional tax is imposed by the state to make total death taxes collected by the state equal to the maximum allowable credit under federal estate tax law.

Gift Tax: None.

KENTUCKY

Inheritance Tax:
  Class A beneficiaries: Spouse, minor child or mentally disabled child, other children, stepchild, stepchild's child, grandchild, parent.
  Class B beneficiaries: Brother or sister, nephew or niece, aunt, uncle, spouse of child.
  Class C beneficiaries: All others.

Amount received by each	Class A	Class B	Class C
To $10,000	2%	4%	6%
From $10,000 to $20,000	2%	5%	8%
From $20,000 to $30,000	3%	6%	10%
From $30,000 to $45,000	4%	8%	12%
From $45,000 to $60,000	5%	10%	14%
From $60,000 to $100,000	6%	12%	16%
From $100,000 to $200,000	7%	14%	16%
From $200,000 to $500,000	8%	16%	16%
From $500,000 and over	10%	16%	16%

(Exemptions: Spouse, $50,000; minor or mentally disabled child, $20,000; all other Class A beneficiaries, $5,000; Class B beneficiaries, $1,000; Class C beneficiaries, $500. The rates shown are for amounts in excess of the exemptions.)

Estate Tax: Equal to federal credit for state death taxes. Thus, if an inheritance tax amounts to less than the maximum credit allowable under federal estate tax law, an additional tax is imposed by the state to make total death taxes collected by the state equal to the maximum allowable credit under federal estate tax law.

Gift Tax: None.

LOUISIANA

Inheritance Tax:

Class 1 beneficiaries: Spouse, direct descendant by blood or affinity, and direct ascendant.

Class 2 beneficiaries: Collateral relation, including brother, sister, nephew and niece by affinity.

Class 3 beneficiaries: State of Louisiana or political subdivision.

Class 4 beneficiaries: All others.

Amount received by each	Class 1	Class 2
To $20,000	2%	5%
From $20,000 and over	3%	7%

Amount received by each	Class 4
To $5,000	5%
From $5,000 and over	10%

(Exemptions: Class 1 beneficiary, $5,000, effective January 1, 1984, $10,000 if death occurs during 1984, $15,000 if death occurs during 1985, $20,000 if death occurs during 1986, $25,000 thereafter; Class 2 beneficiary, $1,000; Class 3 beneficiary, all property; Class 4 beneficiary, $500. The rates shown are for amounts in excess of the exemptions.)

Estate Tax: Equal to federal credit for state death taxes. Thus, if an inheritance tax amounts to less than the maximum credit allowable under federal estate tax law, an additional tax is imposed by the state to make total death taxes collected by the state equal to the maximum allowable credit under federal estate tax law.

Gift Tax: Tax imposed.

MAINE

Inheritance Tax:
  Class A beneficiaries: Spouse, parent, child, stepchild, adoptive parent, grandchild, ancestor, descendant, spouse or surviving spouse of child.
  Class B beneficiaries: Brother, sister, uncle, aunt, nephew, niece, grandnephew or niece, cousin.
  Class C beneficiaries: All others.

Amount received by each	Class A	Class B
To $25,000	5%	8%
From $25,000 to $50,000	5%	10%
From $50,000 to $100,000	6%	10%
From $100,000 to $250,000	8%	12%
From $250,000 and over	10%	14%

Amount received by each	Class C
To $75,000	14%
From $75,000 to $150,000	16%
From $150,000 and over	18%

(Exemptions: Spouse, $50,000; parent, child, stepchild, adoptive parent, grandchild of deceased child per stirpes, $25,000; other Class A beneficiaries, $2,000; Class B and all other beneficiaries, $1,000. The rates shown are for amounts in excess of the exemptions.)

For period July 1981–June 1986, amount of tax calculated above is reduced by following percentages:

1. Death occurring after June 30, 1981, and before July 1, 1982 .... 15%
2. Death occurring after June 30, 1982, and before July 1, 1983 .... 25%
3. Death occurring after June 30, 1983, and before July 1, 1984 .... 35%
4. Death occurring after June 30, 1984, and before July 1, 1985 .... 45%
5. Death occurring after June 30, 1985, and before July 1, 1986 .... 55%

After July 1, 1986, no inheritance tax.

Estate Tax: Equal to federal credit for state death taxes. Thus, if an inheritance tax amounts to less than the maximum credit allowable under federal estate tax law, an additional tax is imposed by the state to make total death taxes collected by the state equal to the maximum allowable credit under federal estate tax law.

Gift Tax: None.

MARYLAND

Inheritance Tax:
 Class 1 beneficiaries: Parent, stepparent, spouse, child, stepchild, descendant.
 Class 2 beneficiaries: All others.

Amount received by each	Class 1	Class 2
Any amount	1%	10%

(Exemptions: Any share that does not exceed $150; jointly-owned property received by spouse; spouse of descendant, first $2,000 of jointly-owned savings accounts taxed at 1%; insurance received by trust or named beneficiary.)

Estate Tax: Equal to federal credit for state death taxes. Thus, if an inheritance tax amounts to less than the maximum credit allowable under federal estate tax law, an additional tax is imposed by the state to make total death taxes collected by the state equal to the maximum allowable credit under federal estate tax law.

Gift Tax: None.

MASSACHUSETTS

Inheritance Tax: None.

Estate Tax:

Amount of taxable estate	Rate
To $50,000	5%
From $50,000 to $100,000	7%
From $100,000 to $200,000	9%
From $200,000 to $400,000	10%
From $400,000 to $600,000	11%
From $600,000 to $800,000	12%
From $800,000 to $1,000,000	13%
From $1,000,000 to $2,000,000	14%
From $2,000,000 to $4,000,000	15%
From $4,000,000 and over	16%

If the estate tax amounts to less than the maximum credit allowable under federal estate tax law, the estate tax shall be increased to equal such maximum credit.

(Exemptions: Every estate is entitled to a $30,000 exemption; if the Massachusetts net estate is $60,000 or less, the exemption is equal to the Massachusetts net estate.)

Gift Tax: None.

MICHIGAN

Inheritance Tax:
   Class 1 beneficiaries: Spouse, grandparent, parent, child, brother, sister, spouse or surviving spouse of son, spouse of daughter, descendant.
   Class 2 beneficiaries: All others.

Amount received by each	Class 1	Class 2
To $50,000	2%	12%
From $50,000 to $250,000	4%	14%
From $250,000 to $500,000	7%	14%
From $500,000 to $750,000	8%	17%
From $750,000 and over	10%	17%

A tax of one-half of 1% is added to the inheritance tax and the estate tax, if applicable.

(Exemptions: Spouse, all property; all other Class 1 beneficiaries, $10,000. The rates shown are for amounts in excess of the exemptions.)

Estate Tax: Equal to federal credit for state death taxes. Thus, if an inheritance tax amounts to less than the maximum credit allowable under federal estate tax law, an additional tax is imposed by the state to make total death taxes collected by the state equal to the maximum allowable credit under federal estate tax law.

Gift Tax: None.

MINNESOTA

Inheritance Tax: None.

Estate Tax:

Amount of taxable estate	Rate
To $25,000	7%
From $25,000 to $50,000	7%
From $50,000 to $100,000	7%
From $100,000 to $200,000	8%
From $200,000 to $300,000	9%
From $300,000 to $500,000	10%
From $500,000 to $1,000,000	11%
From $1,000,000 and over	12%

(Exemption: Spouse, all property.)

If the estate tax amounts to less than the maximum credit allowable under federal estate tax law, the estate tax shall be increased to equal such maximum credit.

Gift Tax: None.

MISSISSIPPI

Inheritance Tax: None.

Estate Tax:

Amount of taxable estate	Rate
To $60,000	1.0%
From $60,000 to $100,000	1.6%
From $100,000 to $200,000	2.4%
From $200,000 to $400,000	3.2%
From $400,000 to $600,000	4.0%
From $600,000 to $800,000	4.8%
From $800,000 to $1,000,000	5.6%
From $1,000,000 to $1,500,000	6.4%
From $1,500,000 to $2,000,000	7.2%
From $2,000,000 to $2,500,000	8.0%
From $2,500,000 to $3,000,000	8.8%
From $3,000,000 to $3,500,000	9.6%
From $3,500,000 to $4,000,000	10.4%
From $4,000,000 to $5,000,000	11.2%
From $5,000,000 to $6,000,000	12.0%
From $6,000,000 to $7,000,000	12.8%
From $7,000,000 to $8,000,000	13.6%
From $8,000,000 to $9,000,000	14.4%
From $9,000,000 to $10,000,000	15.2%
From $10,000,000 and over	16.0%

(Exemptions: Any decedent dying in 1981, $161,563; any decedent dying in 1982 and thereafter, $175,625. These amounts shall be deducted first from above table.)

If the estate tax amounts to less than the maximum credit allowable under federal estate tax law, the estate tax shall be increased to equal such maximum credit.

Gift Tax: None.

MISSOURI

Inheritance Tax: None.

Estate Tax: Equal to federal credit for state death taxes.

Gift Tax: None.

MONTANA

Inheritance Tax:

Class 1 beneficiaries: Spouse; child; minor child to whom decedent stood in acknowledged relationship of parent for at least ten years prior to death, which relationship began when the person was under age 15 years; ancestor; descendant.

Class 2 beneficiaries: Brother and sister or their descendants, spouse of child.

Class 3 beneficiaries: Uncle, aunt, and their children.

Class 4 beneficiaries: All others.

Amount received by each	Class 1	Class 2	Class 3	Class 4
To $25,000	2%	4%	6%	8%
From $25,000 to $50,000	4%	8%	12%	16%
From $50,000 to $100,000	6%	12%	18%	24%
From $100,000 and over	8%	16%	24%	32%

(Exemptions: Spouse and descendants, all property; lineal ancestor, $7,000; Class 2 beneficiaries, $1,000. The rates shown are for amounts in excess of the exemptions.)

Estate Tax: Equal to federal credit for state death taxes. Thus, if an inheritance tax amounts to less than the maximum credit allowable under federal estate tax law, an additional tax is imposed by the state to make total death taxes collected by the state equal to the maximum allowable credit under federal estate tax law.

Gift Tax: None.

NEBRASKA

Inheritance Tax:

Class 1 beneficiaries: Spouse, parent, child, brother, sister, spouse of daughter, spouse of son, descendant.

Class 2 beneficiaries: Aunt, uncle, niece, nephew, or descendant of any of them.

Class 3 beneficiaries: All others.

Amount received by each	Class 1	Class 2	Class 3
To $2,000	0	6%	6%
From $2,000 to $5,000	0	6%	6%
From $5,000 to $10,000	0	6%	9%
From $10,000 to $20,000	1%	6%	12%
From $20,000 to $50,000	1%	6%	15%
From $50,000 to $60,000	1%	6%	18%
From $60,000 and over	1%	9%	18%

(Exemption: Spouse, all property.)

Estate Tax: Equal to federal credit for state death taxes. Thus, if an inheritance tax amounts to less than the maximum credit allowable under federal estate tax law, an additional tax is imposed by the state to make total death taxes collected by the state equal to the maximum allowable credit under federal estate tax law.

Gift Tax: None.

NEVADA

Inheritance Tax: None.

Estate Tax: None.

Gift Tax: None.

NEW HAMPSHIRE

Inheritance Tax: All property received is subject to tax at the rate of 15%.

(Exemptions: Spouse, ancestor, descendant, spouse of ancestor or descendant, all property.)

Estate Tax: Equal to federal credit for state death taxes. Thus, if an inheritance tax amounts to less than the maximum credit allowable under federal estate tax law, an additional tax is imposed by the state to make total death taxes collected by the state equal to the maximum allowable credit under federal estate tax law.

Gift Tax: None.

NEW JERSEY

Inheritance Tax:

Class A beneficiaries: Parent, grandparent, spouse, child, stepchild, descendants.
Class C beneficiaries: Brother, sister, spouse or surviving spouse of child.
Class D beneficiaries: All others.

Amount received by each	Class A
To $15,000	0
From $15,000 to $50,000	2%
From $50,000 to $100,000	3%
From $100,000 to $150,000	4%
From $150,000 to $200,000	5%
From $200,000 to $300,000	6%
From $300,000 to $500,000	7%
From $500,000 to $700,000	8%
From $700,000 to $900,000	9%
From $900,000 to $1,100,000	10%
From $1,100,000 to $1,400,000	11%
From $1,400,000 to $1,700,000	12%
From $1,700,000 to $2,200,000	13%
From $2,200,000 to $2,700,000	14%
From $2,700,000 to $3,200,000	15%
From $3,200,000 and over	16%

Amount received by each	Class C	Class D
To $700,000	11%	15%
From $700,000 to $1,100,000	11%	16%
From $1,100,000 to $1,400,000	13%	16%
From $1,400,000 to $1,700,000	14%	16%
From $1,700,000 and over	16%	16%

(Exemptions: Class A beneficiaries, $15,000 (reflected in above table); all others, $500 if share is less than this amount.)

Estate Tax: Equal to federal credit for state death taxes. Thus, if an inheritance tax amounts to less than the maximum credit allowable under federal estate tax law, an additional tax is imposed by the state to make total death taxes collected by the state equal to the the maximum allowable credit under federal estate tax law.

Gift Tax: None.

NEW MEXICO

Inheritance Tax: None.

Estate Tax: Equal to federal credit for state death taxes.

Gift Tax: None.

NEW YORK

Inheritance Tax: None

Estate Tax:

Amount of taxable estate	Rate
To $50,000	2%
From $50,000 to $150,000	3%
From $150,000 to $300,000	4%
From $300,000 to $500,000	5%

Amount of taxable estate	Rate
From $500,000 to $700,000	6%
From $700,000 to $900,000	7%
From $900,000 to $1,100,000	8%
From $1,100,000 to $1,600,000	9%
From $1,600,000 to $2,100,000	10%
From $2,100,000 to $2,600,000	11%
From $2,600,000 to $3,100,000	12%
From $3,100,000 to $3,600,000	13%
From $3,600,000 to $4,100,000	14%
From $4,100,000 to $5,100,000	15%
From $5,100,000 to $6,100,000	16%
From $6,100,000 to $7,100,000	17%
From $7,100,000 to $8,100,000	18%
From $8,100,000 to $9,100,000	19%
From $9,100,000 to $10,100,000	20%
From $10,100,000 and over	21%

(Exemptions: None; however, there are credits as follows: Tax up to $2,750—credit for entire tax; tax of $2,750 to $5,000—credit for difference between amount of tax and $5,000; tax of $5,000 or more—credit is $500.)

If the estate tax amounts to less than the maximum credit allowable under federal estate tax law, the estate tax shall be increased to equal such maximum credit.

Gift Tax: Tax imposed.

NORTH CAROLINA

Inheritance Tax:

Class A beneficiaries: spouse, issue, stepchild, ancestor, spouse of child where child is not entitled to property of deceased.

Class B beneficiaries: Brother or sister or their issue, aunt or uncle.

Class C beneficiaries: All others.

Amount received by each	Class A	Class B	Class C
To $5,000	1%	4%	8%
From $5,000 to $10,000	1%	5%	8%
From $10,000 to $25,000	2%	6%	9%
From $25,000 to $50,000	3%	7%	10%
From $50,000 to $100,000	4%	8%	11%
From $100,000 to $200,000	5%	10%	12%
From $200,000 to $250,000	6%	10%	12%
From $250,000 to $500,000	6%	11%	13%
From $500,000 to $1,000,000	7%	12%	14%
From $1,000,000 to $1,500,000	8%	13%	15%
From $1,500,000 to $2,000,000	9%	14%	16%
From $2,000,000 to $2,500,000	10%	15%	16%
From $2,500,000 to $3,000,000	11%	15%	17%
From $3,000,000 and over	12%	16%	17%

(Exemptions: None; however, there are credits as follows: Spouse, $3,150; minor children and certain incapacitated children, balance of credit unused by spouse; other Class A beneficiaries, balance of credit unused by spouse and minor children, etc.)

Estate Tax: Equal to federal credit for state death taxes. Thus, if an inheritance tax amounts to less than the maximum credit allowable under federal estate tax law, an additional tax is imposed by the state to make total death taxes collected by the state equal to the maximum allowable credit under federal estate tax law.

Gift Tax: Tax imposed.

NORTH DAKOTA

Inheritance Tax: None.

Estate Tax: Equal to federal credit for state death taxes.

Gift Tax: None.

OHIO

Inheritance Tax: None.

Estate Tax:

Amount of taxable estate	Rate
To $40,000	2%
From $40,000 to $100,000	3%
From $100,000 to $200,000	4%
From $200,000 to $300,000	5%
From $300,000 to $500,000	6%
From $500,000 and over	7%

(Exemptions: $10,000, plus $60,000 to spouse, plus $14,000 to each minor child and $6,000 to each child over 18.) If the estate tax amounts to less than the maximum credit allowable under federal estate tax law, the estate tax shall be increased to equal such maximum credit.

Gift Tax: None.

OKLAHOMA

Inheritance Tax: None.

Estate and Transfer Tax:
Class 1 beneficiaries: Parent, child, child of spouse, descendant.
Class 2 beneficiaries: All others.

Amount of net estate after exemptions received by each beneficiary	Class 1	Class 2
To $10,000	1.0%	2%
From $10,000 to $20,000	2.0%	4%
From $20,000 to $40,000	3.0%	6%

Amount of net estate after exemptions received by each beneficiary	Class 1	Class 2
From $40,000 to $60,000	4.0%	8%
From $60,000 to $100,000	5.0%	10%
From $100,000 to $250,000	6.0%	12%
From $250,000 to $500,000	6.5%	13%
From $500,000 to $750,000	7.0%	14%
From $750,000 to $1,000,000	7.5%	14%
From $1,000,000 to $3,000,000	8.0%	15%
From $3,000,000 to $5,000,000	8.5%	15%
From $5,000,000 to $10,000,000	9.0%	15%
From $10,000,000 and over	10.0%	15%

(Exemptions: Spouse, entire amount; Class 1 beneficiaries, $175,000.)

If the estate tax amounts to less than the maximum credit allowable under federal estate law, the estate tax shall be increased to equal such maximum credit.

Gift Tax: Tax imposed.

OREGON

Inheritance Tax: All amounts, 12%.

This rate is reduced by exemptions as follows: 1981 and 1982, $100,000; 1983 and 1984, $200,000; 1985 and 1986, $500,000; 1987 and thereafter, all property.

A credit is allowed as follows: Spouse, minor, or incapacitated child, 1981 and 1982, $48,000; 1983–1984, $36,00, but not to exceed tax.

Estate Tax: Equal to federal credit for state death taxes. Thus, if an inheritance tax amounts to less than the maximum credit allowable under federal estate tax law, an additional tax is imposed by the state to make total death taxes collected by the state equal to the maximum allowable credit under federal estate tax law.

Gift Tax: Tax imposed.

PENNSYLVANIA

Inheritance Tax: All amounts received by grandparent, parent, spouse, descendant, spouse or surviving spouse of child, 6%. (There is a $2,000 family exemption.) All amounts received by others, 15%.

(Exemption: Property held jointly with spouse.)

Estate Tax: Equal to federal credit for state death taxes. Thus, if an inheritance tax amounts to less than the maximum credit allowable under federal estate tax law, an additional tax is imposed by the state to make total death taxes collected by the state equal to the maximum allowable credit under federal estate tax law.

Gift Tax: None.

RHODE ISLAND

Inheritance Tax: None.

Estate Tax:

Taxable estate	Rate
To $25,000	0
From $25,000 to $50,000	3%
From $50,000 to $100,000	4%
From 100,000 to $250,000	5%
From 250,000 to $500,000	6%
From $500,000 to $750,000	7%
From $750,000 to $1,000,000	8%
From $1,000,000 and over	9%

If the estate tax amounts to less than the maximum credit allowable under federal estate tax law, the estate tax shall be increased to equal such maximum credit.

Gift Tax: Tax imposed.

SOUTH CAROLINA

Inheritance Tax: None.

Estate Tax:

Taxable estate	Rate
To $120,000	0
From $120,000 to $160,000	5%
From $160,000 to $220,000	6%
From $220,000 and over	7%

If the estate tax amounts to less than the maximum credit allowable under federal estate tax law, the estate tax shall be increased to equal such maximum credit.

Gift Tax: Tax imposed.

SOUTH DAKOTA

Inheritance Tax:

Class 1 beneficiary: Spouse.

Class 2 beneficiaries: Issue, child acknowledged as such for ten years provided relationship began prior to child's 15th birthday.

Class 3 beneficiaries: Ancestor.

Class 4 beneficiaries: Brother, sister or issue of either, spouse or surviving spouse of son, spouse of daughter.

Class 5 beneficiaries: Aunt or uncle or issue of either.

Class 6 beneficiaries: All others.

Amount received by each	Class 2
To $30,000	0
From $30,000 to $50,000	3 3/4%
From $50,000 to $80,000	6%
From $80,000 to $100,000	6%
From $100,000 and over	7 1/2%

Amount received by each	Class 3	Class 4
To $500	0	0
From $500 to $3,000	0	4%
From $3,000 to $10,000	3%	4%
From $10,000 to $15,000	3%	4%
From $15,000 to $50,000	7%	10%
From $50,000 to $100,000	12%	16%
From $100,000 and over	15%	20%

Amount received by each	Class 5	Class 6
To $100	0	0
From $100 to $200	0	6%
From $200 to $500	5%	6%
From $500 to $3,000	5%	6%
From $3,000 to $10,000	5%	6%
From $10,000 to $15,000	5%	6%
From $15,000 to $50,000	12 1/2%	15%
From $50,000 to $100,000	20%	24%
From $100,000 and over	25%	30%

(Exemptions: Spouse, all amounts; others reflected in above tables except brother or sister, with respect to property used in business or farming in which brother or sister was continuously engaged with decedent for at least ten years, 3% of first $14,500 above the $500 exemption.)

Estate Tax: Equal to federal credit for state death taxes. Thus, if an inheritance tax amounts to less than the maximum credit allowable under federal estate tax law, an additional tax is imposed by the state to make total death taxes collected by the state equal to the maximum allowable credit under federal estate tax law.

Gift Tax: None.

TENNESSEE

Inheritance Tax:
  Class A beneficiaries: Spouse, descendant, ancestor, brother, sister, stepchild.
  Class B beneficiaries: All others, plus common-law spouse.

Amount passing to class	Class A	Class B
To $10,000	0	0
From $10,000 to $60,000	0	6.5%
From $60,000 to $110,000	0	9.5%
From $110,000 to $120,000	0	12.0%
From $120,000 to $160,000	5.5%	12.0%
From $160,000 to $210,000	6.5%	13.5%
From $210,000 to $360,000	6.5%	16.0%
From $360,000 to $560,000	7.5%	16.0%
From $560,000 and over	9.5%	16.0%

(Exemptions: Reflected in above table.)

Estate Tax: Equal to federal credit for state death taxes. Thus, if an inheritance tax amounts to less than the maximum credit allowable under federal estate tax law, an additional tax is imposed by the state to make total death taxes collected by the state equal to the maximum allowable credit under federal estate tax law.

Gift Tax: Tax imposed.

TEXAS

Inheritance Tax: None.

Estate Tax: Equal to federal credit for state death taxes.

Gift Tax: None.

UTAH

Inheritance Tax: None.

Estate Tax: Equal to federal credit for state death taxes.

Gift Tax: None.

VERMONT

Inheritance Tax: None.

Estate Tax: Equal to federal credit for state death taxes.

Gift Tax: None.

VIRGINIA

Inheritance Tax: None.

Estate Tax: Equal to federal credit for state death taxes.

Gift Tax: None.

WASHINGTON

Inheritance Tax: None.

Estate Tax: Equal to federal credit for state death taxes.

Gift Tax: Tax imposed.

WEST VIRGINIA

Inheritance Tax:
    Class A beneficiaries: Spouse, child, stepchild, parent, grandchild.
    Class B beneficiaries: Brother and sister.
    Class C beneficiaries: Other relations.
    Class D beneficiaries: All others.

Amount received by each	Class A	Class B	Class C	Class D
To $50,000	3%	4%	7%	10%
From $50,000 to $150,000	5%	6%	9%	12%
From $150,000 to $300,000	7%	8%	11%	14%
From $300,000 to $500,000	9%	10%	15%	18%
From $500,000 to $1,000,000	11%	14%	20%	24%
From $1,000,000 and over	13%	18%	25%	30%

(Exemptions: Spouse, $30,000; child, stepchild, parents, $10,000; grandchild, $5,000; brother and sister, $10,000.)

Estate Tax: Equal to federal credit for state death taxes. Thus, if an inheritance tax amounts to less than the maximum credit allowable under federal estate tax law, an additional tax is imposed by the state to make total death taxes collected by the state equal to the maximum allowable credit under federal estate tax law.

Gift Tax: None.

WISCONSIN

Inheritance Tax:

Class A beneficiaries: Descendant, ancestor, mutually acknowledged child and issue of same, spouse or surviving spouse of child.

Class B beneficiaries: Brother, sister or descendant.

Class C beneficiaries: Aunt, uncle, or descendant.

Class D beneficiaries: All others.

Amount received by each other than spouse	Class A	Class B	Class C	Class D
To $25,000	2.5%	5%	7.5%	10%
From $25,000 to $50,000	5.0%	10%	15.0%	20%
From $50,000 to $100,000	7.5%	15%	22.5%	30%
From $100,000 to $500,000	10.0%	20%	30.0%	30%
From $500,000 and over	12.5%	25%	30.0%	30%

Tax rate on amount passing to spouse is 5% on amounts from $250,000 to $500,000 and 6.25% on any excess.

Note: In no event is tax to exceed 20% of any property transferred to any beneficiary.

(Exemptions: Spouse, all property; Class A beneficiaries, $10,000; Class B and C beneficiaries, $1,000; Class D beneficiaries, $500.)

Estate Tax: 80% (plus 30% surtax thereon) of federal credit for state death taxes.

Gift Tax: Tax imposed.

WYOMING

Inheritance Tax: None (effective January 1, 1983).

Estate Tax: Equal to federal credit for state death taxes.

Gift Tax: None.

TABLE 4

State-required Disposition of Property
When Property Not Disposed of by Will or Otherwise

The listings that follow are intended to serve as a guide only, and are not intended to be a complete statement of the applicable laws. For example, the listings do not reflect state variations in defining "child," "children," or "next of kin." Some states include in the definition an adopted child, a stepchild, children of an adopted child, and so on. In some states, relatives of half blood are treated the same as relatives of whole blood (same set of parents) and in some states they are not so treated.

ALABAMA

SPOUSE AND ISSUE: If all the children are those of the surviving spouse, $50,000 plus one-half to spouse, but if any of the children are not those of the surviving spouse, one-half only. Balance to children or their issue *per stirpes*.

SPOUSE AND NO ISSUE: If no parent survives, all to the surviving spouse. If parent survives, $100,000 plus one-half to spouse, balance to parent(s).

NO SPOUSE BUT ISSUE: All to children equally or to their issue *per stirpes*.

NO SPOUSE OR ISSUE BUT PARENTS: All to parents equally or to survivor.

NO SPOUSE, ISSUE, OR PARENTS: All to issue of parents *per stirpes*, and, if none, to grandparents or their issue *per stirpes*, and if none, to deceased spouse's next of kin.

ALASKA

SPOUSE AND ISSUE: If all the children are those of surviving spouse, $50,000 plus one-half to spouse, but if any of the children are not those of the surviving spouse, one-half only. Balance to children or their issue *per stirpes*.

SPOUSE AND NO ISSUE: If no parent survives, all to surviving spouse. If parents survive, one-half to parents or to parent and one-half to surviving spouse.

NO SPOUSE BUT ISSUE: All to children equally or to their issue *per stirpes*.

NO SPOUSE OR ISSUE BUT PARENTS: All to parents equally or to survivor.

NO SPOUSE, ISSUE, OR PARENTS: All to issue of parents *per stirpes*, and, if none, one-half to paternal grandparents or their issue *per stirpes*, and one-half to maternal grandparents or their issue *per stirpes*.

ARIZONA

SPOUSE AND ISSUE: If any issue are not those of surviving spouse, one-half of separate property and none of decedent's one-half interest in community property to spouse. Otherwise all of separate property and one-half of community property to spouse. Balance to children or to their issue *per stirpes*.

SPOUSE AND NO ISSUE: If no parent survives, all to surviving spouse. If parents survive, one-half to parents or to parent and one-half to surviving spouse.

NO SPOUSE BUT ISSUE: All to children equally or to their issue *per stirpes*.

NO SPOUSE OR ISSUE BUT PARENTS: All to parents equally or to the survivor.

NO SPOUSE, ISSUE, OR PARENTS: All to issue of parents *per stirpes*, and, if none, to next of kin.

ARKANSAS

SPOUSE AND ISSUE: Real property—as to one-third, life estate to spouse. Balance to children equally or to their issue *per stirpes*. Personal property—one-third to spouse, balance to children equally or to their issue *per stirpes* (non-community property only).

SPOUSE AND NO ISSUE: One-half to spouse if married to decedent less than three years and balance to parents equally or to survivor or all to spouse if married three years or more. If no parents, to brothers and sisters equally or to their issue *per stirpes*, and, if none, to ancestors (up to great-grandparents) and their issue; and, if none, all to spouse.

NO SPOUSE BUT ISSUE: All to children equally or to their issue *per stirpes*.

NO SPOUSE OR ISSUE BUT PARENTS: All to parents equally or to the survivor.

NO SPOUSE, ISSUE, OR PARENTS: All to issue of parents *per stirpes*, and, if none, to grandparents and their issue.

CALIFORNIA

SPOUSE AND ISSUE: All community property to spouse. As to other property, if only one child or issue of child, one-half to spouse and one-half to child or child's issue. If more than one child or issue of same, one-third to spouse and two-thirds to children or their issue *per stirpes*.

SPOUSE AND NO ISSUE: All community property to spouse. As to other property, one-half to spouse and one-half to parents or their survivor and, if none, to brothers and sisters equally or to their issue *per stirpes*, and, if none, all to spouse.

NO SPOUSE BUT ISSUE: All to children equally or to their issue *per stirpes*.

NO SPOUSE OR ISSUE BUT PARENTS: All to the parents equally or to the survivor.

NO SPOUSE, ISSUE, OR PARENTS: All to issue of parents *per stirpes,* and, if none, to next of kin.

COLORADO

SPOUSE AND ISSUE: If all the children are those of the surviving spouse, $25,000 plus one-half to spouse, but if any of the children are not those of the surviving spouse, one-half only. Balance to children or to their issue *per stirpes.*

SPOUSE AND NO ISSUE: All to spouse.

NO SPOUSE BUT ISSUE: All to children equally or to their issue *per stirpes.*

NO SPOUSE OR ISSUE BUT PARENTS: All to parents equally or to the survivor.

NO SPOUSE, ISSUE, OR PARENTS: All to issue of parents *per stirpes,* and, if none, to grandparents and their issue, and, if none, to nearest lineal ancestors and their issue.

CONNECTICUT

SPOUSE AND ISSUE: If all children are those of the surviving spouse, $50,000 plus one-half to spouse, but if any of the children are not those of the surviving spouse, one-half only. Balance to children or to their issue *per stirpes.*

SPOUSE AND NO ISSUE: $50,000 plus three-fourths of balance to spouse. Balance to parents or surviving parent and, if none, to spouse.

NO SPOUSE BUT ISSUE: All to children equally or to their issue *per stirpes.*

NO SPOUSE OR ISSUE BUT PARENTS: All to parents equally or to the survivor.

NO SPOUSE, ISSUE, OR PARENTS: All to issue of parents *per stirpes,* and, if none, to next of kin.

DELAWARE

SPOUSE AND ISSUE: Real property—a life estate only to spouse. Balance to children or to their issue *per stirpes.* Personal property—if all children are those of the surviving spouse, $50,000 plus one-half of personal property to spouse, but if any of the children are not those of surviving spouse, one-half only. Balance to children or to their issue *per stirpes.*

SPOUSE AND NO ISSUE: Real property—if no parents surviving, all to spouse. If parents surviving, life estate only, balance to parents equally or to the survivor, and, if none, to issue of parents *per stirpes.* Personal property—if no parents surviving, all to spouse. If parents surviving, $50,000 plus one-half of balance. Balance to parents or to survivor of them.

NO SPOUSE BUT ISSUE: All to children equally or to their issue *per stirpes.*

NO SPOUSE OR ISSUE BUT PARENTS: All to parents equally or to the survivor.

NO SPOUSE, ISSUE, OR PARENTS: All to brothers and sisters or to their issue *per stirpes,* and, if none, to next of kin.

DISTRICT OF COLUMBIA

SPOUSE AND ISSUE: Real property—as to one-third, life estate to spouse. Balance to children equally or to their issue *per stirpes.* Personal property—one-third to spouse and balance to children equally or to their issue *per stirpes.*

SPOUSE AND NO ISSUE: Real property—as to one-third, life estate to spouse. Balance to parents or surviving parent and, if none, to issue of parents *per stirpes,* and, if none, to collaterals and, if none, to grandparents and, if none, all to spouse. Personal property—one-half to spouse, balance same as for real property.

NO SPOUSE BUT ISSUE: All to children equally or to their issue *per stirpes.*

NO SPOUSE OR ISSUE BUT PARENTS: All to parents equally or to the survivor.

NO SPOUSE, ISSUE, OR PARENTS: All to brothers and sisters or to their issue *per stirpes,* and, if none, to collaterals, and, if none, to grandparents.

FLORIDA

SPOUSE AND ISSUE: If all children are those of the surviving spouse, $20,000 plus one-half to spouse, but if any children are not those of the surviving spouse, one-half only. Balance to children or to their issue *per stirpes.*

SPOUSE AND NO ISSUE: All to spouse.

NO SPOUSE BUT ISSUE: All to children equally or to their issue *per stirpes.*

NO SPOUSE OR ISSUE BUT PARENTS: All to parents equally or to the survivor.

NO SPOUSE, ISSUE, OR PARENTS: All to brothers and sisters or to their issue *per stirpes,* and, if none, one-half each to maternal and paternal next of kin beginning with grandparents.

GEORGIA

SPOUSE AND ISSUE: Children or their issue share equally with spouse, with widow entitled to at least one-fifth.

SPOUSE AND NO ISSUE: All to spouse.

NO SPOUSE BUT ISSUE: All to children equally or to their issue *per stirpes.*

NO SPOUSE OR ISSUE BUT PARENTS: All to parents, brothers, and sisters equally or to their issue *per stirpes.*

NO SPOUSE, ISSUE, OR PARENTS: All to brothers and sisters or to their issue *per stirpes,* and, if none, to paternal and maternal next of kin.

HAWAII

SPOUSE AND ISSUE: One-half to spouse and one-half to children.

SPOUSE AND NO ISSUE: One-half to spouse and one-half to parents equally or all to survivor of parents and, if none, all to spouse.

NO SPOUSE BUT ISSUE: All to children equally or to their issue *per stirpes.*

NO SPOUSE OR ISSUE BUT PARENTS: All to parents equally or to the survivor.

NO SPOUSE, ISSUE, OR PARENTS: All to brothers and sisters or to their issue *per stirpes,* and, if none, to grandparents, and, if none, to uncles and aunts equally.

IDAHO

SPOUSE AND ISSUE: Community property to spouse. One-half of quasi-community property to spouse and also other one-half if not disposed of by will. If child or children are those of surviving spouse, $50,000 plus one-half of balance to spouse, but if not, one-half to spouse. Balance to surviving child or children or to their issue *per stirpes.*

SPOUSE AND NO ISSUE: Community property to spouse. Quasi-community property as where issue survive. If parents do not survive, all to spouse. Otherwise, $50,000 plus one-half to spouse and balance to parents or to survivor of them.

NO SPOUSE BUT ISSUE: All to children equally or to their issue *per stirpes.*

NO SPOUSE OR ISSUE BUT PARENTS: All to parents equally or to the survivor.

NO SPOUSE, ISSUE, OR PARENTS: To brothers and sisters or to their issue.

ILLINOIS

SPOUSE AND ISSUE: One-half to spouse and one-half to children equally or to their issue *per stirpes.*

SPOUSE AND NO ISSUE: All to spouse.

NO SPOUSE BUT ISSUE: All to children equally or to their issue *per stirpes.*

NO SPOUSE OR ISSUE BUT PARENTS: All to parents, brothers and sisters, or issue of brothers and sisters, *per stirpes.* One surviving parent takes a double share.

NO SPOUSE, ISSUE, OR PARENTS: One-half each to maternal and paternal grandparents equally or to survivor, and, if none, to their issue *per stirpes,* then to great-grandparents, as above, then to next of kin without representation.

INDIANA

SPOUSE AND ISSUE: If any issue but none by spouse, life estate in real property to spouse and balance as below. If one child, one-half to spouse and one-half to child or child's issue. Otherwise, one-third to spouse and two-thirds to children or their issue *per stirpes*.

SPOUSE AND NO ISSUE: If no parents, all to spouse. If parents, one-fourth to parents or survivor of them and three-fourths to spouse.

NO SPOUSE BUT ISSUE: All to children equally or to their issue *per stirpes*.

NO SPOUSE OR ISSUE BUT PARENTS: One-half to parents if both survive or one-fourth to one surviving parent. Balance to brothers and sisters or to their issue *per stirpes*.

NO SPOUSE, ISSUE, OR PARENTS: All to brothers and sisters or to their issue *per stirpes*, and, if none, to grandparents and, if none, to uncles and aunts *per stirpes*.

IOWA

SPOUSE AND ISSUE: Real property—one-third to spouse and two-thirds to children or to their issue *per stirpes*. Personal property—exempt property of decedent plus one-third of balance to spouse. Balance to children or to their issue *per stirpes*.

SPOUSE AND NO ISSUE: Real property—one half to spouse and one-half to parents or survivor and, if none, to their issue *per stirpes*, and, if none, all to spouse. Personal property—exempt property of decedent plus one-half of balance to spouse. Balance to parents or survivor and, if none, to their heirs *per stirpes*, or their issue *per stirpes*, and, if none, all to spouse.

NO SPOUSE BUT ISSUE: All to children equally or to their issue *per stirpes*.

NO SPOUSE OR ISSUE BUT PARENTS: All to parents equally or to the survivor.

NO SPOUSE, ISSUE, OR PARENTS: All to brothers and sisters or to their issue *per stirpes*, and, if none, to ancestors and their issue, and, if none, to spouse or to heirs of spouse.

KANSAS

SPOUSE AND ISSUE: One-half to spouse and one-half to children equally or to their issue *per stirpes*.

SPOUSE AND NO ISSUE: All to spouse.

NO SPOUSE BUT ISSUE: All to children equally or to their issue *per stirpes*.

NO SPOUSE OR ISSUE BUT PARENTS: All to parents equally or to survivor.

NO SPOUSE, ISSUE, OR PARENTS: All to issue of parents *per stirpes*.

KENTUCKY

SPOUSE AND ISSUE: Real property—life estate in one-third of real property of which decedent was seized of fee simple estate during marriage and one-half of surplus real estate and balance to children equally or to their issue *per stirpes*. Personal property—one-half to spouse and one-half to children equally or to their issue *per stirpes*.

SPOUSE AND NO ISSUE: One-half to spouse and one-half to parents equally or to survivor but if neither parent survives, their one-half to their issue *per stirpes*, and, if none, to spouse.

NO SPOUSE BUT ISSUE: All to children equally or to their issue *per stirpes*.

NO SPOUSE OR ISSUE BUT PARENTS: All to parents equally or to the survivor.

NO SPOUSE, ISSUE, OR PARENTS: To brothers and sisters or to their issue *per stirpes*, and, if none, one-half to maternal next of kin and one-half to paternal next of kin. Distribution to grandparents first and, if none, to uncles and aunts or their issue *per stirpes*.

LOUISIANA

SPOUSE AND ISSUE: All community property to descendants *per stirpes*, subject to a usufruct interest in the spouse unless spouse remarries. All separate property passes to children equally or to their issue *per stirpes*.

SPOUSE AND NO ISSUE: All community property to spouse. As to separate property to brothers and sisters or to their issue *per stirpes*, if no brothers and sisters or their issue survive, all to the parents. If none of the above survive, to spouse.

NO SPOUSE BUT ISSUE: All to children equally or to their issue *per stirpes*.

NO SPOUSE OR ISSUE BUT PARENTS: All to brothers and sisters or to their issue *per stirpes*, and, if there are none, all to parents.

NO SPOUSE, ISSUE, OR PARENTS: All to brothers and sisters equally or to their issue *per stirpes*, and, if none, to more remote next of kin.

MAINE

SPOUSE AND ISSUE: If all children are those of the surviving spouse, $50,000 plus one-half to spouse, but if any children are not those of surviving spouse, one-half only. Balance to children or their issue *per stirpes*.

SPOUSE AND NO ISSUE: $50,000 plus one-half to spouse, balance to parents or to survivor of them or to their issue *per capita*, and, if none, one-half to paternal grandparents or to their issue *per capita*, and one-half to maternal grandparents or to their issue *per capita*.

NO SPOUSE BUT ISSUE: All to children equally or to their issue *per stirpes*.

NO SPOUSE OR ISSUE BUT PARENTS: All to parents or to the survivor of them.

NO SPOUSE, ISSUE, OR PARENTS: One-half to paternal grandparents or to their issue *per capita*, and one-half to maternal grandparents or to their issue *per capita*.

MARYLAND

SPOUSE AND ISSUE: If minor child survives, one-half to spouse and one-half to children equally or to their issue *per stirpes*, but if no minor child, additional $15,000 to spouse.

SPOUSE AND NO ISSUE: $15,000 plus one-half to spouse and one-half to parents or to the survivor and if neither parent survives, all to spouse.

NO SPOUSE BUT ISSUE: All to children equally or to their issue *per stirpes*.

NO SPOUSE OR ISSUE BUT PARENTS: All to parents or to surviving parent.

NO SPOUSE, ISSUE, OR PARENTS: All to brothers and sisters equally or to their issue *per stirpes*, and, if none, to collateral next of kin.

MASSACHUSETTS

SPOUSE AND ISSUE: One-half to spouse and one-half to children equally or to their issue *per stirpes*.

SPOUSE AND NO ISSUE: $50,000 plus one-half of the balance to spouse and other half to parents equally or to the survivor, but if neither parent survives, then one-half to brothers and sisters equally or to their issue *per stirpes*, and, if none, to next of kin. If no next of kin, all to spouse.

NO SPOUSE BUT ISSUE: All to children equally or to their issue *per stirpes*.

NO SPOUSE OR ISSUE BUT PARENTS: All to parents equally or to the survivor.

NO SPOUSE, ISSUE, OR PARENTS: All to brothers and sisters equally or to their issue *per stirpes*, and, if none, to next of kin.

MICHIGAN

SPOUSE AND ISSUE: $60,000 plus one-half to surviving spouse and the balance to surviving issue *per stirpes*, but if any of the issue are not issue of surviving spouse, surviving spouse does not get the $60,000.

SPOUSE AND NO ISSUE: $60,000 plus one-half the balance to surviving spouse and the balance to parents equally or to the survivor, and if there are no parents, all to spouse.

NO SPOUSE BUT ISSUE: All to the children equally or to their issue *per stirpes*.

NO SPOUSE OR ISSUE BUT PARENTS: All to parents equally or to survivor.

NO SPOUSE, ISSUE, OR PARENTS: All to brothers and sisters equally or to their children *per stirpes,* and, if none, one-half to maternal grandparents and one-half to paternal grandparents or to their issue *per stirpes.*

MINNESOTA

SPOUSE AND ISSUE: If only one child, then one-half to spouse and one-half to child or issue of such child, but if more than one child, then one-third to spouse and two-thirds to children equally or to their issue *per stirpes.*

SPOUSE AND NO ISSUE: All to spouse.

NO SPOUSE BUT ISSUE: All to children equally or to their issue *per stirpes.*

NO SPOUSE OR ISSUE BUT PARENTS: All to parents equally or to survivor.

NO SPOUSE, ISSUE, OR PARENTS: All to brothers and sisters equally or to their issue *per stirpes,* and, if none, to next of kin.

MISSISSIPPI

SPOUSE AND ISSUE: Property is divided into the number of shares equal to the number of children (or issue of a child) and spouse living, and each takes an equal share.

SPOUSE AND NO ISSUE: All to spouse.

NO SPOUSE BUT ISSUE: All to children or to their issue *per stirpes.*

NO SPOUSE OR ISSUE BUT PARENTS: All to parents, brothers, and sisters equally or to issue of brothers and sisters *per stirpes.* If no brothers or sisters or their issue, all to parents equally or to survivor.

NO SPOUSE, ISSUE, OR PARENTS: All to brothers and sisters equally or to their issue *per stirpes,* and, if none, to grandparents, uncles, and aunts equally or to their issue *per stirpes,* and, if none, to next of kin.

MISSOURI

SPOUSE AND ISSUE: If all the children are those of surviving spouse, $20,000 plus one-half to spouse, but if any children are not those of surviving spouse, one-half only. Balance to children or to their issue *per stirpes.*

SPOUSE AND NO ISSUE: $20,000 plus one-half of balance to spouse and the other half to parents or to the survivor of them, and, if none, all to spouse.

NO SPOUSE BUT ISSUE: All to children equally or to their issue *per stirpes.*

NO SPOUSE OR ISSUE BUT PARENTS: All to parents, brothers, and sisters equally or to their issue *per stirpes,* and, if none, all to parents or to survivor.

NO SPOUSE, ISSUE, OR PARENTS: All to brothers and sisters equally or to their issue *per stirpes*, and, if none, to grandparents, uncles and aunts and their issue *per stirpes*, and, if none, to nearest lineal ancestor and their issue.

MONTANA

SPOUSE AND ISSUE: All to surviving spouse if child or children are those of surviving spouse; if only one child, one-half to spouse and one-half to child. If more than one child, one third to spouse and the balance to children.

SPOUSE AND NO ISSUE: All to spouse.

NO SPOUSE BUT ISSUE: All to children equally or to their issue *per stirpes*.

NO SPOUSE OR ISSUE BUT PARENTS: All to parents equally or to survivor.

NO SPOUSE, ISSUE, OR PARENTS: All to brothers and sisters equally or to their issue *per stirpes*, and, if none, one-half to paternal grandparents or to their issue *per stirpes*, and one-half to maternal grandparents or to their issue *per stirpes*.

NEBRASKA

SPOUSE AND ISSUE: $50,000 plus one-half to spouse. If any of the children are not children of the surviving spouse, only one-half to spouse and the balance to children or to their issue *per stirpes*.

SPOUSE AND NO ISSUE: All to spouse but if any parent survives, $50,000 plus one-half to spouse and the balance to parents equally or to survivor.

NO SPOUSE BUT ISSUE: All to children equally or to their issue *per stirpes*.

NO SPOUSE OR ISSUE BUT PARENTS: All to parents equally or to survivor.

NO SPOUSE, ISSUE, OR PARENTS: All to brothers and sisters equally or to their children *per stirpes*, and, if none, one-half to paternal next of kin and one half to maternal next of kin.

NEVADA

SPOUSE AND ISSUE: All community property to spouse. As to other property, if only one child or its issue survive, one-half to spouse and one-half to such child or such child's issue, but if there is more than one child or issue, then one-third to spouse and the balance to such children or to their issue *per stirpes*.

SPOUSE AND NO ISSUE: All community property to spouse. As to other property, one-half to spouse and one-half to parents equally or to the survivor, but, if none, to brothers and sisters equally or to their children *per stirpes*, and, if none, all to spouse.

NO SPOUSE BUT ISSUE: All to children equally or to their issue *per stirpes*.

NO SPOUSE OR ISSUE BUT PARENTS: All to parents equally or to survivor.

NO SPOUSE, ISSUE, OR PARENTS: All to brothers and sisters equally or to their issue *per stirpes,* and, if none, to next of kin.

NEW HAMPSHIRE

SPOUSE AND ISSUE: $50,000 plus one-half to spouse, but if any of the children are not children of surviving spouse, only one-half. The balance to children or to issue of a child *per stirpes.*

SPOUSE AND NO ISSUE: $50,000 plus one-half to spouse and balance to parents equally or to the survivor and if there is none, all to spouse.

NO SPOUSE BUT ISSUE: All to children equally or to their issue *per stirpes.*

NO SPOUSE OR ISSUE BUT PARENTS: All to parents equally or to survivor.

NO SPOUSE, ISSUE, OR PARENTS: All to brothers and sisters equally or to their issue *per stirpes,* and, if none, one-half to paternal next of kin and one-half to maternal next of kin *per stirpes.*

NEW JERSEY

SPOUSE AND ISSUE: $50,000 plus one-half to spouse but if any of the children are not children of the surviving spouse, only one-half. The balance to children or to issue of a child *per stirpes.*

SPOUSE AND NO ISSUE: $50,000 plus one-half to spouse and the balance to parents equally or to the survivor and if there is none, all to spouse.

NO SPOUSE BUT ISSUE: All to children equally or to their issue *per stirpes.*

NO SPOUSE OR ISSUE BUT PARENTS: All to parents equally or to survivor.

NO SPOUSE, ISSUE, OR PARENTS: All to brothers and sisters equally or to their issue *per stirpes,* and, if none, one-half to maternal grandparents or to their issue and one-half to paternal grandparents or their issue.

NEW MEXICO

SPOUSE AND ISSUE: All community property to spouse. As to other property, one-fourth to spouse and three-fourths to children equally or to their issue *per stirpes.*

SPOUSE AND NO ISSUE: All to spouse.

NO SPOUSE BUT ISSUE: All to children equally or to their issue *per stirpes.*

NO SPOUSE OR ISSUE BUT PARENTS: All to parents equally or to survivor.

NO SPOUSE, ISSUE, OR PARENTS: All to brothers and sisters equally or to their issue *per stirpes*, and, if none, one-half to maternal grandparents or to their issue and one-half to paternal grandparents or their issue.

NEW YORK

SPOUSE AND ISSUE: If one child and no descendants of predeceased child, $4,000 plus one-half to spouse and the balance to the child or such child's issue. If more than one child or one child and descendants of predeceased child, $4,000 plus one-third to spouse and balance to children or to their issue *per stirpes*.

SPOUSE AND NO ISSUE: $25,000 plus one-half to spouse and the balance to parents equally or to the survivor, and if there is none, all to spouse.

NO SPOUSE BUT ISSUE: All to children equally or to their issue *per stirpes*.

NO SPOUSE OR ISSUE BUT PARENTS: All to parents equally or to survivor.

NO SPOUSE, ISSUE, OR PARENTS: All to brothers and sisters or to their issue *per stirpes*, and, if none, to grandparents equally or to their issue *per capita*, and, if none, to next of kin.

NORTH CAROLINA

SPOUSE AND ISSUE: If one child, $15,000 of personalty (if any) plus one-half to spouse and balance to child or such child's issue. If more than one child, $15,000 of personalty (if any) plus one-third to spouse and balance to children or to their issue *per stirpes*.

SPOUSE AND NO ISSUE: $25,000 of personalty (if any) plus one-half to spouse and balance to parents equally or to the survivor, and if there is none, all to spouse.

NO SPOUSE BUT ISSUE: All to children equally, or to their issue *per stirpes*.

NO SPOUSE OR ISSUE BUT PARENTS: All to parents equally or to survivor.

NO SPOUSE, ISSUE, OR PARENTS: All to brothers and sisters equally or to their issue *per stirpes*, and, if none, one-half to maternal grandparents or to their issue, and one-half to paternal grandparents or to their issue.

NORTH DAKOTA

SPOUSE AND ISSUE: $50,000 plus one-half to spouse. If any of the children are not children of surviving spouse, only one-half to spouse and the balance to children or to their issue *per stirpes*.

SPOUSE AND NO ISSUE: All to spouse but if any parent survives, $50,000 plus one-half to spouse and the balance to parents or to survivor.

NO SPOUSE BUT ISSUE: All to children equally or to their issue *per stirpes.*

NO SPOUSE OR ISSUE BUT PARENTS: All to parents or to survivor.

NO SPOUSE, ISSUE, OR PARENTS: All to brothers and sisters equally or to their children *per stirpes,* and, if none, one-half to paternal next of kin and one-half to maternal next of kin.

OHIO

SPOUSE AND ISSUE: $30,000 if spouse is natural or adoptive parent of any child, but, if not, $10,000. In addition, one-half to spouse if there is only one child or issue of a child; otherwise, one-third to spouse. The balance to child or children or to their issue *per stirpes.*

SPOUSE AND NO ISSUE: All to spouse.

NO SPOUSE BUT ISSUE: All to children equally or to their issue *per stirpes.*

NO SPOUSE OR ISSUE BUT PARENTS: All to parents equally or to the survivor.

NO SPOUSE, ISSUE, OR PARENTS: All to brothers and sisters or to their issue *per stirpes,* and, if none, one-half to maternal grandparents or to the survivor of them or to their issue *per stirpes,* and one-half to paternal grandparents or to the survivor of them or to their issue *per stirpes,* and, if none, to next of kin.

OKLAHOMA

SPOUSE AND ISSUE: If one child, one-half to spouse and one-half to child or child's issue; otherwise, one-third to spouse and two-thirds to children or to their issue *per stirpes.*

SPOUSE AND NO ISSUE: One-half to spouse and one-half to parents equally or to the survivor, but, if none, to brothers and sisters equally or to their children *per stirpes,* and, if none, all to spouse.

NO SPOUSE BUT ISSUE: All to children equally or to their issue *per stirpes.*

NO SPOUSE OR ISSUE BUT PARENTS: All to parents equally or to survivor.

NO SPOUSE, ISSUE, OR PARENTS: All to brothers and sisters equally or to survivor *per stirpes,* and, if none, to next of kin.

OREGON

SPOUSE AND ISSUE: One-half to spouse and one-half to children or to their issue *per stirpes.*

SPOUSE AND NO ISSUE: All to spouse.

NO SPOUSE BUT ISSUE: All to children equally or to their issue *per stirpes.*

NO SPOUSE OR ISSUE BUT PARENTS: All to parents equally or to survivor.

NO SPOUSE, ISSUE, OR PARENTS: All to brothers and sisters equally or to their issue *per stirpes*, and, if none, to next of kin.

PENNSYLVANIA

SPOUSE AND ISSUE: $30,000 plus one-half to surviving spouse and the balance to the surviving issue *per stirpes*, but if any issue are not issue of surviving spouse, surviving spouse does not get the $30,000.

SPOUSE AND NO ISSUE: $30,000 plus one-half of the balance to surviving spouse and the balance to parents equally or to survivor, and if there are no parents, all to spouse.

NO SPOUSE BUT ISSUE: All to the children equally or to their issue *per stirpes*.

NO SPOUSE OR ISSUE BUT PARENTS: All to parents equally or to survivor.

NO SPOUSE, ISSUE, OR PARENTS: All to brothers and sisters equally or to their issue *per stirpes*, and, if none, one-half to maternal grandparents and one-half to paternal grandparents or to survivor of them, and, if none, to aunts and uncles or to their issue.

RHODE ISLAND

SPOUSE AND ISSUE: Real property—life estate to spouse. Balance to children equally or to their issue *per stirpes*. Personal property—one-half to spouse and one-half to children equally or to their issue *per stirpes*.

SPOUSE AND NO ISSUE: Real property—life estate to spouse plus, in discretion of court, $25,000; balance to parents equally or to survivor, and, if none, to brothers and sisters equally or to survivor, and, if none, one-half to maternal grandparents and one-half to paternal grandparents or to survivor, and, if none, to aunts and uncles equally or to their issue *per stirpes*, and, if none, to next of kin, and, if none, to spouse. Personal property—$50,000 and one-half to spouse. Balance to parents equally or to survivor and, if none, to brothers and sisters equally or to their issue *per stirpes*, and, if none, one-half to maternal grandparents and one-half to paternal grandparents, and, if none, to next of kin, and, if none, to spouse.

NO SPOUSE BUT ISSUE: All to children equally or to their issue *per stirpes*.

NO SPOUSE OR ISSUE BUT PARENTS: All to parents equally or to survivor.

NO SPOUSE, ISSUE, OR PARENTS: All to brothers and sisters equally or to their issue *per stirpes*, and, if none, one-half to maternal grandparents and one-half to paternal grandparents, and, if none, to next of kin.

SOUTH CAROLINA

SPOUSE AND ISSUE: If one child, one-half to spouse and one-half to child or child's issue. If more than one child, one-third to spouse and two-thirds to children equally or to their issue *per stirpes.*

SPOUSE AND NO ISSUE: One-half to spouse and one-half to parents, brothers, and sisters, in equal shares, or to their issue *per stirpes,* and, if no parents, one-half to brothers and sisters *per stirpes,* and, if no brothers and sisters, to parents equally or to survivor, and, if none, one-half to lineal ancestors, and, if none, to spouse.

NO SPOUSE BUT ISSUE: All to children equally or to their issue *per stirpes.*

NO SPOUSE OR ISSUE BUT PARENTS: To parents equally or to survivor if no brothers and sisters.

NO SPOUSE, ISSUE, OR PARENTS: All to brothers and sisters *per stirpes,* and, if none, to lineal ancestors equally or to survivor, and, if none, to aunts and uncles equally or to their issue, and, if none, to next of kin.

SOUTH DAKOTA

SPOUSE AND ISSUE: If one child, one-half to spouse and one-half to child or such child's issue. If more than one child, one-third to spouse and two-thirds to children equally or to their issue *per stirpes.*

SPOUSE AND NO ISSUE: $100,000 plus one-half to spouse, balance to parents equally or to survivor, and, if none, to brothers and sisters equally or to their issue *per stirpes,* and, if none, to spouse.

NO SPOUSE BUT ISSUE: All to children equally or to their issue *per stirpes.*

NO SPOUSE OR ISSUE BUT PARENTS: All to parents equally or to survivor.

NO SPOUSE, ISSUE, OR PARENTS: All to brothers and sisters equally or to their issue *per stirpes,* and, if none, to next of kin.

TENNESSEE

SPOUSE AND ISSUE: Homestead and year's support allowance plus child's share but not less than one-third if issue survive. Balance to children equally or to their issue *per stirpes.*

SPOUSE AND NO ISSUE: All to spouse.

NO SPOUSE BUT ISSUE: All to children equally or to their issue *per stirpes.*

NO SPOUSE OR ISSUE BUT PARENTS: All to parents equally or to survivor.

NO SPOUSE, ISSUE, OR PARENTS: All to brothers and sisters equally or to their issue *per stirpes*, and, if none, one-half to maternal grandparents, one-half to paternal grandparents or to survivor, and, if none, to their issue *per stirpes*.

TEXAS

SPOUSE AND ISSUE: One-half of community property to spouse and one-half to children equally or to their issue *per stirpes*. As to separate real property, life estate in one-third to spouse. As to separate personal property, one-third to spouse. Balance of real property and personal property to children equally or to their issue *per stirpes*.

SPOUSE AND NO ISSUE: All community property and personal property to spouse. As to other property, one-half of realty and all of personalty to spouse and balance to parents equally, but if only one parent, one-half (of such balance) to such parent and one-half to brothers and sisters equally or to their issue *per stirpes*, and if there are none, the entire one-half to surviving parent, but if there is no parent, to brothers and sisters or to their issue *per stirpes*. If there are none, to grandparents and their descendants, and, if none, to spouse.

NO SPOUSE BUT ISSUE: All to children equally or to their issue *per stirpes*.

NO SPOUSE OR ISSUE BUT PARENTS: All to parents equally if both survive, or one-half to one surviving parent and one-half to brothers and sisters equally or to their issue *per stirpes*, and, if none, to surviving parent.

NO SPOUSE, ISSUE, OR PARENTS: All to brothers and sisters equally or to their issue *per stirpes*. If none, one-half to maternal grandparents and their issue and one-half to paternal grandparents and their issue.

UTAH

SPOUSE AND ISSUE: $50,000 plus one-half to surviving spouse and the balance to surviving issue *per stirpes*, but if any issue are not issue of surviving spouse, surviving spouse does not get the $50,000.

SPOUSE AND NO ISSUE: $100,000 plus one-half of the balance to surviving spouse and the balance to parents equally or to survivor, and if there are no parents, all to spouse.

NO SPOUSE BUT ISSUE: All to children equally or to their issue *per stirpes*.

NO SPOUSE OR ISSUE BUT PARENTS: All to parents equally or to survivor.

NO SPOUSE, ISSUE, OR PARENTS: All to brothers and sisters equally or to their issue *per stirpes*, and, if none, one-half to maternal grandparents or their descendants and one-half to paternal grandparents or their descendants *per stirpes*, or all to survivor of them and, if none, to next of kin.

VERMONT

SPOUSE AND ISSUE: If one child, with respect to real property, one-half to spouse and one-half to child or such child's issue, and one-third of personal property to spouse and two thirds to children equally or to their issue *per stirpes*. If more than one child, one-third to spouse and two-thirds to children equally or to their issue *per stirpes*.

SPOUSE AND NO ISSUE: $25,000 plus one-half to spouse and the balance to parents equally or to survivor, and, if none, to brothers and sisters equally or to their issue *per stirpes*, and, if none, to next of kin, and, if none, to spouse.

NO SPOUSE BUT ISSUE: All to children equally or to their issue *per stirpes*.

NO SPOUSE OR ISSUE BUT PARENTS: All to parents equally or to survivor.

NO SPOUSE, ISSUE, OR PARENTS: All to brothers and sisters equally or to their issue *per stirpes*, and, if none, to next of kin.

VIRGINIA

SPOUSE AND ISSUE: Real property—life estate in one-third to spouse, balance to children equally or to their issue *per stirpes*. Personal property—one-third to spouse and balance to children equally or to their issue *per stirpes*.

SPOUSE AND NO ISSUE: All to spouse.

NO SPOUSE BUT ISSUE: All to children equally or to their issue *per stirpes*.

NO SPOUSE OR ISSUE BUT PARENTS: All to parents equally or to survivor.

NO SPOUSE, ISSUE, OR PARENTS: All to brothers and sisters equally or to their issue *per stirpes*, and, if none, one-half, or all if there is no maternal next of kin, to paternal next of kin, and one-half, or all if there is no paternal next of kin, to maternal next of kin, but first to grandparents or to survivor or to their issue.

WASHINGTON

SPOUSE AND ISSUE: All the community property to spouse. As to other property, one-half to spouse and one-half to children equally or to their issue *per stirpes*.

SPOUSE AND NO ISSUE: All community property to spouse. As to other property, three-fourths to spouse and one-fourth to parents equally or to survivor or their issue, and, if none, all to spouse.

NO SPOUSE BUT ISSUE: All to children equally or to their issue *per stirpes*.

NO SPOUSE OR ISSUE BUT PARENTS: All to parents equally or to survivor.

NO SPOUSE, ISSUE, OR PARENTS: All to brothers and sisters equally or to their children *per stirpes*, and, if none, to grandparents or to their issue.

WEST VIRGINIA

SPOUSE AND ISSUE: Real property—life estate in one-third to spouse and balance to children equally or to their issue *per stirpes*. Personal property—one-third to spouse and balance to children equally or to their issue *per stirpes*.

SPOUSE AND NO ISSUE: All to spouse.

NO SPOUSE BUT ISSUE: All to children equally or to their issue *per stirpes*.

NO SPOUSE OR ISSUE BUT PARENTS: All to parents equally or to survivor.

NO SPOUSE, ISSUE, OR PARENTS: All to brothers and sisters equally or to their issue *per stirpes*, and, if none, one-half, or all if there is no maternal next of kin, to paternal next of kin, and one-half, or all if there is no paternal next of kin, to maternal next of kin but first to grandparents or to survivor, then uncles and aunts or their issue.

WISCONSIN

SPOUSE AND ISSUE: If all children are those of surviving spouse, $25,000 plus one-half of the estate if only one child, or one-third of the estate if more than one child. If any child is not that of surviving spouse, one-half of the estate to surviving spouse if only one child or one-third of the estate if there is more than one child, and the balance to the surviving children or their issue *per stirpes*.

SPOUSE AND NO ISSUE: All to spouse.

NO SPOUSE BUT ISSUE: All to children equally or to their issue *per stirpes*.

NO SPOUSE OR ISSUE, BUT PARENTS: All to parents equally or to survivor.

NO SPOUSE, ISSUE, OR PARENTS: All to brothers and sisters equally or to their issue *per stirpes*, and, if none, all to grandparents or survivor, and, if none, all to next of kin.

WYOMING

SPOUSE AND ISSUE: One-half to spouse and one-half to children equally or to their issue *per stirpes*.

SPOUSE AND NO ISSUE: $20,000 plus three-fourths to spouse. One-fourth to parents equally or to survivor, and, if none, to brothers and sisters equally or to their issue *per stirpes*, and, if none, to spouse.

NO SPOUSE BUT ISSUE: All to children equally or to their issue *per stirpes*.

NO SPOUSE OR ISSUE BUT PARENTS: All to parents, brothers and sisters equally, or to issue of a brother or sister *per stirpes*.

NO SPOUSE, ISSUE, OR PARENTS: All to brothers and sisters equally or to their issue *per stirpes*, and, if none, to grandparents, uncles, and aunts, or their issue *per stirpes*.

TABLE 5

Requirements for Wills, by State

State	Minimum Age	Number of Witnesses
ALABAMA	Real Estate, 19; other, 18	2
ALASKA	18	2
ARIZONA	18	2
ARKANSAS	18	2
CALIFORNIA	18	2
COLORADO	18	2
CONNECTICUT	18	2
DELAWARE	18	2
DISTRICT OF COLUMBIA	18	2
FLORIDA	18	2
GEORGIA	14	2
HAWAII	18	2
IDAHO	18; emancipated child, any age	2
ILLINOIS	18	2
INDIANA	18	2
IOWA	18	2
KANSAS	18	2
KENTUCKY	18	2
LOUISIANA	16	2
MAINE	18	2
MARYLAND	18	2
MASSACHUSETTS	18	2
MICHIGAN	18	2
MINNESOTA	18	2
MISSISSIPPI	18	2
MISSOURI	18	2
MONTANA	18	2

State	Minimum Age	Number of Witnesses
NEBRASKA	18	2
NEVADA	18	2
NEW HAMPSHIRE	18; married any age	3
NEW JERSEY	18	2
NEW MEXICO	18	2
NEW YORK	18	2
NORTH CAROLINA	18	2
NORTH DAKOTA	18	2
OHIO	18	2
OKLAHOMA	18	2
OREGON	18; married any age	2
PENNSYLVANIA	18	2
RHODE ISLAND	18	2
SOUTH CAROLINA	18	3
SOUTH DAKOTA	18	2
TENNESSEE	18	2
TEXAS	18; married now or previously or member of U.S. Armed Forces or Merchant Marine, any age	2
UTAH	18	2
VERMONT	18	3
VIRGINIA	18	2
WASHINGTON	18	2
WEST VIRGINIA	18	2
WISCONSIN	18	2
WYOMING	18	2

TABLE 6

Compensation Allowed to Executors and Trustees, by State

The listings that follow are intended to serve as a guide only and are not intended to be a complete statement of the applicable laws.

In many states, local court rules fix the amount of compensation. In many states custom prevails as to the amount of compensation. The reader is urged to consult with local counsel to determine the appropriate compensation.

Also, in virtually every state the compensation may be varied by special circumstances, such as by extended litigation.

Compensation of Fiduciaries

State	Executor, Administrator, or Personal Representative	Trustee under Will
Alabama:	Just and fair but not in excess of 2 1/2% of disbursements.	No statutory provision.
Alaska:	$200 plus 2% of excess of estate over $4,000.	No statutory provision.
Arizona:	Reasonable compensation.	Reasonable compensation.
Arkansas:	Reasonable compensation not to exceed $300 plus 3% of excess of personal property over $5,000. Compensation for legal services not to exceed 5% of value of real and personal property up to $5,000; 4% of next $20,000; 3% of next $75,000; 2 3/4% of next $300,000; 2 1/2% of next $600,000; and 2% of balance.	No statutory provision.

State	Executor, Administrator, or Personal Representative	Trustee under Will
California:	Commissions and fees of attorneys are each 4% of $15,000; 3% on next $85,000; 2% on next $900,000; and 1% on excess over $1,000,000.	Reasonable compensation.
Colorado:	Reasonable compensation.	Reasonable compensation.
Connecticut:	No statutory rates provided. Customarily based on percentage of gross estate administered.	Reasonable compensation.
Delaware:	Provided by Rules of Court and based on value of gross estate. In summary as follows: $10,000, $800; $60,000, $2,850; $15,000, $5,400; $300,000, $8,700; $500,000, $12,500.	No statutory provision.
District of Columbia:	Reasonable compensation of between 1% and 10% of gross estate.	No statutory provision.
Florida:	Reasonable compensation.	No statutory provision.
Georgia:	2 1/2% on money received and 2 1/2% on money paid out. On property distributed in kind, reasonable fee not to exceed 3%.	Same as for executors, etc.
Hawaii:	On income, 7% on first $5,000 and 5% on excess. On principal, 5% on first $1,000, 4% on next $9,000, 3% on next $10,000, 2% on excess over $20,000.	On income, same as executors, etc. On principal, 1% at inception; 1/10 of 1% on final distribution; 2 1/2% received after inception; 2 1/2% on payments before termination.
Idaho:	Reasonable compensation.	Reasonable compensation.
Illinois:	Reasonable compensation.	Reasonable compensation.
Indiana:	Reasonable compensation.	Reasonable compensation.

State	Executor, Administrator, or Personal Representative	Trustee under Will
Iowa:	Reasonable compensation not to exceed 6% on first $1,000, 4% on next $4,000, 2% on excess. Attorney fees based on above.	Reasonable compensation.
Kansas:	Reasonable compensation.	Reasonable compensation.
Kentucky:	Not to exceed 5% of personal estate plus 5% of income.	5% of income plus 1/5 of 1% of principal annually, or at option of fiduciary 5% of principal when distributed.
Louisiana:	2 1/2% of gross estate.	Reasonable compensation.
Maine:	Not exceeding 5% of gross estate.	Same as executors, etc.
Maryland:	Reasonable compensation not exceeding 10% of first $20,000 of gross estate plus 4% of excess.	6% on income of real estate. Other income: 6 1/2% on first $10,000, 5% on next $10,000, 4% on next $10,000, 3% on excess. Annual principal commissions, 4/10 of 1% on $250,000, 1/4 of 1% on next $250,000, 3/20 of 1% on next $250,000, 1/10 of 1% on excess. 1/2 of 1% on final distribution.
Massachusetts:	Reasonable compensation but following not considered unreasonable, 2 1/2% to 3% of first $500,000 and 1% on excess.	Reasonable compensation.

State	Executor, Administrator, or Personal Representative	Trustee under Will
Michigan:	Reasonable compensation.	Reasonable compensation.
Minnesota:	Reasonable compensation.	Reasonable compensation.
Mississippi:	Not to exceed 7% of gross estate.	Reasonable compensation.
Missouri:	5% on first $5,000; 4% on next $20,000; 3% on next $75,000; 2 3/4% on next $300,000; 2 1/2% on next $600,000; 2% on excess.	Reasonable compensation.
Montana:	Reasonable compensation not to exceed 3% of first $40,000, 2% on excess. Attorney's fees not to exceed 1 1/2 times above.	Reasonable compensation.
Nebraska:	Reasonable compensation.	Reasonable compensation.
Nevada:	6% on first $1,000; 4% on next $4,000; 2% on excess.	Reasonable compensation.
New Hampshire:	Reasonable compensation.	Reasonable compensation.
New Jersey:	On income, 6%. On principal, 5% up to $100,000 and on excess up to 5% in discretion of court. On distribution of principal, 2% if within 5 years of receipt, 1 1/2% if within 5–10 years of receipt, 1% above.	On income, 6%. On principal, annually, 5/10 of 1% on first $100,000, 3/10 of 1% on next $100,000, 2/10 of 1% on excess.
New Mexico:	Reasonable compensation.	Reasonable compensation.

State	Executor, Administrator, or Personal Representative	Trustee under Will
New York:	For receiving and paying out first $25,000, 4%; next $125,000, 3 1/2%; next $150,000, 3%; over $300,000, 2%. Also, 5% of gross rents on real property. If gross estate is $200,000 or more, each fiduciary (up to 3) allowed full commission; if $100,000 to $200,000, each fiduciary (up to 2) allowed full commission.	Annual commissions of $7 per $1,000 on first $300,000 of principal; $3.75 per $1,000 on next $500,000; $2.50 per $1,000 on balance. For paying out principal 1%. On income, 2% on first $25,000, 1% on balance. Also, 6% of gross rents on real property. Same provisions as for executors, etc., for allocation where more than one trustee.
North Carolina:	In discretion of clerk of court, not to exceed 5% of receipts and expenditures fairly made.	Same as for executors, etc.
North Dakota:	Reasonable compensation.	Reasonable compensation.
Ohio:	On personal property, real property sold and income, 4% on first $100,000, 3% on next $300,000, 2% on balance. Plus 1% on real estate subject to Ohio estate tax and not sold, other than jointly-owned.	Reasonable compensation.
Oklahoma:	5% on first $1,000; 4% on next $4,000; 2 1/2% on excess.	Reasonable compensation.
Oregon:	On estate, including income, 7% on first $1,000; 4% on next $9,000; 3% on next $40,000; 2% on excess. Plus, 1% on other property subject to estate taxation.	Reasonable compensation.

State	Executor, Administrator, or Personal Representative	Trustee under Will
Pennsylvania:	Reasonable compensation but custom is to allow 5% on small estates (not defined) and 3% on large estates.	Reasonable compensation.
Rhode Island:	Reasonable compensation.	Reasonable compensation.
South Carolina:	2 1/2% on assets received and paid. 10% on interest received on money loaned.	Same as executors, etc.
South Dakota:	5% on first $1,000; 4% on next $4,000; 2 1/2% on excess. Real property included in above when sold; otherwise, just compensation.	Reasonable compensation.
Tennessee:	Reasonable compensation.	Reasonable compensation.
Texas:	5% on sums paid in cash and 5% on sums received in cash, other than cash on hand.	Reasonable compensation.
Utah:	Reasonable compensation.	Reasonable compensation.
Vermont:	Reasonable compensation (minimum of $4 per day).	Reasonable compensation.
Virginia:	Reasonable compensation.	Reasonable compensation.
Washington:	Reasonable compensation.	Reasonable compensation.
West Virginia:	Reasonable compensation.	Reasonable compensation.
Wisconsin:	2% of estate.	Reasonable compensation.
Wyoming:	10% on first $1,000; 5% on next $4,000; 3% on next $15,000; 2% on excess.	Reasonable compensation.

INDEX

INDEX

Scott, Foresman and the American Association of Retired Persons have joined together to create . . . AARP BOOKS

These comprehensive guides, written by experts, will help you manage your money, choose where to live, plan your estate, save on insurance, and help those you care about to live a better life.

What to Do with What You've Got: The Practical Guide to Money Management in Retirement Here's a wealth of information on how to identify, protect and increase your assets. Turn investments into money producers. Figure your net worth. Cut your expenses (without cutting back). Complete with detailed worksheets. Highly recommended. $7.95

Planning Your Retirement Housing Should you own or rent? Move or stay put? Buy land? A condo? This book covers everything from Caribbean real estate to retirement communities to mobile homes. You'll find out how to cash in on your present home's equity. Save on energy and repairs. Take advantage of tax breaks. Secure financing. Protect your rights as a tenant. $8.95

Policy Wise: The Practical Guide to Insurance Decisions for Older Consumers Avoid being under-insured as well as over-insured by evaluating what your needs really are. Includes helpful checklists for policy comparison. Written by a consumer protection attorney and former counsel to the Federal Trade Commission. $5.95

It's Your Choice: The Practical Guide to Planning a Funeral A practical and sensitive volume on how to make the proper arrangements, protect your legal rights, avoid excessive expense. The planning you do now will make it easier for your family to fulfill your wishes. A personal planning form is included. $4.95

Join AARP today and enjoy valuable benefits!

Join the American Association of Retired Persons, the national organization which helps people like you, age 50 and over, realize their full potential in so many ways! The rewards you'll reap with AARP will be many times greater than your low membership dues. And your membership also includes your spouse!

Your AARP benefits...

- Modern Maturity magazine
- Legislative work benefiting mature persons
- Nonprofit Pharmacy Service
- Quality Group Health Insurance
- Specially priced Motoring Plan
- Community Volunteer Activities
- Hotel & Car Rental Discounts
- Travel Service
- Tax-Aide Program to help with your taxes

☐ one year/$5
☐ three years/$12.50 (saves $2.50)
☐ ten years/$35 (saves $15)
☐ Check or money order enclosed, payable to AARP. DO NOT SEND CASH.
☐ Please bill me.

Name (please print)

Address   Apt.

City

State   Zip

Date of Birth _____ mo/ . . . . day/ _____ year

LTAA

55% of dues is designated for Association publications. Dues outside continental U.S.: $7 one year, $18 three years. Please allow 3 to 6 weeks for receipt of membership kit.

The Over Easy Foot Care Book Advice from Dr. Timothy P. Shea, podiatrist for the Over Easy program on PBS: how to know when the shoe fits; running vs. walking; the right way to treat corns; the effectiveness of over-the-counter remedies; how back pain relates to feet . . . plus much more! Diagrams and exercises included. $6.95

Name of book(s)	Price:
_____	_____
_____	_____
_____	_____
_____	_____
	subtotal: _____

ORDER INFORMATION
Complete the following information and return it **along with your name and address** (be sure to include ZIP code) to the address below. All orders must be prepaid.

add $1.45 shipping and handling   per order: $1.45

total: _____

List extra titles on separate sheet of paper

Check method of payment:

☐ Check   ☐ Money Order
   (make payable to AARP Books)
☐ Visa   ☐ MasterCard

AARP *Information* BOOKS *you can count on*

_____
Card Number   Expiration Date

AARP Books, Dept. EGW
400 South Edward Street
Mount Prospect, IL 60056

AARP Books are also available in your local bookstore, distributed by Farrar, Straus and Giroux.

- -

BUSINESS REPLY CARD

FIRST CLASS   PERMIT NO. 3132   LONG BEACH, CA

POSTAGE WILL BE PAID BY ADDRESSEE

American Association of Retired Persons
Membership Processing Center
215 Long Beach Boulevard
Long Beach, CA 90801

NO POSTAGE
NECESSARY
IF MAILED
IN THE
UNITED STATES